R 8 00
  ———
  nph

EEE

F

THE
VISUAL
ARTS

Authors: **Maurice K. Symonds** B.A.
Principal Lecturer, Head of Art Department,
Alexander Mackie College of Advance Education,
N.S.W.

Coll Portley A.Ed.
Lecturer in Art, Kelvin Grove Teachers College,
Queensland

Ralph E. Phillips Dip. Fine Art
(Painting)
Lecturer in Painting and History of Art, Salisbury
Teachers College, South Australia

Contributors: Dr S. M. MEAD
HAMISH KEITH
KEN REINHARD
MARGEL HINDER
PETER NEWELL

THE
VISUAL
ARTS

**A world survey from prehistoric times
to the present, with special reference
to Australia and New Zealand.**

THE JACARANDA PRESS

First published 1972 by
JACARANDA PRESS PTY LTD
46 Douglas Street, Milton, Q.
32 Church Street, Ryde, N.S.W.
37 Little Bourke Street, Melbourne, Vic.
142 Colin Street, West Perth, W.A.
154 Marion Road, West Richmond, S.A.
57 France Street, Auckland, N.Z.
P.O. Box 3395, Port Moresby, P.N.G.
122 Regents Park Road, London NW1
70A Greenleaf Road, Singapore 10
P.O. Box 239, Makati, Rizal, Philippines

Type set in Australia by
Queensland Type Service Pty Ltd, Brisbane
Printed in Hong Kong

© Maurice K. Symonds
  Coll Portley
  Ralph E. Phillips
  1972

National Library of Australia
Card Number and ISBN 0 7016 0337 2

Contents

Foreword

Educators of the present are aware of the need for students to range widely in their experiences and to select some areas of interest for concentrated, specialized study. In ranging widely, it is important that students become aware of the most significant concepts and achievements of the past, and gain an understanding and appreciation of their cultural heritage. It is also important that they should come into contact with the cultural developments of their own time and place, and see these in the broader context of developments throughout the world.

Thus, as many of the secondary school courses created in recent years, and particularly the art courses, emphasize both survey studies and in-depth studies, there has developed a need for student reference materials which reflect and facilitate these approaches.

This book, as its title so clearly indicates, is designed to meet such a need. The range of material included is wide, effectively covering the development of the Western visual arts from their roots in the achievements of ancient civilizations through to the *avant-garde* of the early 1970s. The contributions to world art of Asian and African cultures are given prominence as well. In one major respect this book is significantly different, in that the authors have invited dominant figures on the contemporary scene in both Australia and New Zealand to relate local works and personalities to the overall art survey.

The text is suitably brief yet pertinent and factual, but even more importantly, the book is liberally furnished with illustrations of works which, in themselves, supply much information as well as lending support to the text.

Although the emphasis in this book has been properly placed on the works of artists, the text gives insight into artists as people. It does not fall into the error of becoming merely an entertaining résumé of anecdote about them, but rather, each artist is presented in his social and cultural context.

In its organization, inclusions and approaches the book provides a particularly sound basis for worthwhile study, and it should encourage students to undertake further research.

Robert B. Winder
Inspector of Schools (Art), N.S.W.
Professional Assistant to the Director-General of
Education, N.S.W.

Contributors

Ken Reinhard

Born at Mudgee, N.S.W., in 1936, Ken Reinhard is a practising artist and teacher who holds a Diploma in Art (Education) from Sydney Teachers College, and a Graduate Diploma in Industrial Design from the University of N.S.W. His works have been featured in numerous one-man and group exhibitions both in Australia and overseas, and among his many art awards was the Marland House Sculpture Prize in 1971.

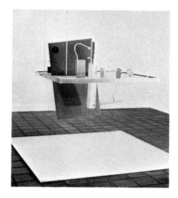

Reinhard: *Horizontal Hanging Picture*, mixed media, 1967. 122 x 124 x 124 cm. Mildura Art Centre, Victoria

Peter Newell F.R.A.I.A., A.C.I.V.

Born at Melbourne, Victoria, in 1916, Peter Newell qualified as an architect in 1941. He is at present the director of an architectural company with offices in the Queensland cities of Brisbane and Townsville, and is actively involved in writing, lecturing and TV programmes on architectural subjects. He is the author of the following 'Sketchbooks' in the series published by Rigby Limited: *Brisbane*, *Gold Coast and Green Mountains*, *New England*, *Darling Downs*, and *Tropical Queensland*.

St Matthew's Church at Mundingburra, Townsville, Queensland. Architects Ford, Hutton and Newell, 1957

Margel Hinder

Sculptor, born New York, U.S.A., 1906. Married Australian artist Frank Hinder and arrived in Australia in 1934. Margel Hinder taught at the National Art School, Sydney, from 1949. Among her larger works are abstract, free-standing sculptures in welded copper for Sydney's Western Assurance Building (1960) and the Commonwealth Reserve Bank (1964), in addition to the Newcastle Civic Park Fountain illustrated here.

Hinder: *Civic Park Fountain*, welded copper, 1966. 15.25 x 4.5 x 7.5 metres. Newcastle, N.S.W.

S. M. Mead M.A., Ph.D.

Born 1927. At present Senior Lecturer in Maori Studies in the Department of Anthropology, University of Auckland, N.Z., Dr Mead's special interests lie in the fields of Maori language and Maori art and craft. His main publications include *Taaniko Weaving*, 1952, *We Speak Maori*, 1959, *The Art of Maori Carving*, 1961, *Selected Readings in Maori* (with B. Biggs and P. Hohepa), 1963, *The Art of Taaniko Weaving: Its Cultural Context, Style and Development*, 1968, and *Traditional Maori Clothing*, 1969.

Hamish Keith

Graphic designer, art historian, critic, writer and broadcaster, born Dunedin, N.Z., 1936. A graduate of the Canterbury University School of Fine Arts, Hamish Keith was Keeper of the Auckland City Art Gallery from 1965 to 1970. He writes a weekly column in the *Auckland Star* and a regular column in the *Christchurch Press*, the *New Zealand Listener* and *Arts and Community*. Published works include *New Zealand Painting 1827-1870*, 1968, and *An Introduction to New Zealand Painting 1827-1967* (with Gordon H. Brown), 1969. Among his works in preparation are monographs on Don Binney and William Strutt, and a survey of the last ten years in New Zealand painting and sculpture.

Preface

This book has been designed as an introductory study to the mainstreams of painting, sculpture and architecture from prehistory to the present, with some reference to the indigenous art forms of Australia and New Zealand, as well as the subsequent manifestations of Western culture in both countries.

While it is hoped that this survey will serve as a valuable background to the study of art in secondary schools, we submit it also as an introduction for those whose school experiences have not included a study of the visual arts.

A survey which embraces at its extreme points some 40,000 years has obvious limitations: the necessary concentration on painting, architecture and sculpture in the post-Christian period has largely precluded reference to interior design and the wealth of domestic artifacts and ornament generally. Similarly, within the survey of the twentieth century visual art forms, film and photography have both been by-passed. Then, too, the constraints on space available to treat the highly complex achievements of various cultures and artists — as well as the limits on available reproductions — give rise to both unavoidable omission and generalization.

Yet it is hoped that this work will not only encourage the subsequent study of definitive volumes on the various movements and personalities involved, but that it will lead to the first-hand understanding and enjoyment of the visual arts in Australasia, and eventually of art achievements in countries overseas.

We should like to pay tribute to the contributors in Australia — Mrs Margel Hinder, Mr Ken Reinhard, Mr Peter Newell — and in New Zealand to Dr Sid Mead and Mr Hamish Keith. To Mr Harold Greenhill, too, we record our thanks for his insightful reading of the text and for the many valuable suggestions which he offered.

Maurice K. Symonds
Coll Portley
Ralph E. Phillips

Acknowledgments

The authors and publisher wish to thank the museums, galleries and private collectors indicated in the captions to illustrations for permitting the reproduction of works from their collections. Throughout this book, photographs have been provided by the owners or custodians of the works, except for the following photographers and agencies, whose assistance is gratefully acknowledged:

Aerofilms Ltd, London **4, 190**
Agence Top, Paris **57**
Alinari-Anderson, Florence **34, 35, 120**
All Saints' Parish Church, Earls Barton **51**
Montserrat Blanch Almuzara **80**
John Baker, London **312**
Joachim Blauel, Munich **242, 249**
E. Boudot-Lamotte, Paris **67**
Brompton Studio, London **240, 260, 279**
J. Allan Cash, London **78, 79, 320**
L. C. Clarke, Sydney **344**
Commissariat Général au Tourisme, France **38**
Durham Dean and Chapter **53**
Giraudon, Paris **66, 70, 75, 77, 218, 219, 221**
The Green Studio Ltd, Dublin **59**
Hamlyn Group Picture Library, London **105, 106, 107, 110, 111, 225, 252, 254, 265, 266, 276**
Gregory Heath, Sydney **332, 333, 334, 335, 336, 337, 340, 341**
J. Henshaw, Sydney **342**
Colorphoto Hans Hinz SWB, Basle **1, 32, 241**
Max Hirmer Fotoarchiv, Munich **23, 25**
Michael Holford, London **29, 62, 64 (lower), 91, 138, 140, 145, 153, 171, 211**
Illustrative Photography Ltd, Auckland **323, 329**
A. Irvine, London **310, 311, 318**
Japanese Embassy, Canberra **99**
Jarrold and Sons, London **65**
A. F. Kersting, London **36, 39, 45, 52, 54, 189**
Keystone Press Agency Ltd, London **319**
Mansell Collection, London **14a, 24, 27, 34, 37, 42, 85**
Erwin Meyer, Vienna **2, 48**
Antony Miles Ltd, Salisbury **64 (upper)**

David Moore, Sydney **343, 346**
Hans Nölter, Hanover **269**
Novosti Press Agency, London **50**
Orion Press, Tokyo **101**
Photographic Library of Australia, Sydney **93, 112, 113, 114**
Picturepoint Ltd, London **5, 17, 20, 21, 98, 104**
Paul Popper Ltd, London **6, 28**
J. Powell, Rome **87, 88, 90**
Presseamt der Stadt, Gelsenkirchen **308**
Gerhard Reinhold, Leipzig-Molkau **188, 221**
Ritter-Jeppesen Pty Ltd, Melbourne **331**
H. Roger-Viollet, Paris **69, 314**
E. R. Rotherham, Melbourne **339**
Jean Roubier, Paris **55, 56, 226**
Sakamoto, Tokyo **100, 102**
Scala, Florence **26, 41, 43, 44, 46, 49, 71, 72, 73, 74, 76, 121, 122, 123, 124, 125, 126, 127, 129, 130, 131, 132, 133, 134, 135, 136, 137, 139, 141, 143, 144, 146, 148, 150, 152, 154, 155, 156, 157, 158, 159, 161, 162, 165, 166, 169, 170, 172, 173, 186, 191, 212, 215, 216**
Elton Schnellbacher, Pittsburgh **275**
C. A. Schollum, Auckland **116, 117, 118, 119**
Tom Scott, Edinburgh **232**
Dr Franz Stoedtner, Düsseldorf **317, 321**
Ezra Stoller Associates, New York **322**
Eric Sutherland, Minneapolis **305**
Charles F. Uht, New York **307**
Malcolm Varon Associates, New York **285**
Victoria and Albert Museum, London **309**
S. Walker, Arcadia **347**
Woodmansterne Ltd, London **31, 61, 63, 68**
Alfred J. Wyatt, Philadelphia **262, 280**

The publishers also gratefully acknowledge the consent of the following for permission to reproduce subjects in this book:
© A.D.A.G.P., Paris, 1971 **274**
© S.P.A.D.E.M., Paris, 1971 **250, 251, 273**

PREHISTORIC ART

Prehistory refers to the period of human history before the invention of writing. Recent scientific research has shown that the world is about 4500 million years old, but man has only been on the scene for the last half million years.

Earliest man had no tools and built no shelters: apart from a few pieces of bone which have been unearthed, little is known about him. However, quite a considerable amount is known of man in later Palaeolithic times when glaciers from the north pole threatened his existence. During these glacial periods — four in all — man had to acquire vital skills in order to overcome the hazards of his environment. He needed clothing for protection from the freezing weather, and so had to learn the art of hunting large furred animals such as bears and bison. Thus man evolved a wide range of weapons — clubs, axes, knives and spears; later, spear-throwers were used to gain extra thrust. The word Palaeolithic ('old stone') refers to the symmetrical but roughly chipped stone implements produced at this early stage. With these tools, hundreds of which have been found in caves where he lived, man, being resourceful, survived the ice ages.

It was during this period about 40,000 years ago that man began to draw and paint. Whether his first efforts were accidentally, playfully or consciously wrought cannot be known, but it is widely accepted that prehistoric paintings and drawings are of a remarkably high artistic standard; in the twentieth century they have proved of great interest to artists and historians.

In prehistoric society, art and magic were very closely allied. To men's minds, a supernatural affinity existed between things that resembled each other; for example, the painted representation of an animal had the power to attract its live counterpart. The more accurately the image of the reindeer, bison, horse or mammoth painted on the cave wall resembled the actual animal, the more powerful the magic would be.

Frequently the cave artists painted arrows and spearheads on or near the animals which they depicted, indicating that prehistoric hunters may have carried out death-magic ceremonies prior to hunting. This magical aspect of prehistoric art is shown in [1], in which a flight of arrows converges on the galloping horse.

[1] Lascaux cave painting: horse with arrows, length 142 cm, *c.* 15,000-10,000 B.C.

[3] Painted Samarra pottery, fifth millennium B.C. British Museum, London

[4] Stonehenge, height above ground 4 metres, c. 1800-1400 B.C.: ground-level view from the east; aerial view from the north-north-west ▶

[2] 'Venus of Willendorf', limestone, height 11.5 cm, c. 15,000-10,000 B.C. Naturhistorisches Museum, Vienna

Most of the paintings that have been discovered have been located in caves which are almost inaccessible, generally deep underground, where no natural light penetrated. A possible explanation could be that the prehistoric artist did not want the animal or the spirit of the animal watching when he painted its image by grease-lamp or torch light; also, as some of the animals seem to move out of deeper recesses of the caves, the artists could have been interpreting the creation by the 'mother earth' of animals important to them.

Probably the best-known prehistoric art 'galleries' are to be found at Lascaux in France and Altamira in Spain. At Lascaux drawings and paintings reveal various stages in the development of Palaeolithic art, climaxing in the brilliant polychrome examples of horses and large bulls; at Altamira this development includes the use of relief surfaces to advance the thought that the bison painted on the cave ceilings are solid as well as vital. The prehistoric artist used natural earth colours — yellow and red ochres, and black made from carbon possibly mixed with animal fat. This aspect of prehistoric painting is discussed relative to the Australian Aborigine on page 57.

Apart from painting, prehistoric man carved in the round in ivory and stone, and engraved animals of the hunt on spear-throwers and other weapons. A significant piece of figure sculpture is the 'Venus of Willendorf' [2], a tiny 11·5 cm statuette carved in limestone. When the prehistoric artist carved the human body he was not as completely concerned with accurate or realistic representation as he was when he painted animals, and thus his own feelings determined the sculpture's form and significance. The 'Venus' has no facial details and only rudimentary arms; the emphasis is placed on the exaggerated breasts and hips, symbols of propagation of the race. It seems reasonable to assume that the 'Venus' was carved as a fertility charm.

The period which followed the last ice age about 10,000 B.C. is called the Neolithic '(new stone'), for ground and polished stone implements were now produced in contrast to the cruder artifacts of Palaeolithic times. Game was abundant and man adopted a more localized existence by building houses, domesticating animals, tilling the soil, weaving textiles and making pottery; artists decorated their pots by painting and incising them with geometric patterns. Neolithic pottery generally displays an appropriateness of decoration to form and of form to function, and the pots from Samarra in modern-day Iraq [3], made about 6000 years ago, exhibit superb craftsmanship and most effectively painted decoration.

From the first cave magic of Palaeolithic times to the

Neolithic period there evolved a religion based on the sun and heavens in relation to the earth and the elements; man was dependent on the sun, rain and seasons for food production, and it was therefore natural that he began constructing buildings to worship them. Perhaps the most famous example of Neolithic architecture is located at Stonehenge [4] on Salisbury Plain in England. Stonehenge, which was built about 4000 years ago, originally consisted of an outer circle, an inner circle and an inner horseshoe shape of upright stones. The enormity of the task of construction can be appreciated when it is considered that some of the stones had to be transported nearly 300 kilometres to the site on rafts, barges and sledges on rollers. While no satisfactory theory exists relative to the identity of the builders of Stonehenge, there seems to be conclusive evidence that it was a kind of astronomical calendar which forecast the seasons, moon phases, eclipses and other phenomena. Certain stones outside the perimeter of the main circle have been associated with the sun, and on Midsummer Day the sun always rises over the hele or sun stone.

Greater leisure time, mainly because of the development of agriculture and methods of storing food, allowed Neolithic man to use his mental capacities more and more. He learnt the art of combining copper and tin to make bronze, and later the use of iron was discovered. These and other innovations born out of necessity thus paved the way for greater achievements in succeeding ages.

EGYPTIAN ART

Prehistoric man's need for food constantly drove him to seek places where it was plentiful. If anything resembling a civilization was to be possible, it would have its beginning in those areas where there was sufficient food to support a large, stable community.

Because of the fertility of the Nile valley, and because of its isolated geographical position which protected its inhabitants from constant invasion, Egypt was able to develop a civilization thousands of years before our ancestors of the Western world even contemplated such things as the use of the wheel or living in houses. The Egyptians were sophisticated farmers, using irrigation to bring water to their crops; they invented a calendar with which they were able to measure time, and their buildings, many of which survive to the present day, prove their excellence in the field of architecture. However, perhaps the greatest achievement of the ancient Egyptians was the invention of writing. The civilizations of Egypt and Mesopotamia accomplished this at roughly the same time, and it enabled records of their knowledge and culture to be passed on to future generations.

The ancient Egyptian hieroglyphics ('sacred carvings') were made in picture form, and it was not until one of Napoleon's officers found the now famous Rosetta stone while repairing a fort in the Nile delta that the basic principles of the script were able to be worked out. With the solution of the mystery of hieroglyphic writing the world was able to read an almost uninterrupted record of 4000 years of ancient Egyptian history.

Prehistoric man was not able to devote much time to creating works of art or thinking about problems associated with his environment because the greater part of each day was spent in an endless search for food. It was only when man had leisure time that problems could be pondered and solutions to those problems sought. The ancient Egyptians living in the fertile Nile valley were among the first men to enjoy leisure periods, partly because of the benevolent nature of the river, which every year flooded and covered the river plain with rich silt; thus, until the water fell again, the land could not be worked.

Because the Egyptians were now not solely concerned with the problems of eating, sleeping and survival, they had time to consider things that were not strictly involved with self-preservation. They made objects that were ornamental and not useful or functional in the sense that weapons and tools were. They began to wonder about the world around them and their relation to the universe.

The men who attempted to solve problems of this nature, and who soon developed and stored a great body of knowledge on behalf of the community, were called priests. They were highly learned and greatly respected men who became guardians of thought and whose sacred task was to keep written records. The priests were also guardians of religion and performed ceremonies in the many temples scattered throughout the land. The ancient Egyptians believed in a life after death, where the soul after judgment entered the realm of Osiris who was ruler of both the living and the dead. The Egyptians also believed that no soul could enter the kingdom of Osiris without the possession of its earthly frame, so great pains were taken to preserve the body after death.

After a person died, the embalmed and heavily bandaged body was placed in a special coffin and housed in a tomb together with pieces of furniture, food supplies, musical instruments and little statues of attendants to make life more pleasant in the next world. Usually one or more statues of the deceased were also placed in the tomb to act as substitutes if the mummy was destroyed, because the Egyptians believed that the soul could move about freely and be transferred to an image of the dead person.

Just as religious customs dominated life in ancient Egypt, so religion was the chief influence in art. This is not to say that the only buildings constructed, sculptures carved and pictures painted were of a religious nature and concerned with preparation for the life hereafter; but most of the artistic achievements that have survived the ravages of time and looters have been those associated with religion, for example temples and tombs.

However, art forms not connected solely with religion have been found in tombs — pieces of sculpture, furniture, pottery, glassware, jewellery and personal trinkets. These reveal the tastes and interests of well-to-do Egyptians, while pictures and stories painted on tomb walls give us a good idea of contemporary Egyptian life.

Architecture

Early Egyptian houses were made of wood and thatch or dried mud bricks, and these have long since disappeared. The greatest of their buildings, many of which are still in remarkably good repair, were made of stone. Limestone and granite were readily available from the high cliffs on the Nile and vast resources of manpower were on hand during the annual flooding of the river when workers were unemployed.

Pyramid construction was one of the Egyptians' major engineering and architectural achievements. There are about thirty of these colossal tomb structures which rise impressively from the flat sands of the desert. The pyramid probably evolved from the mastaba (an arabic word meaning 'little bench'). This had a square base and sloping sides but was truncated, thus finishing in a flat or bench-like top. As additional height was given to the basic shape of the mastaba, it developed into the stepped pyramid, and this type of tomb structure was gradually modified until the strictly defined 'classical' pyramid design was arrived at. The core of the pyramid was made of limestone blocks and was faced with polished red granite slabs which reflected the sun's rays; the sun was an important religious emblem and assisted in reflecting the power and wealth of the pharaoh throughout the land. A system of inner chambers with false passageways and secret entrances was designed to protect the body and belongings from robbers and vandals. These measures largely failed, however, as most Egyptian tombs were plundered in ancient times.

The great pyramids are masterpieces of engineering; as far as we know, hand labour was used exclusively, and yet measurements vary only by millimetres over their vast dimensions. The line drawing [5b] shows the largest of the pyramids, the Great Pyramid of Cheops at Giza near Cairo, which was constructed almost 5000 years ago. It is solid except for the burial chamber of the king, the sloping corridor often called the grand gallery, two ventilation shafts and two smaller chambers. The Great Pyramid covers an area of 5·25 hectares and originally was 146 metres high; it is estimated that almost 2,500,000 blocks of stone went into its construction, which took 20 years; a work force of 100,000 men was used for 3 months every year during the annual Nile flood.

Echoing the stability, strength and mystery of the pyramids is the Sphinx [5a], which is in the form of a human-headed recumbent lion carved out of solid rock (with some stone blocks added). Although the Sphinx has been mutilated over the centuries it still stands as a grand monument. The small open temple between its paws indicates that it was used for religious purposes.

The Egyptian religion did not require vast spaces for congregations inside the temples, since only priests and kings were permitted to enter the sanctuary which housed the shrine and statue of the particular god to whom the temple was dedicated. The ancient Egyptians built in the trabeated (post and lintel) style, and because of the huge number of supports required to hold up a tremendously heavy, flat stone roof the interior of an Egyptian temple was virtually a forest of columns. An illustration of this is the enormous hypostyle (inner columned) hall of the Great Temple of Amon at Karnak [6], built by Rameses II. The gigantic columns shown are 3·6 metres thick and

[5a] The Sphinx (height 20 metres, c. 2530 B.C.) and the Great Pyramid of Cheops (c. 2570 B.C.), Giza

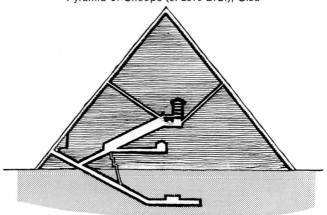

[5b] Sectional view of the Great Pyramid

[6] Hypostyle hall of the Great Temple of Amon at Karnak, c. 1260 B.C.

[7] Seated scribe, limestone, height 43.2 cm. *c.* 2400 B.C. Egyptian Museum, Cairo

[8] King Menkure and his queen, slate schist, height 138.4 cm. *c.* 2599-2571 B.C. Museum of Fine Arts, Boston

nearly 22 metres high; the incised hieroglyphics can still be seen clearly, and originally the columns were brightly painted. Notice that the columns end in a swollen capital or head; these particular capitals are in the shape of the lotus flower which grew in the Nile. The Persians, Greeks and Romans also used natural forms such as leaves, shells and plants in their column designs.

Sculpture

Because of the death cult where kings became gods after death, the builders of the ancient Egyptian monuments mastered the difficulties of working stone early in their history, and this subsequently led to the development of sculpture. The tombs erected to honour and protect the dead were generally huge, and sculpture was closely fused with architecture. Early Egyptian sculptures were carved from the front and side in much the same manner as a carved monumental building, and consequently most individual free-standing sculptured figures convey an impression of not having been completely freed from their stone bonds; they retain the solidity and stability of the original stone blocks from which they were cut.

Since the pharaoh was a god, statuary designed to perpetuate his soul was highly idealized: all lines of human weakness and deformity were removed and there was no suggestion of movement to conflict with the statue's serene monumentality. However, in the reign of the pharaoh Akhenaton, when the god-cult was abandoned, the recording of the royal family in painting and sculpture was realistic. Statuary of people other than the pharaoh-god sometimes revealed the reality of the human form and the inevitable ravages of life.

Another rule that had to be observed was that of 'frontality' in portraying the human figure. The body, whether seated or standing, was always represented in a symmetrical position; a line drawn vertically through the middle of the figure from head to groin divided it into two equal parts. These rules or conventions that applied to sculpture imposed a strict discipline on the artist and resulted in few technical changes in this art form over thousands of years.

Considering the limitations imposed on the Egyptian sculptor, it is remarkable that some statues could look so life-like and dynamic. The painted limestone statue of a scribe [7] portrays an educated man, a government official of ancient Egypt, seated cross-legged with his roll of papyrus (paper) resting on his knee, ready to take down his master's dictation. The face, framed by a wig, is most

6

[9] Amenemheb of Thebes, his wife and daughter fowling in the marshes, tomb painting, *c.* 1400 B.C. British Museum, London

lively. This liveliness is intensified by the eyes; engraved in copper, they hold an iris of clear quartz which reflects the light, and the whites are made of white limestone. Careful attention was paid to the modelling of the detail of the human figure, as the mouth, cheeks, arms, hands and chest demonstrate. The figure is symmetrically posed and the scribe embodies a remarkable expression of intelligence and alertness.

A sculpture of King Menkure and his wife, who reigned in Egypt over 4000 years ago, is portrayed in [8]. Although the pose is characteristically frontal and rigid, the sculptor working within very narrow conventions has managed to express the spirit of his royal subjects, thus rendering a highly personal portrait group. The figure of Menkure exhibits tension which is the result of the conventional pose — arms held stiffly by the sides with hands clenched. Menkure's wife seems more relaxed because her left forearm stretches horizontally across her body, thus breaking the rigid vertical. Note that the left legs of the couple are advanced and that all feet are placed firmly on the ground. This was another convention to be observed when sculpting free-standing figures. 'King Menkure and Wife' is carved in slate which is a very hard and very durable material intended to last throughout eternity. Although the sculpture is immobile and rigid in gesture, its combination of simplicity of form and spiritual intensity makes it a masterpiece of Egyptian art.

Painting

Painted reliefs were used to decorate the walls of palaces and tombs, their chief purpose being to supply the needs of the dead in the images that were represented. Although, as in sculpture, the artists followed strict conventions, Egyptian relief paintings display much more movement than sculpture, are more lively, and give a vivid impression of the busy life of the times. They often represented sowing, reaping, hunting in the papyrus swamps, fishing in the Nile and the preparation of food.

The fowling scene in [9] depicts Amenemheb of Thebes hunting in a papyrus swamp, accompanied by his wife and daughter. Amenemheb is painted much taller than his wife, and the child is dwarfed by comparison. This was a convention: Amenemheb was more important than both of them, so he was drawn larger. This painting also shows clearly the Egyptian formula for representation of the human figure. The shoulders and eye are portrayed as if seen from the front, the head and legs as if seen from the side. This formula was followed not because Egyptian artists could not draw skilfully, but possibly because this kind of portrayal created a more complete image of the person represented. By combining both profile and frontal views, the painting would have maximum effect on the spirits in the hereafter.

7

MESOPOTAMIAN ART

The valley of the Nile had attracted people to Egypt because abundant supplies of food were available for the minimum expenditure of labour. To the north-east of Egypt in western Asia (now Iran and Iraq) was another fertile valley between two great rivers, the Tigris and the Euphrates; this, the paradise of the Old Testament, was Mesopotamia, a Greek word meaning 'the country between the rivers'.

Although Mesopotamia was a tremendously rich agricultural area which enabled its people to develop civilizations at an early date, its central location made it a target for constant invasion from all sides by varied racial groups. This was a different story from that of Egypt, which was relatively isolated and generally free from invasion. Consequently the state of flux which was an ingredient of Mesopotamian culture had a marked effect on artistic expression.

The Mesopotamian story is one of ceaseless warfare and conquest. Because of the constant rivalry for possession of the most productive land it was largely a matter of survival of the fittest, and this is why the country produced such strong, dynamic people. The area was first controlled by the Sumerians, from the mountains of the north, forty centuries before the birth of Christ. The Sumerians were afterwards defeated by the Akkadians, and Mesopotamia was later variously inhabited by the Babylonians, Chaldeans, Hittites, Hebrews, Assyrians, Persians and others.

Mesopotamia lacks the great architectural ruins of Egypt because the vast supplies of stone required for massive buildings were not available in the region. Palaces and temples were built of sun-dried or baked bricks which disintegrated or were destroyed by conquering races over the centuries, and thus our knowledge of Mesopotamian architectural styles depends on archaeological restorations.

Besides availability of materials, environment is one of the most important factors which governs the style of architecture used in any country. The Mesopotamian region was damp, hot and subject to flooding, so all important buildings were constructed on high platforms.

Climatic conditions in Mesopotamia also played a significant part in the formation of religious beliefs, particularly those concerned with the idea of immortality of the body. While the dry climate of Egypt was one of the factors responsible for a cult preoccupied with life in the hereafter and corporeal immortality, the damp climate of Mesopotamia might have precluded the development of similar concepts. This may be why the tomb did not exist as a dominant architectural form in Mesopotamia.

Architecture

The outstanding type of architectural structure in Mesopotamia was the palace, with its temple tower or ziggurat. The Sumerians came from the mountains and had been used to worshipping their gods on the tops of hills, so after they entered the land between the rivers they constructed artificial hills on the summits of which they built their altars. These early ziggurats were not unlike the stepped pyramids of Egypt and the much later pyramids of Central America. In the reconstruction of the Ziggurat of Ur [10], notice the use of ramps to connect one level to the next — you may have recognized that this device is used in modern buildings such as railway stations and sporting stadiums. In addition, excavations at Ur have revealed long stairways to the top of the first platform.

Mesopotamian cities had impressive gates. These too were made of unbaked bricks, and like the buildings were faced with glazed ceramic tiles. This decoration not only added brilliance to the surface but also had the functional purpose of shedding water which would erode the structure. The most famous city gate constructed in the history of Mesopotamia was the Ishtar Gate, dedicated by the Babylonians to Ishtar, the goddess of love. The gate, and the walls of the Royal Processional Street into which it led, were covered with turquoise-blue tiles and adorned with golden lions and griffins [11]. The Babylonians succeeded the Assyrians as masters of Mesopotamia; as well as the Ishtar Gate, Nebuchadnezzar, King of Babylon, built a temple tower (the Tower of Babel of the Old Testament), and the famous Hanging Gardens where exotic vines and flowers cascaded from arched balconies. The Mesopotamians used and developed the arch, dome and vault, and so were pioneers in the use of these architectural devices that influenced later building throughout the world.

Sculpture

Because most stone had to be imported it was greatly prized, and because of the great distances involved there was a limit to the size of stones that could be transported to the region; thus most Mesopotamian stone sculpture is small. Since the sculptors lacked granite or marble they mostly turned to metal, bronze, gold, silver and ivory. Mesopotamian sculpture generally is more emotionally expressive than the symbolic sculpture of Egypt, but it still echoes the formality, frontality and highly stylized techniques of contemporary Egyptian work.

[10] Sumerian architecture: reconstruction of the Ziggurat of Ur, *c.* 3000 B.C. University Museum, Philadelphia

[11] Babylonian sculpture: lion from the Royal Processional Street, Babylon, glazed brick relief, 106.7 x 228.6 cm, *c.* 604-561 B.C. Museum of Fine Arts, Boston. Maria Antoinette Evans Fund

[12a] Akkadian sculpture: head of an Akkadian ruler from Nineveh, bronze, height 30.5 cm, *c.* 2300-2200 B.C. Iraq Museum, Baghdad

[12b] Sumerian sculpture: Gudea, governor of Lagash, diorite, height 76.8 cm, *c.* 2290-2255 B.C. British Museum, London

The symmetrically balanced head of an Akkadian ruler [12a] was cast in bronze after having first been modelled in clay, and the inherent plastic quality of the original material has been retained. Note the detailed modelling of the perfectly groomed beard, the stylized herringbone eyebrows and fastidious hairstyle. The sculpture displays a sheer delight in pattern and shows great skill in organization; above all, it is a significant achievement as an interpretation of the human head. The Sumerian sculptor who carved the diorite figure of Gudea [12b] has balanced the formality of presentation with a dignified expressiveness, created by the strong and highly-finished modelling of the features in this intractable stone medium.

[14a] Assyrian sculpture: dying lioness, limestone relief from the palace of Assurbanipal at Nineveh, height of figure 34.9 cm, c. 668-662 B.C. British Museum, London

[14b] Assyrian sculpture: lion hunt, seventh century B.C. British Museum, London ►

[15] Persian lion roundel, gold, diameter 10.5 cm, fifth-fourth century B.C. Oriental Institute, University of Chicago ►

[16] Persian ibex head, bronze, sixth-fifth century B.C. Metropolitan Museum of Art, New York. Fletcher Fund, 1956 ►

[13] Assyrian sculpture: winged guardian bull from the gate of the palace of Assurnasirpal II at Nimrud, alabaster, height 262·9 cm, ninth century B.C. Metropolitan Museum of Art, New York. Gift of John D. Rockefeller Jr, 1932

Perhaps the most powerful and dynamic people to rule Mesopotamia were the Assyrians, who built great cities like Nimrud and Nineveh. The Assyrians lined the walls of their palaces with stone reliefs, and carved, human-headed, winged bulls flanked their entrance gates to act as guardians. The huge stone monster illustrated in [13] stood guard over the palace of Assurnasirpal II at Nimrud. It is made of alabaster and carved partly in the round and partly in high relief. Two legs can been seen from the front and four from the side, but when viewed diagonally, five legs appear. This was done so that it was possible to get a complete view either way. The winged bull is highly conventionalized in style, and the feathers, beard, hair and muscles are fashioned into patterns very similar to those of the head in [12a], though they are less exaggerated.

One of the Assyrians' favourite sports was hunting lions with bows and arrows, and it was in the field of animal sculpture that the Assyrian sculptor was most proficient. Among the numerous hunting reliefs from the Assyrian period, the most powerful and most harrowing is that showing the dying lioness [14a]. It has tremendous emotional impact, and we feel much sympathy for the lioness; mortally wounded by three arrows, one of which has smashed her spine, she drags her paralyzed body forward defiant to the last. In [14b] this dynamic force is again apparent, despite the formal nature of the composition. For vitality, movement and power in portraying animals in action, the Assyrians have few equals.

The Persians, although contemporaries of the Greeks and great admirers of their art, were uninfluenced by them, preferring to borrow early Mesopotamian art forms and motifs. The Persians perfected the techniques of metal casting and produced magnificent objects in gold, silver and bronze. Two such examples of their craftsmanship are illustrated here. The lion roundel or medallion [15] was designed as a personal ornament, and its winged, prancing stance reflects the influence of the Assyrians and Babylonians. The wonderfully sensitive bronze ibex head [16] again reflects the formality and eye for pattern, most delicate in this case, of the older Mesopotamian cultures.

AEGEAN ART

Before the rise of Greece, two great civilizations flourished in the Aegean world, one on the island of Crete and the other on the Greek mainland at Mycenae. For centuries, the cities of these civilizations provided the background to the legends of King Minos, the Labyrinth, the Minotaur and the famous hero, Theseus. However, it was not until the latter part of the nineteenth century and the early part of this century that archaeologists uncovered the ruins of these civilizations and provided a basis of reality for the legends.

The culture of the Cretans (or Minoans, after the legendary King Minos) reflects an almost totally different attitude to life from that of the Egyptians and Mesopotamians. This attitude is revealed in their works of art: the fresco paintings on the palace walls are of sunny landscapes, joyous processions, dancing scenes and athletic contests, and there is a complete absence of the violence, warfare and bloodshed which was a major preoccupation of Mesopotamian art.

One of the reasons why Cretan art is so cheerful and does not exhibit the gloom prevalent in much Egyptian and Mesopotamian art was that the Cretans lacked the artistic restrictions imposed by a dominant priest class. Thus, the Cretans were not greatly concerned with the building of temples and tombs associated with religion and death, and their art was secular and worldly. This worldliness or sophistication was gleaned from many sources, for the island of Crete was strategically placed as the centre of trade in the Aegean, and the Cretans travelled in their ships far and wide trading with their neighbours. As a result they grew wealthy and powerful, so powerful in fact that at the height of their civilization they controlled the whole of the Aegean region.

According to legend, the mainland city of Athens was required to send King Minos a yearly tribute of youths and maidens, who were then shut up beneath the palace in the complex of passages called the Labyrinth, with the half-human, half-bull monster known as the Minotaur. The Greek hero Theseus came to Crete as one of the sacrificial youths, and killed the Minotaur with the help of Ariadne, daughter of King Minos. The foundations of this legend are readily apparent when one considers the complex layout of the 'Palace of Minos' at Knossos, and the frequent appearance of the bull motif in the wall paintings.

Some idea of the style of palace architecture created by the Cretans can be gained from [17]. Painted, tapering wooden pillars supported wooden beams and flat stone roofs, and brightly coloured frescoes adorned painted stucco walls. The whole effect is one of light, space and colour. Modern conveniences such as running water and baths were incorporated and almost total emphasis was placed on interior comfort and convenience. Decorative wall paintings indicate that the Cretans were slender, graceful, and elegant in their dress and manners. They took great pains over their clothes and hairstyles, and present a very stylish appearance to modern eyes.

Even the containers in which they transported olive oil and wine to their customers in the Mediterranean world were a delight to the eye. The containers the Cretans used were beautiful pottery vessels like the jars shown in [18a and b], ranging from delicate thin shapes to man-sized storage jars. The maritime influence on Crete (and the island's strong artistic influence on mainland Mycenae) can be seen in the recurrence of decorative marine motifs, either naturalistically or conventionally designed, on Cretan and Mycenaean pottery. The naturalistically painted nautilus and the dolphin on the jars illustrated here are beautifully arranged so that their forms naturally and gracefully follow the curved surface of the vessels.

Although the Cretans had no hierarchical priesthood, built no temples and created no monumental religious sculpture, they did make offerings to fertility gods who provided crops and attended to the change of seasons. In Crete the main deity was the snake goddess, a statuette of whom is illustrated in [19]. This tiny figurine with two serpents coiled up its arms is made of ivory and gold. One of the chief religious symbols of both the Cretans and the people of the mainland city of Mycenae was the downward-tapering pillar. The Cretans used this 'mushroom-shaped' pillar in their architectural forms (refer back to the illustration of the palace of Knossos), as well as in isolation. In the Lion Gate at Mycenae [20], this pillar is carved on a triangular stone slab above the main gateway to the city, and it is faced by two guardian lions whose paws rest on its base.

The athletic Cretans' most popular religious ritual probably took place in the bull ring, where gymnastically inclined youths and maidens performed bull dances. From the fresco illustrated in [21] and from written sources, it would appear that teams competed in this ritual. Their aim was to complete a handspring over the charging animal, using the horns to obtain leverage. As the bull lowered its head to gore the competitor he grasped the horns, and when the animal thrust its head upward the athlete would vault over its back. The performer was

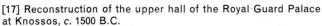

[17] Reconstruction of the upper hall of the Royal Guard Palace at Knossos, c. 1500 B.C.

[18a] False-necked jar with dolphin and shells, Late Minoan, c. 1300 B.C. British Museum, London

[18b] Jar with nautilus and rocks, Mycenaean, 1500-1400 B.C. British Museum, London

[19] Minoan snake goddess, ivory and gold, height 22.9 cm, c. 1500 B.C. Museum of Fine Arts, Boston

steadied on landing by a supporter who ran in behind the bull. All such Cretan murals as 'Bull Dancers' were executed in the true fresco technique, in which the colour and design were applied directly to the wet plaster. This technique requires rapid execution and confidence, because when the wall dries no changes can be made; perhaps this factor contributed to the animation and spontaneity of Cretan paintings.

Eventually the magnificent civilizations of the Aegean peoples came to an end. Invaders from the mainland and earthquakes probably accounted for the decline of Crete, and Mycenae was destroyed by the Dorians from the north.

[20] Lion Gate, Mycenae, 1350-1300 B.C.

[21] 'Bull Dancers' fresco from the palace of
Knossos, height approx. 60 cm, *c.* 1500 B.C.
Iraklion Museum, Crete

GREEK ART

The Dorians wiped out all memory of Cretan and Mycenaean culture; with the Ionians, another Indo-European race, they resettled the Greek mainland and Crete, and moved as far east as Asia Minor. These invaders were wanderers, and since Greece is divided by mountains and seas into fairly isolated valleys and numerous small islands, the Greek or Hellene society became fragmented. Although it lacked the general stability and unification that were characteristic of the two great empires of Egypt and Mesopotamia, Greece was marked from its earliest days by a powerful spirit of independence and individual aspiration; this applied in all fields of human endeavour — art, religion, philosophy, politics and commerce. The Greeks were the first people to experiment with self-government and it is from them that we learned the meaning of democracy — government by the *demos* or people.

The Greek ideal of life was moderation in all things. Their houses were very plain, lacking the comforts that today we regard as essential. Their foods were simple and spare, for they regarded eating as a necessary function and not in the main a pleasurable activity. What was important, though, in connection with food was the discussion that accompanied it. They dressed very simply and personal ornaments were kept to a minimum.

This ideal of moderation which pervaded all Greek thought forced them to strive for perfection, and they believed that perfection was not possible without moderation. Consequently, in their artistic endeavours the Greeks avoided ostentation, working on a scale that related to man and with forms that they attempted to refine towards perfection.

After the destruction of the Cretan and Mycenaean civilizations, many centuries passed before old artistic freedoms were revived or rediscovered. By about the seventh century B.C. a style that is now called Archaic had evolved. This style was primitive by later standards, but attempts at naturalistic expression are obvious. By the early fifth century B.C. Archaic characteristics were refined and a Transitional period (between Archaic and Classic) was evidenced.

It is important to realize that this evolution was gradual and varied between different areas; the dates and time spans mentioned here must be regarded as being flexible, for no firm line of demarcation can be drawn between the end of one period and the beginning of another.

The culmination of Hellenic ideals was realized in the Classic age, or the Golden Age of Athens, a very brief period in world history but one which had far-reaching effects and whose spirit has been a source of inspiration to most Western cultures ever since.

Although the last period of Greek art, the Hellenistic, lacks pure Hellenic features, it is very important for it marked the wide dissemination of Greek culture with the establishment of a Greek world empire. During the Hellenistic period, true Greek art became mingled with Oriental and 'barbarian' styles. In Italy it became known as Graeco-Roman, in Egypt, Ptolemaic, and in Mesopotamia, Seleucid. It took a particularly strong hold in the Roman world and consequently was transmitted to Western Europe.

Archaic Age

The most obvious influence on Archaic art seems to have been that of geometry, but this is understandable when one considers that Pythagoras was formulating his geometric theories during this period. Archaic buildings were heavy-looking, simple and formal, perhaps partly influenced by Egyptian temples, and sculptures appear to have been marked out precisely in sections before carving. Even the paintings on pottery are precise and seem to have been based on geometrical concepts.

The statue of a goddess with pomegranate [22], a votive-offering figure (korai), is an example of this influence in sculpture in which the figure has been thoughtfully considered as a geometric unit. The clothing falls in ornamental geometric patterns and the hair is carved in balanced curls. To achieve a certain amount of human expression, the sculptor has curved the eyes upwards and the lips are drawn back into what is now called an 'Archaic smile'.

The tiny Treasury of the Athenians [23] is a stone building; although stiff and primitive by later Greek standards, it represents the first attempts at the monumental architecture which attained perfection during the Classic period.

Archaic potters were also conscious of geometry. In [24] can be seen a painted drinking cup by Exckias, showing Dionysus sailing the sea; rhythmically leaping dolphins, subtly spaced, develop the quality of movement in the kylix. The curve of the ship's sail is balanced by the curve of the keel, and from the sail spring vines laden with grapes, symbolic of Dionysus, the god of wine. The painting is composed with a strong feeling for decorative pattern.

[22] Goddess with pomegranate from Keratea, Attica, marble, height 196.2 cm, sixth century B.C. Staatliche Museum, Berlin

[23] Treasury of the Athenians at Delphi, 515 B.C.

[24] Interior of a cup by Exekias showing Dionysus crossing the sea, diameter 30.5 cm, c. 535 B.C. Antikensammlungen, Munich

[25] Apollo: central figure from the west pediment of the Temple of Zeus at Olympia, marble, over life-size, c. 465-457 B.C. Olympia Museum

Transitional Period

This period is marked by a gradual refinement of the primitive features of the Archaic, and it produced forms that we associate today with the Classic age of Greek art. In sculpture, facial expression changed from the Archaic smile to an expression of serene dignity. Much of the statuary still exhibits the tension of Archaic sculpture, but now the gods are more human and the humans more god-like.

The central figure of Apollo [25] from the pediment of the Temple of Zeus at Olympia illustrates these properties. Tension is apparent, but the techniques of stone carving are obviously more refined, knowledge of human anatomy is greatly advanced, and the facial expression is not forced.

One of the best examples of this period and one of the best-known of all Greek sculptures is the statue of a discus thrower by Myron [26]. It represents an athlete poised and momentarily balanced at the end of a backward swing during the throwing of the discus: the facial expression is rather passive — a feature in keeping with the restraint of traditional Classic sculpture. The creation of this statue marked an innovation in Greek sculpture in that it was an experiment aimed at depicting complete freedom of action, while still retaining equilibrium. This was made possible by the perfection of the technique of bronze

[26] 'The Discus Thrower' by Myron: life-size Roman copy in marble of the bronze original of c. 450 B.C. National Museum, Rome

casting; the original was cast in bronze, but this has unfortunately been lost and the statue illustrated here is a marble copy which is now in Rome.

When we think of Greek sculpture we generally think of carved marble statues, but the bulk of Greek sculptures were cast in bronze. Because bronze sculptures were cast hollow, they were fairly light and were easily carried off by plunderers to be melted down for various purposes; thus there are relatively few bronze sculptures from ancient Greece in existence.

Classic Age

The culmination of the Greek style of architecture and sculpture occurred under the leadership of the eminent statesman Pericles, when the Acropolis at Athens was rebuilt after having been destroyed by the Persians. Pericles directed the famous sculptor Phidias to gather the best artisans in the country for the project.

The Acropolis [27] was built on a flat-topped hill which towers above Athens, and featured many temples associated with Athenian religious festivals and processions. The chief building was the Parthenon [28], a shrine dedicated to the maiden Athena, the patroness of Athens.

The primary purpose of Greek temples was the protection of sacred carved statues. In the case of the Parthenon, it was a statue of Athena made of ivory and gold, 12 metres high, that was to be suitably housed. As the Greeks were vitally concerned with moderation and perfection in all things, their temples (including the Parthenon) were comparatively small in scale. Since their religious worship took place outside the temples, there was no need for them to accommodate large assemblies. Because the temple was to be viewed by the majority from the outside, much attention was given to its position and its external appearance.

Greek architecture was based on the simplest form of building, the trabeated principle of construction, in which the roof was supported by beams (the entablature) and the beams were supported by piers or columns. The use of the column became the most distinctive feature of Greek architecture, and Greek architects concerned themselves with the relationships between columns and structure. The Greeks discovered some fascinating solutions to the problem of optical illusion, and incorporated these refinements in their buildings in an attempt to achieve aesthetic perfection. They made the shafts of columns swell slightly, the distortion increasing upwards to a maximum at half of the height, and then decreasing; this swelling is called 'entasis' and was used to counteract the suggestion of concavity which results from straight-sided columns. Similarly, horizontal lines were curved upwards a little

[27] Reconstruction of the Acropolis, Athens

to counteract their apparent sag. Note that practically all Classic columns have 'diminution': their diameters diminish as the shafts rise.

Every Greek temple was built according to one of three architectural plans or 'orders'. An order consists of three parts: a base, columnar supports, and a superstructure of lintels and sloping roof. Three orders evolved in the Greek style — the Doric, the Ionic and the Corinthian — differing from each other in the type of column capital and in the proportions of the three parts. The Parthenon was designed in the Doric order, like the Treasury of the Athenians [23].

To understand and appreciate Greek architecture, especially the Parthenon, more fully, it is necessary to know some terminology associated with the style. The walled-in or solid part of the temple is a rectangular chamber called the cella, functioning as a naos or shrine room. Its walls are extended at one end to form the pronaos or anteroom, and this porch was usually repeated at the other end as a rear portico (opisthodomus). To support the roof, larger temples sometimes had a single or double row of columns in the cella, while the whole temple was often surrounded by a continuous row of columns (a colonnade or peristyle). Facing out above the porticos at each end are triangular spaces created by the shape of the gable roof; these are called pediments, and they were filled with free-standing sculptures.

As mentioned previously, the most important element in Greek construction was the column. The shafts of stone columns were fluted (grooved), and were composed of a series of drums usually held together by metal dowels or clamps as no mortar was used. Doric order shafts rest directly on the upper step or stylobate of the triple-stepped base. The superstructure which rests on top of the column is called the entablature and comprises three distinct parts; the lower member is called the architrave, the next is the frieze, and above these two horizontal sections is a heavily projecting moulding called a raking cornice.

The Parthenon [28] is the finest example of the Doric order and is one of the most perfectly proportioned buildings ever erected. Iktinos and Kallikrates, the two architects who designed the Parthenon, built it so that it dominated the highest part of the Acropolis and its continuous colonnade could been seen from any point in Athens. The rectangular plan of the temple shows a double cella: one room, the naos, served to protect the statue of Athena, while the other housed treasures of the temple. It has a portico at each end and is completely surrounded by columns. Eight columns can been seen from the ends and seventeen from the sides.

The Parthenon exhibited a superb union of architecture and sculpture. Free-standing sculptures were located in the triangular pediments at each end of the building. Ninety-two metopes carved in high relief dominated the outer frieze which is part of the entablature, and an inner frieze carved in low relief ran right around the top outer walls of the double cella, just behind the columns. The inner low-relief frieze represented the procession from the Great

18

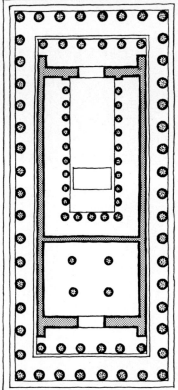
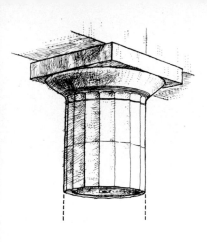

[28] The Parthenon, Athens, 448-432 B.C.

Panathenaic ('all Athens') festival, which took place every four years in honour of Athena.

A portion of this processional frieze, showing youths on prancing horses, is illustrated in [29]. This frieze was located inside the colonnade away from the bright sunlight which bathed the outer sculptures. The carving is in low relief because this technique presents more flat surface area and fewer shadows are cast, so that details are clearly defined by light reflected from the temple's base.

On the other hand, the sculpture of the Three Fates [30] stood in sunlight on the east pediment. Pedimental sculptures were carved in the round and strong contrasts of light and shade enhanced their three-dimensional form. In this group, note the magnificent handling of the drapery; this was carved to produce a masterly pattern of flowing grace and yet achieve the reality of a covering for solid flesh, as it appears to cling like wet material to a living form.

A detail of a very famous building on the Acropolis, the Erechtheum, is shown in [31]. Because the Greeks were deeply concerned with the representation of the human figure in sculpture, and since the column was a very important feature in architecture, it is not surprising that some imaginative architect eventually experimented with a 'human' column. In the Porch of the Maidens [31], female forms (caryatids) are used to support the entablature. These figures bear the weight elegantly and effortlessly, as each stands relaxed with one knee slightly bent.

[29] Parthenon frieze: horsemen in the Panathenaic procession, marble, height 101.6 cm, c. 440 B.C. British Museum, London

[30] The Three Fates, from the east pediment of the Parthenon, marble, over life-size, c. 438-432 B.C. British Museum, London

19

[31] Porch of the Maidens, Erechtheum, c. 421-405 B.C.

Greek painting is known to us almost exclusively from pottery. Pots were produced in a wide variety of shapes for many purposes. In keeping with the Greek ideal of simplicity, basic colour schemes were used; the chief wares produced were black-figured and red-figured. Black-figured pottery was decorated with black designs outlined on a red clay body. Red-figured pots were produced by covering red-bodied clay vessels with black slip (semi-liquid clay), and scraping away parts of it to expose the red undersurface.

A beautiful example of black-figured pottery of the fifth century B.C. is a vase on which is painted Achilles slaying the queen of the Amazons, Penthesilea [32]. The painter has arranged the forms of the ruthless Achilles, the resigned victim and the accompanying figures to conform to the shape of the vessel.

Hellenistic Period

The Hellenistic world of the Greek empire brought wealth, an international outlook, and the wide dissemination of Greek ideas. It was also marked by the sacrifice of the Classic ideals of harmony and perfection to expression and heightened naturalism. This, however, was a natural consequence of the Hellenistic mastery of techniques and increased knowledge of the physical world. Thus, armed with this knowledge and technical expertise, Hellenistic artists explored the whole spectrum of human experience — love, hatred, suffering, sleep, old age, death — subjects that would not have interested or appealed to Classic artists.

The result of this new outlook was a more individualized form of expression, intense, realistic and unrestrained. The best artists produced magnificent works, but less disciplined artists produced highly exaggerated, laboured pieces which only have technical dexterity to commend them.

The 'Mosaic of Dionysus' [33] is part of a large design which was set into the floor of the House of the Masks on the island of Delos in the Aegean Sea. This mosaic depicts the god holding a tambourine in one hand and his thyrsus (staff) in the other, mounted sideways on a fierce leopard; despite the stiffness and rigidity that are generally associated with mosaics, this example reflects a remarkable degree of vitality and realism.

[32] 'The Death of Penthesilea', vase painting, diameter 45.7 cm, c. 460 B.C. Antikensammlungen, Munich

[33] 'Mosaic of Dionysus', second century B.C.

ETRUSCAN AND ROMAN ART

ETRUSCAN ART

The Etruscans probably settled in western and central Italy about the tenth century B.C., and they came to dominate most of the country before being conquered by the Romans. It seems that the Etruscans migrated to Italy from the Aegean area. They were great sailors and traders like their Aegean ancestors, and had much contact with Greece and Asia Minor. It was natural, therefore, that Etruscan art would be influenced by art forms from these countries. Although it does exhibit both Greek and Oriental characteristics, the Etruscans never slavishly copied or imitated and their art retained a distinctive flavour of its own.

No Etruscan buildings survive because they built mainly in wood, which is an impermanent material; however, remnants of semicircular arches, some stone constructions and underground tombs remain. The Romans later used Etruscan building techniques, chiefly the arch, in their architecture.

The most significant works of Etruscan art that have come down to us are stone, terracotta and metal sculptures, and vivid tomb wall paintings. The Etruscans seem to have preferred working in terracotta and bronze rather than in stone for their sculptures. A delightful life-size terracotta couple that surmount the lid of a sarcophagus or carved stone coffin are shown in [34]. As well as ordinary burial the Etruscans practised cremation, and the ashes of cremated persons were placed in decorated funerary urns. The Etruscans believed that the soul survived death, and care was taken to suitably enshrine either the ashes or the body of the deceased. The smiling faces of this couple resemble those of the Archaic period of Greek sculpture, and they have a marked Mesopotamian appearance. This was due to the influence, as mentioned before, of both Greece and Asia Minor on Etruscan art.

The 'Capitoline Brutus' [35], a bronze portrait, is a fine example of the quality of realistic portrayal attained by Etruscan artists in this medium. The rhythmic details of hair, eyebrows and beard contrast strongly with the firmness of the nose and the penetrating eyes. The genius with which Etruscan artists could express such forceful individual personalities greatly impressed the Romans, who later excelled in the art of portraiture.

[34] Etruscan sculpture: painted terracotta sarcophagus, length 2 metres, sixth-fifth century B.C. Villa Giulia, Rome

[35] Etruscan portraiture: 'Capitoline Brutus', bronze, height 32 cm, third century B.C. Palazzo dei Conservatori, Rome

[36] Colosseum, Rome, A.D. 72-80

[37] Baths of Caracalla, Rome, A.D. 211-217

ROMAN ART

Rome had become the cultural centre of the Mediterranean world by about 146 B.C. and remained so until the fourth century A.D. Before the emergence of Rome as a world power, the Etruscans had been the chief disseminators of Hellenic ideas in Italy. The Romans were greatly impressed by Greek art and absorbed all they could find. But eventually the dynamic and progressive Romans evolved their own style, although Greek influence, particularly that of the Hellenistic period, remained strong.

Conquest opened the way for the spread of Rome's civilization. Cities sprang up in Spain, France and England, and Roman government, language and customs were imposed on the indigenous cultures. The successful administration of the great empire required the building of roads, bridges, sewers, aqueducts and public buildings, and the Romans' most important contribution to the history of art probably lies in their architectural engineering.

Architecture

Of all styles of architecture, the Roman ideal is nearest to the modern in its emphasis on utility, massiveness and magnificence, and in its adaptability to fulfil the needs of later civilizations. The great buildings of the Romans were made possible by the development of engineering principles which included the use of the arch and the vault, and the discovery of concrete.

The Romans' chief engineering problem was how to enclose and roof a vast space to contain crowds without cluttering up the interior with columns, as in Egyptian and Greek buildings. Obviously a flat-roofed structure provided no answer. The problem was solved by the use of the arch. The Romans joined together a succession of arches resting directly on the side walls and made the simplest arch system, the barrel vault. Barrel vaults were made of stone masonry, brick or concrete. The method of concreting was similar to that used today. A framework of wooden scaffolds held the mass of concrete in place until it set. Variations on the same theme included the groined vault, which resulted when barrel vaults were set at right angles to each other, and the dome. Buildings constructed in this fashion presented rough or raw surfaces, so they were faced with stucco, sheets of marble or bronze, and elaborate floor mosaics were laid. This method of facing concrete work is still used in building today. Public utilities — paved roads, bridges, aqueducts, tunnels, sewers and canals — were constructed solidly.

The Colosseum [36] is perhaps the most famous of all Roman ruins. It was an amphitheatre which comfortably seated about 50,000 people while they watched 'games' which included bloodthirsty gladiatorial contests and

[38] Pont du Gard, Nîmes, height 48.8 metres, 27 B.C.-A.D. 14

[39] Arch of Constantine, Rome, A.D. 312-315

[40] The interior of the Pantheon, Rome, A.D. 118-125: painting by Giovanni Panini (c. 1740). National Gallery of Art, Washington D.C. Kress Collection

possibly sea battles. The vaults were made of poured concrete and the three tiers of arches were framed on the exterior by the three classical Greek orders, the Doric, Ionic and Corinthian, in ascending order. Under the arena was a maze of cells, passages and dens for wild animals used in the spectacles.

Another building that was designed for mass accommodation and entertainment and which employed concrete vault construction was the Baths of Caracalla [37]. The illustration shows that groined vaults were used to create a vast interior space, and the huge columns served to emphasize the interior height. The vaults were faced with coloured marble and stucco ornamentation and the floors were patterned with mosaic, which gave tremendous richness to the design.

Perhaps the greatest structural achievements of the Romans were those that were designed for pure utility: roads, bridges and aqueducts. The Pont du Gard [38], one of the finest Roman aqueducts, is located near Nîmes in southern France. With its three tiers of rhythmically repeating arches, it has a powerful visual impact on the spectator. Aqueducts carried water to cities by gravity flow and were made of solid stone; no mortar was used to join the masonry. These utilitarian structures are among the most beautiful of all Roman constructions, yet they were designed from a purely functional viewpoint and not an aesthetic one.

The Arch of Constantine [39] was built to commemorate the military triumphs of the emperor of that name. It is an ornate monument; low relief carvings recounting the victories of Constantine and his deeds of chivalry cover almost its entire surface. Triumphal arches and columns were often erected to glorify military leaders and their victories abroad.

The most important temple constructed by the Romans was the Pantheon [40], which embodies all the finest aspects of Roman architecture and is the best preserved of all ancient monuments. The Pantheon is a circular building with walls 6 metres thick supporting a dome, at the top of which there is an opening (oculus or eye) 8·5 metres in diameter. It is said that the eye is symbolic in that it opens to the heavens, the home of the numerous gods to whom the temple was dedicated. It provides a source of light, but allows rain to enter (the water, however, flows away through gratings in the floor). In the illustration the niches provided for statues of the gods can be seen. Most impressive is the underside of the dome with its five ranges of square coffers; the coffers derived their shape from the way the dome was constructed, concrete having been poured into a framework of brick squares.

[43] 'Hercules Finding his Son Telephos' fresco from Herculaneum, first century A.D. Museo Nazionale, Naples

[42] 'Marcus Aurelius Receiving Conquered Barbarians', A.D. 161-180, Palazzo dei Conservatori, Rome

[41] Portrait of the emperor Augustus, marble, height 2.03 metres, *c.* 10 B.C. Vatican Museum, Rome

Sculpture

The Romans were realists by nature, and Roman sculpture is characterized by intense realism. As mentioned previously, Greek ideals of beauty first came to the Romans via the Etruscans, and with the conquest of Greece in 146 B.C. huge numbers of Greek works of art were brought to Rome as plunder. So popular did Greek art become that Greek artists were imported to make copies of great masterpieces to adorn the homes of wealthy Romans. Ancestor-worship made the demand for portrait busts and statues great, and sculptors could scarcely keep up the supply.

Illustrated in [41] is a very dignified statue of the emperor Augustus; although it shows the classical Greek traits of naturalism and idealism it also displays the Roman characteristic of individualism. The stance of Augustus, with one foot advanced and right arm raised, suggests that he is addressing his army. The absence of footwear and helmet symbolizes courage, and the tiny carved figure by his leg represents Aphrodite, the goddess of love from whom the imperial Roman dynasty was supposed to have descended.

One of the most intelligent and just rulers of the Roman empire was Marcus Aurelius, depicted in [42] receiving conquered barbarians. Nearly 200 years separate the creation of this relief sculpture from the statue of Augustus. The most striking feature of this work is its realism: it does not exhibit the idealism that marks the portrayal of Augustus; far from being idealized, Marcus Aurelius is a little 'paunchy' and battle weary. Note the attempt made in this relief to achieve greater realism by representing space. Although the human figures are very prominent and practically fill the foreground, they are arranged so that they recede into deep space. This is achieved by overlapping the figures and horses in four or five ranges.

Painting

Roman painting continued the fluid style developed in the late Classic and Hellenistic Greek periods, and many of the masterpieces that remain are to be found on the walls of villas in Pompeii and Herculaneum.

Roman painters experimented with three-dimensional effects, and the artist who painted the picture of Hercules finding his son Telephos [43] was concerned with the same problems of spatial representation as the sculptor who carved the Marcus Aurelius relief. The solid, sculptural treatment of the figures, the heightened emotional expression, and the concern for the atmospheric treatment of space in this painting were to influence later periods of art.

24

EARLY CHRISTIAN AND BYZANTINE ART

EARLY CHRISTIAN ART

The inevitable decline and disintegration of the Roman empire saw the gradual ascendancy of the Christian church, whose spiritual impetus had been greatly strengthened by persecution during the previous centuries. In A.D. 313 the emperor Constantine was converted and official toleration was secured for Christianity, so that eventually it was established as the state religion of the Roman empire.

During the period when Christians were persecuted they met secretly for worship in the catacombs, which were a series of narrow underground galleries and tomb chambers beneath the city of Rome. On wall surfaces that were generally covered in stucco, they drew in charcoal and painted in earth colours pictures of gospel stories and martyred Christians. In [44] is illustrated the raising of Lazarus from the dead. The technique is very sketchy and tentative since the painter was almost certainly not a trained artist, and as you might anticipate, the figure of Christ reflects contemporary Roman fashions in clothing and hairstyle.

When Christians were allowed to build public places of worship, the need to accommodate growing congregations created an unprecedented church building boom. Unlike the pagans, who concentrated on exterior beauty in their religious buildings, the early Christians emphasized the beauty of the interior, and it was not until the Gothic period at the end of the Middle Ages that the ideal of external as well as internal beauty was fully realized.

The interior of St Paul's Outside the Walls at Rome is shown in [45]. This basilica was rebuilt on the site of

[44] 'The Raising of Lazarus from the Dead', catacomb wall painting, Rome, *c.* 80 x 110 cm, late third century A.D.

[45] Interior of St Paul's Outside the Walls, Rome, rebuilt 1823 from original begun in A.D. 386

[46] 'The Good Shepherd', marble, Lateran Museum, Rome

the original church over the tomb of St Paul. The nave or centre aisle walls rest on Corinthian columns and rise higher than the side walls, forming a clerestory for lighting and leaving a wall space between the arcade and the windows. This space is decorated with mosaic portraits of saints and other religious personages.

The rhythmic repetition of the nave arcade leads the eye to the semicircular apse which contains the altar, where the most important part of the Christian ritual takes place. The apse of the early Christian basilica had no windows and was a very effective location for mosaics, which glowed out of the gloom.

Most early Christian sculpture was crude by classical standards and dimensionally was small (see the half life-size statue of the Good Shepherd [46], representing Christ as a youth). These features are attributable to the poverty of the early Christians and to the association of monumental sculpture with pagan graven images, which later proved to be a controversial issue in the early church. Some of the most important examples of early Christian sculpture are found on sarcophagi executed in the Roman and Etruscan tradition but using Christian symbols and narrative.

BYZANTINE ART

Before Christianity officially became the Roman state religion, vigorous Christian communities flourished in the eastern half of the empire. The emperor Constantine selected the wealthy and powerful city of Byzantium as the capital of the eastern empire, and in A.D. 330 it was renamed Constantinople in his honour.

It was here that Greek, Roman and Eastern artistic influences amalgamated to form what is known as Byzantine art, the Christian art of the East. In the Byzantine civilization the emperor had supreme authority over the army, government and church. Everyone and everything had to serve the throne, in much the same way as all things were subservient to the state in ancient Egypt. Now, just as artistic expression in ancient Egypt was restricted for this reason, Byzantine art also manifests similar rigid, unyielding characteristics.

Architecture

The Byzantine empire reached its first great peak of power, its first Golden Age, in the sixth century A.D. during the reign of Justinian, when many of the great buildings in Constantinople and in the Byzantine outpost of Ravenna in Italy were constructed. From the Romans, Byzantine architects derived the use of the arch, the dome and concrete construction; from the Greeks, conscious awareness of the great classical tradition was gained, and

Eastern influences are apparent in the preferences for square or central plans and in the handling of colour. However, the Byzantine architecture of Ravenna in Italy followed the traditional basilican rectangular shape and plan.

Because they preferred central plans for their churches, the Byzantines were confronted with the architectural and engineering problem of constructing a circular dome on a square base of columns and arches. This was solved by the use of pendentives, which are triangular corner pieces resembling the groined vaults of Roman constructions.

The most impressive of Byzantine buildings, the cathedral of Hagia Sophia [47] dedicated to the Holy Wisdom of Christ, was the greatest built during the reign of Justinian. With its magnificent dome and rather bulky stone exterior it has been likened to the Pantheon [40]. Although there are resemblances, the Pantheon had a very thick circular wall and the dome rested directly on it. In Hagia Sophia, the dome is supported by pendentives which rest on four enormous piers in each corner of the square, central part of the building. The weight of the dome is therefore concentrated on these four points, thus creating a large unbroken space inside the church. (See the accompanying sketch.)

These four supporting piers are heavily buttressed on the exterior of the north and south sides, and on the east and west façades the dome receives additional support from a series of half and quarter domes which transfer the downward thrust in stages to the ground.

The interior of Hagia Sophia glowed with mosaics which were illuminated by a multitude of windows in the walls and in the base of the dome itself. These mosaics were painted over by Moslem conquerors who added the minarets, or slim, lofty towers. In recent years the mosaics have been restored to their former brilliance, and Hagia Sophia is now recognized as one of the world's major architectural achievements.

[47] Hagia Sophia, Istanbul, A.D. 532-537

[48] Portrait of a Byzantine empress, ivory, c. A.D. 800. Kunsthistorisches Museum, Vienna

Sculpture

During the Iconoclastic Controversy in the eighth and ninth centuries the worship of images was considered idolatrous, so the representation of man in religious art was forbidden. Since three-dimensional sculpture was discouraged, Byzantine works were flat and served a largely decorative function.

Reliefs in ivory like the portrait of a Byzantine empress [48], which are more closely related to drawings in relief than sculpture, were not outlawed, and this example typifies the artistic marriage of Eastern and Western styles. The canopy is supported by debased Graeco-Roman Corinthian columns, but the staring, oval-faced, bejewelled figure is Oriental in style.

[49] 'The Betrayal', mosaic, sixth century A.D.
San Apollinare Nuovo, Ravenna

[50] 'Virgin of Vladimir', tempera on wood, 100 x 70 cm,
c. A.D. 1125. Tretyakov Gallery, Moscow

Mosaics

A mosaic is a surface design of small pieces of stone and glass called tesserae, pressed into a background of cement; because of the nature of the medium, mosaics are assembled rather than drawn and are made up of coloured patches rather than lines. Some of the best-known mosaics are in the churches and tombs of Ravenna, which as mentioned before was an outpost of the Byzantine empire in Italy.

The early sixth century mosaic panel illustrating the Betrayal [49] is from the nave of the church of San Apollinare Nuovo, and is one of a series of mosaics depicting episodes from the life of Christ. The betrayal of Christ is shown in stark narrative form with two groups confronting each other. Judas is shown leaning forward to kiss Christ, while Peter grasps the hilt of his sword to cut off the ear of Malchus.

The Byzantine tradition did not end with the fall of Constantinople in the fifteenth century. Elements of the style survived in Central and Eastern Europe and in Russia until the revolution of 1917. In [50] is illustrated a marvellous Byzantine icon, the 'Virgin of Vladimir', now in Russia. The Byzantine artist who painted this icon in the twelfth century has imbued the Virgin with tenderness, grief and a humanity that marks a change from the rather forbidding holy figures of an earlier era.

THE EARLY MIDDLE AGES
AND ROMANESQUE ART

While the Byzantine empire progressed independently in the east, the close of the fifth century marked the final disintegration of the Roman empire in the west. The Germanic peoples, who had acquired much of the imperial Roman domains, had largely been converted to Christianity, and the early church assumed the leading role in European society. The amalgamation of the church, the former barbarians and the remnants of the old Roman empire was the basis for the civilization of the Early Middle Ages in Western Europe. Thus the art of the Medieval period reflects the mingling of these disparate elements — Christianity, barbarism, and remnants of Graeco-Roman culture. The barbarians were nomads and their art forms were, of necessity, portable; basically their contribution could be of a decorative nature only, and it is seen in their personal ornaments, weapons and harness trappings. The church, however, was primarily interested in increasing the Christian population; since prospective Christians were illiterate barbarians, the church was more concerned with utilizing art as a vehicle of propaganda to teach the gospel than it was with 'art for art's sake'.

During the Dark Ages monumental sculpture and painting almost vanished, and since city life had practically disappeared, architecture was of a minimal standard. In the period of Charlemagne and the Holy Roman empire, the arts were temporarily revived; the most striking example of Carolingian architecture in England is the west tower of All Saints', Earl's Barton [51], built around A.D. 930. However, in the ninth and tenth centuries Western Europe was again plunged into darkness and chaos. Foreign trade was cut off by the Moslem blockade of the Mediterranean, and a series of terrible invasions by the Norsemen, Slavs and Magyars saw the collapse of the Holy Roman empire and the birth of a monastic-feudal culture.

In this culture the Christian monasteries were the strongholds of learning and art. During the eleventh century, church construction was revived after a lapse of some centuries. (One reason given for this is that people became interested in the future again, since the prophesied end of the world in the year 1000 did not eventuate.) The power and wealth of the church made it the only organization that could give large architectural commissions. This growing awareness of the plastic arts in the later Medieval period resulted in techniques of the classical past being relearned or rediscovered; the architectural style that emanated from the period is called Romanesque, a term which originated from the use of the true round-headed or Roman arch and is generally applied to art

[51] Western tower of All Saints', Earl's Barton, Northamptonshire, c. A.D. 930

forms of the eleventh and twelfth centuries. However, Romanesque was not a standardized style and it varied widely in the Western European countries — Italy, France Germany, Spain, Norway and England — because of differing geographical, religious, political and social conditions.

Architecture

In England, the Romanesque style was introduced in 1066 by William the Conqueror, and thus it was called Norman. William built many sturdy castles and inaugurated a vast church-building programme using Saxon labour. One of

29

[52] St John's chapel in the White Tower of the Tower of London, 1087

his projects was the magnificent St John's chapel [52] in the Tower of London, constructed in 1087. The illustration shows clearly the massive solidity of Norman architecture, as exemplified in the thick walls and huge supporting columns.

The Normans built mainly with small stones, and construction methods relied purely on the dead weight of the walls to take the sideways thrust of the roof structure. In addition, Norman walls and cylindrical columns were not solid, for they had an outer facing of stone and were filled with rubble.

One of the finest and most dynamic of all English Romanesque buildings is Durham cathedral [53], built between the years 1093 and 1133. Some idea of its size may be gauged from the three-storeyed building in the illustration, which is dwarfed by comparison. Durham's high location and massive twin towers add to its fortress-like appearance. It stood, in common with all Romanesque churches, as a bastion of faith against the evils of the world. Many cathedrals and churches had sections built on to them in subsequent years, and the tall square tower that can be seen behind the twin towers was added to Durham in the fifteenth century. The towers, which are impressive features of Norman cathedrals, housed bells to ring the hours of worship or warnings of flood, fire or invasion.

In Italy, Romanesque builders often constructed the bell tower or campanile apart from the church itself. The most famous bell tower in the world is the Leaning Tower of Pisa [54], built in the twelfth and thirteenth centuries.

[53] Durham cathedral, 1093-1133: view from the River Wear

[54] Pisa: the Leaning Tower and the cathedral, from the east

Sculpture and the Crafts

There is little sculpture of the Romanesque period that can be discussed in isolation, for it is closely wedded to architecture. During the Dark Ages, practically all artistic techniques including sculpture had been lost. When churches started to be built again sculpture was needed to enrich them; but the tradition of monumental sculpture had died, and the stone carvers generally turned to illustrated manuscripts in the monasteries for both subject matter and methods of treatment. Thus most of the early Romanesque sculpture was of a decorative and ornamental nature; however, it abounded in invention and vitality as it sought to master long-lost sculptural techniques.

Although the huge cushion capitals of the columns in St John's chapel in the Tower of London are fairly plain, others like the beautiful winged monster capital from Chauvigny [55] are highly decorative. This capital in a French Romanesque church could almost be a caricature of an Assyrian guardian bull [13], but it was probably based on a winged lion pattern from China. The influence of these non-European cultures is attributable to pilgrimages to the Holy Land, and the fact that many people, including sculptors, travelled far from Europe. This monster, symbolizing evil, would probably have been really terrifying to an illiterate twelfth century peasant.

One function of Romanesque sculpture was to teach the gospels and to graphically emphasize the message that without the church's help man was condemned to the horrors of hell. The most impressive sculpture of every church was generally carved on the tympanum or semicircular area over the main entrance. Perhaps the finest of the great Romanesque tympanums or portals is in the church of La Madeleine at Vézelay, showing the Pentecost when the Holy Spirit descended on the apostles [56]. Here the majestic figure of Christ offers a welcome to the passerby and the lines which radiate from his right hand symbolize the promise of divine mercy. The figures in the box-like compartments above the apostles represent the people of all nations with whom the apostles were able to speak, because of the miraculous gift of tongues at Pentecost. In the same chapter from this gospel is a prophecy of the world's doom and salvation for the faithful: the small figures carved on the lintel at the bottom of the picture represent the procession of souls coming to judgment.

Some of the best surviving examples of figure sculpture from this period are in wood, like the little statue of St Foy [57]. The wood was covered with beaten silver and gold and encrusted with precious stones. This reliquary encloses a fragment or relic of the saint's body, and in Medieval times would have drawn pilgrims from afar to pay homage.

[55] *Left:* Winged monster capital from Chauvigny, twelfth century

[56] *Below left:* Tympanum in the narthex of La Madeleine at Vézelay, showing the Pentecost, *c.* 1125-30

[57] *Below:* Reliquary statue of St Foy, wood covered with gold and silver, height 85 cm, tenth century. Abbey of Conques, Aveyron

[58] Walebone carving of the Adoration of the Magi, English, height 35 cm, early twelfth century. Victoria and Albert Museum, London

[59] Initial page from the Book of Kells, parchment, 33 x 24 cm, eighth century. Library of Trinity College, Dublin

Ivory and whalebone carvings were made in England in the Romanesque period and one of these, showing the Adoration of the Magi, is illustrated in [58]. You will probably notice a resemblance between this twelfth century English carving and the ninth century 'Byzantine Empress' ivory [48]. During the Iconoclastic Controversy of the eighth and ninth centuries a great number of Byzantine priests and artists were forced into exile, and many of them settled in England where they exerted a considerable influence on the religious arts. The 'Adoration of the Magi' is less Oriental than the 'Empress', but still exhibits the round face and bulging eyes of its Eastern relative.

Irish Manuscript Ornamentation

In the fifth century A.D. the Angles, Saxons and Jutes invaded England, scattered the Celtic Britons and drove their priests and monks to Ireland. During the Dark Ages, Ireland became a refuge for Christianity and many monasteries were founded there; the writings of the church fathers were studied and preserved for posterity, and one of the most famous and most extravagantly ornamented manuscripts produced in Ireland is the Book of Kells from the eighth century. In [59] can be seen an initial from the gospel of St Matthew. The other three gospels also have highly decorative initial pages, and these dynamic designs are among the most intricate ever produced. Many of the motifs have Eastern origins, and their incorporation into the traditional Celtic patterns produced some of the finest examples of decorative art.

The Bayeux Tapestry

The Bayeux Tapestry is not really a tapestry, but is an embroidery in wool on a linen strip about 50 cm wide and 70 metres long. It recounts the events that led to William the Conqueror's victory over the Anglo-Saxons in 1066. It was made in either England or Normandy, and derives its name from Bayeux cathedral in Normandy where it was exhibited for centuries after the Battle of Hastings.

Technically it is a masterpiece, and historically it is very important for it tells us much about the ship design, costumes, armour and warfare of the period. Designed like a cartoon strip, it was easily 'read' by the illiterate, while the Latin phrases appealed to the educated. The detail illustration in [60] shows the Norman invasion fleet crossing the English Channel in boats with prows carved like Viking longships.

[60] Bayeux Tapestry, wool embroidery on linen, c. 1073-1083: the Norman invasion fleet crossing the Channel. Bayeux Museum

GOTHIC ART

During the later Romanesque period, feudalism as a system of government grew weaker while individual kings grew more powerful. This trend was intensified by the Crusades, which both strengthened national identities and united many kingdoms in Western Europe as they made a concerted effort to defeat the infidel Moslem and to extend Christianity.

During the Crusades (1096-1291), Europe came into contact with Byzantium and the Near East; the Crusaders brought back wonderful tales of wealth, exotic foods and spices as well as art and learning. Curiosity about these fabled lands resulted in voyages of discovery like Marco Polo's expedition to China, India and Persia, and new trade routes over land and sea hastened the growth of towns which became very prosperous. However, many of the nobles who had taken part in the Crusades returned to their estates penniless: they found a new town life firmly entrenched and many of the town traders more wealthy than themselves. Further, the towns offered better social conditions and employment opportunities to the oppressed peoples of the feudal system, and this resulted in the formation of a new cultural climate.

The Gothic Cathedral

The spirit that marked the growth of the towns is reflected in the growth of thought and learning of the age. Universities were established and new ideas flourished; the greatest expression of this awakened intellectual, spiritual and social freedom was the Gothic cathedral. (The term 'Gothic', first used during the Renaissance, was intended as an expression of contempt for the 'barbarity' of the style.) The cathedral became the focal point and showpiece of the new, independent and vigorous town. In fact, so intense was the enthusiasm of the people that everyone from prince to peasant helped in some way in its construction.

The cathedral was not only the spiritual centre — it was the community social centre as well. It was large enough to house the population of the entire town for special occasions such as Christmas and Easter. The market place was nearby, mystery plays were performed before it, and it was a source of instruction for the illiterate: stories from the Bible and local history were dramatically presented in carved stone and stained glass. One of the most spectacular of the Gothic cathedrals is at Chartres [61], 80 kilometres from Paris. Begun in the twelfth century, it is considered to have the finest examples of stained glass in Europe, as well as thousands of superb pieces of sculpture. Some of these are illustrated in [66] and [70].

The growing religious freedom and unfettered spirit of the Gothic age led to a new concept in church architecture. Gothic builders strove to achieve a more open, better lighted and taller structure that would match the new aspirations and idealism of the period. To achieve previously undreamed-of heights (see [62] showing the interior of Amiens cathedral where the vault is 42 metres high), a new method of construction had to be invented, because the stone barrel vaults of Romanesque churches exerted so much downwards and outwards thrust that walls had to be made extremely thick, thus limiting the interior height.

During the Crusades much was learnt about Eastern, particularly Saracen, engineering and this helped European engineers to understand properly the thrusts set up inside a structure based on arches. The innovations that enabled Gothic builders to erect towering churches were the pointed arch and the flying buttress. The drawing on page 34 illustrates how in pointed arch construction the weight of the stone vaulting is concentrated on four corner piers from which the vaults spring. These points were heavily buttressed to take the downwards thrust, and because there was no downwards pressure exerted between the arches, Gothic craftsmen were able to fill wall spaces between the buttresses with large windows of stained glass.

The thrust from vaulting is not only downward but outward as well. The outward thrust had to be met by a counterthrust if the thin walls were not to be pushed outwards. The function of the flying buttress was to supply this counterthrust by taking the weight of the nave roof and vaulting, and passing it downwards and outwards to the massive outer buttresses rising from the ground. In the illustration of Chartres cathedral [61] you can see how flying buttresses functioned.

A fascinating internal buttress arrangement can be found in Wells cathedral in England; [63] shows one of the unusual buttress arches at the crossing of the nave and transept. This clearly demonstrates how the weight of the square tower is transferred to the ground via these beautiful arches placed point to point. English Gothic cathedrals like Wells and Salisbury [64] were lower and narrower than their French counterparts, because English builders were less interested in thrust and abutment, relying more on thick walls to support the vaulting, as did Romanesque builders before them. Thus the buttress, especially the

[61] Cathedral of Chartres, begun *c.* 1145, rebuilt 1194-1220: view from the south-east

[62] Interior of Amiens cathedral, begun 1220: the nave, looking east

[63] Wells cathedral (*c.* 1230-1260 and later): inverted arches at the crossing, from the south transept (arches added *c.* 1340)

flying buttress, never developed in England as it did in France.

As mentioned before, most cathedrals do not belong strictly to any one period. Many took several generations to complete, and the transition from one period to another was gradual; thus many cathedrals exhibit features of several styles. Salisbury cathedral, however, was completed in the short span of thirty-eight years (1220-1258) and is constructed entirely in the 'Early English' style, except for the spire which was completed in the later 'Decorated' period. The cathedral is situated away from the bustle of the town, and its noble appearance and serenity are enhanced by the spacious areas of trees and grass. In the aerial photograph you can see the enormous square tower and crowning spire, the tallest and most beautiful in England. Also visible on the left is the cloister or covered walk which encloses an open courtyard, and behind the cloister is situated the octagonal chapter house where the business of the cathedral is transacted.

In the climax of the English Gothic period — the 'Perpendicular' style — the vaulting system becomes so complicated that it is difficult to distinguish between the functional and purely decorative ribs. The vaulting of King's College chapel, Cambridge, is shown in [65]; here, however, the solidly built vault is above this fan-like surface which is purely ornamental.

Sculpture

The growing spiritual and intellectual freedoms of the Gothic period are exhibited in cathedral sculptures whose aim was to present the entire Christian panorama. Many of the churches of the Gothic period are overwhelmingly sculptural; Chartres, for example, has more than 8000 stone sculptures. One would think that churches displaying so much sculpture would appear outrageously ornate, but the concentration of sculpture around the portals is just as well integrated into the overall design as the arches and flying buttresses.

Naturally the earliest sculptural attempts were rigid, like the kings and queens of the Old Testament [66] from the west portal of Chartres, which seem to be stone copies after drawings in manuscripts. People entering the church had to pass these majestic figures which, despite their integration with the architectural setting, still maintain a degree of independence. Although the stylized drapery and hairstyles and the stiff, unnatural poses closely resemble the Romanesque, their softened forms and expressions reflect the new humanity of the period.

Gothic figures are far from the ideal beauty created by the Greeks, but they have a special beauty all their own that is often more intimate and more human. The smiling angel from Reims cathedral [67] typifies this. The figure is relaxed and animated by a friendly and intriguing smile,

[64] Salisbury cathedral, 1220-1258 (tower and spire, 1334-c. 1350)

[65] Fan vaulting at King's College chapel, Cambridge, 1508-1515

35

[66] **Kings and queens of the Old Testament, from the west portal of Chartres, c. 1145-1170**

differing from the strained and haunted figures of the Romanesque period.

Although most sculpture that adorned Gothic cathedrals was religious in theme, many of the decorated capitals represented the everyday life of the local people; the subject could be as incidental as stealing apples, or as human as the man with toothache in a carved capital from Wells cathedral [68]. How marvellously touching he appears with this perennial complaint, and how wonderfully the carver has incorporated him into the capital: the figure is not an addition but part of the overall design, and is as involved in the Gothic cathedral's decoration as the many saints.

The dominating image of the whole of Gothic art was the Virgin Mary to whom many cathedrals were dedicated, and usually one entrance was adorned with a representation of her. The Resurrection of the Virgin [69] was carved in the tympanum of Senlis cathedral in France at the end of the twelfth century. This is a good example of the progress in style and technique of Gothic sculpture when it is compared with the kings and queens of the Old Testament [66] from Chartres of the early part of the same century. It is obvious that as the style progressed sculptors grew freer with their tools and ideas, and began to base their designs upon subjects and actions from their own observations and not from manuscript drawings. Figures began to come to life away from the walls where they had been closely attached, and move about freely in a defined space, like these angels from Senlis cathedral which move gracefully and rhythmically round the Virgin.

[67] **Smiling angel from the west front, Reims, c. 1225-1245**

[68] **'Man with a Toothache', carved capital from the south transept of Wells cathedral, c. 1190**

[69] 'Resurrection of the Virgin' from the tympanum of Senlis cathedral, late twelfth century

Stained Glass

The structural methods of Gothic builders obviated the need for solid walls and gave Gothic craftsmen the opportunity to incorporate large stained glass windows into cathedral designs, thus linking the interior and exterior with a partly translucent wall, which provided luminous colour inside the church. The huge size of many stained glass windows called for glass painting in strong colours, and the windows of Chartres cathedral, considered to be the most impressive in Europe, are composed of small pieces of coloured glass, predominantly red and blue. The size of the pieces, the irregularities in thickness, and the bubbles and impurities contained in them produce a muted but vibrant radiance inside the cathedral.

One of the most celebrated examples from Chartres is 'Notre Dame de la Belle Verrière' [70]. The black lead strips holding the small pieces of glass in place, and the reinforcing bars, serve to emphasize the jewel-like brilliance of the translucent stained glass.

Painting

The development of humanistic expression that we have surveyed mainly in French sculpture in the preceding pages is also apparent in Italian paintings of the Gothic period. There are some reasons for this humanistic approach in Italy. Firstly, in the thirteenth century, two monks founded orders whose philosophy was based on humanity, love and gentleness; one of these monks, St Francis of Assisi, had such feelings of love and kindness that he called people, animals and the elements his brothers, while the other, St Dominic, founded a monastic order which trained the sons of the nobility and made the pursuit of education a noble undertaking. Secondly, Italy had never been cut off from the Mediterranean civilizations of Byzantium and Islam, and the influences from these regions, particularly the former, gave impetus to the pictorial arts.

[70] 'Notre Dame de la Belle Verrière', upper section of stained glass window from the choir of Chartres cathedral, 1194-1220

[71] Duccio: *The Maestà*, tempera on wood, 1308-11. Height 2.1 metres. Museo del' Opera del Duomo, Siena

[72] Simone Martini: *The Annunciation*, tempera on wood, 1333. 2.64 x 3.05 metres. Uffizi, Florence

The pioneer paintings have a strong Byzantine flavour, but a gradual evolution towards the representation of space and humanistic expression is obvious. We shall look at some paintings from Florence and Siena, the main centres of Italian Gothic painting.

Siena in the fourteenth century was a Medieval town where the Byzantine style of icon painting was strong. From the Greek traditions in Byzantine painting the Sienese developed a love for the graceful line, and the Oriental traditions are manifest in the richness of colour, particularly in the gold backgrounds and red and green garments. These characteristics are very clearly illustrated in Duccio's *Maestà* [71], which lyrically depicts Mary seated in majesty as Queen of Heaven, surrounded by her court of saints and angels. This painting was so well received that it was carried by the townspeople in joyful procession from Duccio's studio to the high altar of the cathedral.

Duccio's pupil, Simone Martini, advanced further his master's style, and his crowning achievement was the *Annunciation* [72], a two-dimensional, highly decorative linear masterpiece. Note the attention that the artist has paid to the rendering of intricate details of clothing, the Gothic arches which frame the group, and the so-called 'Gothic swing' in the depiction of the Virgin.

In Florence the first attempts in the 'new painting' were made by Cimabue, who still employed many of the elements of Byzantine icon painting, but who instilled into his figures a fresh humanity. On first observation the *Virgin and Child Enthroned* [73] looks very much like Duccio's *Maestà*, but this painting is a little softer and Cimabue has managed to represent a greater though still very limited sense of space.

The painter who finally broke through the 'Byzantine barrier' and whose discoveries changed the whole concept of painting was Giotto. By carefully observing men, women, animals, birds, hills and trees he drew them with less convention and greater insight, and when painting human beings in particular, he considered not only their form but their emotional reactions and gestures. In his fresco illustrating the flight into Egypt [74], the three-dimensional figures are placed in a defined space. Note particularly their gestures and the emotions conveyed by the various individuals in this drama, and you will see how very different this picture is from all of the Gothic paintings previously illustrated in this chapter.

[73] Cimabue: *Virgin and Child Enthroned*, tempera on wood, *c.* 1280-90. 3.85 x 2.24 metres. Uffizi, Florence

[74] Giotto: *The Flight into Egypt*, fresco, *c.* 1305-9. Arena chapel, Padua

[75] The Limbourg brothers: 'The Month of February', from *Les Très Riches Heures du Duc de Berry*, painting on vellum, page 29 x 21 cm, 1413-6. Musée Condé, Chantilly

International Gothic

At the end of the fourteenth century, artists travelled widely from one European country to another absorbing and exchanging different ideas, and soon it became increasingly difficult to distinguish an artist's national style. Art adopted a somewhat international character with an increased and sophisticated elegance and greater richness of detail. With the spread of literacy among the aristocracy there was a great demand for books illustrated with scenes mainly of contemporary life, and the greatest of the Gothic illustrators were the Limbourg brothers who worked for the Dukes of Berry and Burgundy.

Shown in [75] is a page from the Book of Hours, illustrating the month of February. It is an ambitious work; it depicts both interior and exterior activities that occur in winter, and contrasts the snugness of the peasant farmer's house with the bleakness outside. In an effort to give the picture depth, the Limbourg painters used converging lines in buildings, and painted figures smaller as they recede in the background. This is a very important work, for apart from its own artistic worth it exhibits acute observations of nature which make it a pioneer in the landscape tradition of painting.

Perhaps the greatest of all Gothic artists was Gentile da Fabriano, and one of the finest of all Gothic paintings is the *Adoration of the Kings* [76], which he painted early in the fifteenth century. Meticulous attention has been paid to details of costume and pattern, and it glows like an exotic tapestry. Although the processional figures in the background are smaller in scale than those occupying the foreground and the figures, including the animals, have solidity, Gentile was not overly concerned with these three-dimensional effects: he was more interested in rendering detail and decorative surface design, as this altarpiece illustrates.

Religious subjects painted in a naturalistic setting still predominated in the International Gothic period, but there was also a growing interest in portrait painting. Frequently these two elements were combined in 'donor' portraits, where the patron or donor appeared with Christ, the Virgin Mary or the saints. The donor portrait seen in [77] is the *Madonna of Chancellor Rolin*, painted by Jan van Eyck of Flanders. Flemish painters were preoccupied with the representation of space and naturalistic detail, and this very serious painting incorporates both these elements. The effect of depth in the picture is gained by the use of linear perspective, by the converging floor lines, and by aerial perspective where distant objects diminish both in size and in intensity of colour. One can see, almost feel, that in the middle of the composition there is a vertical axis, on the left and right of which van Eyck has balanced his subject materials.

[76] Gentile da Fabriano: *The Adoration of the Kings*, panel, 1423. 3.0 x 2.82 metres. Uffizi, Florence

[77] Jan van Eyck: *The Madonna of Chancellor Rolin*, panel, *c.* 1435. 66 x 62 cm. Louvre, Paris

ISLAMIC ART

During the Dark Ages of Western Europe when cultural activities were practically at a standstill, the Islamic empire flourished and at the height of its power extended from India in the east to western Africa and Spain in the west. The Islamic civilization was contemporaneous with the Byzantine, and Western Europe owes possibly as much to its influence as it does to the Byzantine.

The Islamic empire was established in the seventh century by the Arabian prophet Mohammed, who preached a religion based on submission (Islam) to the will of one god (Allah); its followers became known as Mohammedans or Moslems. Mohammedanism combined elements of Judaism and Christianity as well as some Persian and Arabic religions, and its scriptures were set out in the Koran. The remarkable success of the widely propagated Islamic religion was partly due to the simplicity of its clearly defined precepts, which the common man could follow without the assistance of numerous clergy (as was required in the case of Christianity). In addition, the influence of the Christian church was weakened at the time by a series of schisms or divisions owing to differences of opinion on doctrine, for these confused the ordinary man. Economic and political considerations were also significant in the spreading of Islamic influence; the Arabs wanted more land, and they had an efficient military force to fight for it.

As a result of their liberal attitudes in conquest, they mixed with other civilizations, absorbing and translating their cultures; thus Islamic art, indeed their whole culture, was eclectic in that it borrowed elements from all the civilizations on to which it was grafted.

The Moslems were not prejudiced against pagan learning like the Medieval Christians and were willing to learn from every source, so that when Baghdad became the centre of Islam, scholars representing all countries and religions were invited to study there. Ancient Greek philosophic and scientific texts, as well as mathematical and medical treatises, were translated into Arabic, the official language of Islam, by Arab, Syrian, Jewish and Persian scholars. It was from the Islamic universities and centres of research, especially those in Spain, that a vast body of knowledge was transmitted to Western Europe, via Jewish researchers who translated Arabic writings into Latin for Western scholars. It was only through Islamic theologians that St Thomas Aquinas in the Middle Ages was able to formulate a Christian philosophy.

Architecture

Because of the restrictions placed on the Islamic artist by religious texts that forbade the reproduction of animate forms (though this was not enforced in Persia and India), architecture and its decoration became the important Islamic art forms. Both of these were greatly influenced by the various cultures that the Moslems embraced, as these semi-nomadic people had no established architectural tradition.

[78] Minaret of Samarra mosque, Iraq, height 49 metres, tenth century A.D.

[79] The Taj Mahal, Agra, India, 1630-48

[80] Cappella del Mihrab, Umayyad mosque, Cordova, founded by Abd al-Rahman I in A.D. 785

[81] Carved wood panel from a caliph's palace, Fatimid period, Egypt. Cairo Museum

[82] Fragment of a Persian tomb cover or shroud: double-face compound twill weave silk textile showing a procession of ibexes, Buyid period (dated A.D. 998). 78.1 x 66 cm. Cleveland Museum of Art. Purchase from the J. H. Wade Fund

The minaret of Samarra mosque [78] illustrates how the Moslems utilized their Mesopotamian heritage in the construction of this prayer tower; with its spiral stairway which rises gently around a core of brick, it is reminiscent of the ramped stairways of the ancient Ziggurat of Ur [10].

Another example of the synthesis of Moslem and indigenous styles, and one of the most famous buildings in the world, is the Taj Mahal in India [79]. The Moslem Moguls from Persia conquered India in the sixteenth century, and it became customary for a Mogul emperor to build an impressive palace which would also serve as a mausoleum after his death. The Taj Mahal was built in the seventeenth century by Shah Jahan in memory of his wife and is situated in a magnificent setting of pools and gardens. The huge, lacy, bubble dome, the smaller subordinate domes and the delicate minarets at the corners of the building are features reminiscent of the Turkish-Moslem adaptations made to Hagia Sophia in Constantinople in the fifteenth century (see [47]).

In Spain the Islamic invaders were called Moors; one of the most famous examples of Moorish architecture is the mosque of Cordova, begun in the eighth century; [80] is a detail from this mosque, the Cappella del Mihrab, and could well be a setting from the *Arabian Nights* with its exotic Oriental richness. The Arabs loved the bright designs of Sumeria and the flowing, twining lines of Greek and Coptic Egyptian art, and they combined these elegant 'arabesques' or lace-like ornaments with strong contrasts of colour and shadow.

Sculpture

Although largely restricted in the realistic portrayal of living things, the Moslems created a highly ornamental system of geometric devices and made lavish use of animal, vegetable, floral and even human forms in carving. These decorative forms were not carved in the round as this was forbidden, so every figure was reduced to a two-dimensional surface. This can be seen in [81], which shows a wood panel from a caliph's palace in Egypt, carved in the eleventh century; the flat, symmetrically balanced human figures that stand out in silhouette are part of the overall design of intricate scrolls and twining leaves.

Textiles

Persian carpets are associated with wealth, splendour and colour, and have been imbued in stories with the magical property of being able to fly; however, the magical property of the magnificent tapestry illustrated in [82] is one of design. The central motif of the twin, stationary ibexes is beautifully balanced by a border of smaller, mobile ibexes,

44

[83 Persian manuscript painting:
'A Polo Game', Bokhara school,
manuscript of the Bustan by Sa'di,
sixteenth century A.D. Metropolitan
Museum of Art, New York.
Hewitt Fund, 1911

[84] Persian minai ceramic bowl,
decorated with underglaze colours and
enamels, late twelfth-early thirteenth
century A.D. British Museum, London

displaying a variety of attitudes as they prance along. The
design is full of vitality, and illustrates the creator's careful
observation of this animal's natural and varied movements.

Painting

In the sixteenth century, Islamic book illustration reached
its peak with results as bold and brilliant as any Persian
carpet. The manuscripts of Persia and India dealt with
scientific material, history, scenes of war, the hunt and
court life. The Persian manuscript painting illustrated in
[83] depicts a polo game. The figures are deliberately
painted flat and the whole scene is two-dimensional, linear

and decorative in character. Note also how the three panels
of abstract cursive lettering contrast without conflict with
the human and animal forms.

Pottery

The refined and rhythmical qualities of line and colour,
as well as seeming spontaneity, are also evidenced in Persian
ceramic forms. The bowl shown in [84] dates from the
twelfth century; notice how magnificently the artist has
placed the figures within a limited space and yet has not
overcrowded the design, and how masterfully they are
linked to one another by the decorative elements.

INDIAN ART

The art of India is as old as that of any other nation and its earliest expressions bear striking resemblances to the art of Mesopotamia, as these two nations bordered each other in the north-west. Besides being subjected over the centuries to such external modifiers as Greek Hellenistic influence with the invasion of Alexander the Great, and Islamic influences with the Moslem Moguls from Persia in the sixteenth century, India was the birthplace of many Oriental art styles just as Greece was the birthplace of Western art.

You will have observed that two of the greatest influences in the formation of an artistic style are philosophy and religion, which are closely interrelated; an understanding of these two factors is necessary for an appreciation of Indian art, because it is so different from the Western art with which we are generally acquainted.

The Indian artist was not so much concerned with the visual appearance of objects as with the feelings and ideas that objects conveyed. In other words, Indian art is more concerned with 'inner' rather than 'outer' vision. The Greeks, you remember, worked from nature and idealized it to produce artistic forms, considering all the while such things as realistic representation and proportion. Indian art forms, however, were the result of much contemplation of objects, usually by means of yoga; hence the Indian artist worked not from a series of visual images as did the Greeks, but from a series of mental images.

These conceptual or mental operations in the creation of Indian art forms functioned to express certain conditions or ideas in the minds of spectators. For example, in [91] is illustrated the dancing figure of Shiva. This was not simply created to represent a figure dancing, but is an attempt to express the condition or the state of dancing itself. This is a fairly subtle concept, but one that must be borne in mind when looking at Indian art. Art in India is not representational, nor is it idealistic. It is not 'art for art's sake', but functions in a very practical manner for the purpose of producing a desired mental or physical state.

As mentioned at the outset, religion as well as philosophy played an important role in the formation of artistic styles, and Indian art tells the stories of two important religious systems, the Hindu and the Buddhist. The Hindu religion developed first, while in the sixth century B.C. Buddhism was founded and its influence spread to Ceylon, Siam, Burma, Tibet, China and Japan. Many centuries later, however, Buddhism was replaced by a revival of Hinduism.

Architecture

We usually associate places of worship with churches which can accommodate large congregations, but many places of worship in India are solitary shrines where individual pilgrims pay homage. The stupa at Sanchi shown in [85] is one of eight funerary monuments in which the ashes of Buddha ('the enlightened one') were placed. A stupa is a large earth mound surrounded by a stone wall and carved stone gates. This stupa was built in the first century B.C. when Buddha was still considered too holy to portray

[85] *below left:* A stupa at Sanchi, early first century B.C.

[86] Bas-relief sculpture: 'The Gift of Amrapali' from Gandhara, second-third century A.D. British Museum, London

[87] Temple of Kandariya Mahadeo, Khajuraho, eleventh century A.D.

[88] Surya the sun god riding in his chariot, Konarak, thirteenth century A.D.

[89] Head of Buddha from Gandhara, Romano-Buddhist style, fourth-fifth century A.D. Victoria and Albert Museum, London

[90] 'The Descent of the Ganges': relief carving on a cliff at Mamallapuram, seventh century A.D.

in sculpture, so there are no images of him carved in this shrine. It was not until the second century A.D. that images of Buddha appeared in human form, as in 'The Gift of Amrapali' from Gandhara [86], a bas-relief sculpture which shows the early influence of Hellenism in north-west India. Prior to this time, Buddha was symbolized by animal forms.

With the revival of Hinduism, temple building flourished. Hindu temples are ornate, intricately constructed and present a grand effect, like the Temple of Kandariya Mahadeo at Khajuraho [87], built at the beginning of the eleventh century. Observe the small replicas of the temple itself repeated and grouped one above the other, following the upward surge of the main tower.

Sculpture

The three chief Hindu gods were Brahma the creator, Vishnu the preserver and Shiva the destroyer, and these gods took on many forms, both animal and human; much sculpture, which is the major art of India, was concerned with the portrayal of these gods in their various forms as well as numerous nature spirits. Illustrated in [88] is the magnificent Vishnu appearing as Surya the sun god riding in his chariot. The hierarchical relationship between the serenely majestic god and the attendant figures recalls the convention observed in the Egyptian fowling scene [9].

During the first century of the Christian era great trade routes carrying silk, gold and spices passed through the northern Indian domains on their way to the west, and sculptures of the period have a definite Roman or, more accurately, a Hellenistic flavour. The head of Buddha [89] clearly displays this classical influence. Note also the third eye of wisdom between his brows, the lump of knowledge that rises from his head and the long ear lobes — physical characteristics which Buddha was thought to have possessed.

Buddhist shrines like the stupa were relatively simple sculptural constructions, but the Hindu shrine was much more complicated, as in the relief carving of the Descent of the Ganges [90], dedicated to Vishnu. In [88] this god was carved as Surya the sun god, but here he appears as the Ganges River flowing down from heaven to water the earth. This illustration is only part of the whole complex sculpture which was carved on seven large granite boulders. Surrounding the gigantic elephants are carved thousands of figures and animals which do not appear to follow any set plan, unlike the sculptural decoration on Western shrines or churches. Compare this with the La Madeleine tympanum in [56].

Shiva, another Hindu god illustrated in [91] as Nataraja, lord of the dance, represented the darker powers of nature, yet paradoxically he was a creator as well as a

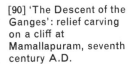

47

[91] Siva Nataraja, lord of the dance, South Indian bronze, eleventh century A.D. Height 95 cm. Musée Guimet, Paris

[92] Detail of fresco painting from Cave 1 at Ajanta, c. A.D. 600-64

destroyer. Shiva's four arms are required for the four functions he performs. In one hand he holds a flame, a symbol of destruction, and in another hand is a tiny drum to tap out the rhythm of things being born again. A third hand is held up as a gesture of reassurance, while the fourth points down to a dwarf on which Shiva dances, symbol of the many evils in the world.

Painting

The 'great' period of Indian history and art was the Gupta dynasty from the fourth to the sixth century A.D. This period has been likened to the Early Gothic period in Western art, because just as Gothic art created the typical Western image of Christ, so Gupta art determined the image of Buddha; the head of Buddha in [89] is a Gupta carving. One of the few paintings from this period that has survived the ravages of time is the fresco painting from a cave at Ajanta [92], which has nevertheless deteriorated over the centuries. The Bodhisattva ('Buddha-to-be'), depicted holding a lotus in his right hand, is surrounded by light-skinned and dark-skinned female figures, dwarfs and monkeys; their presence helps to emphasize the serene spirituality so characteristic of Buddhist works of the Gupta period. The fresco was originally painted with clear, bold lines (now rather faded) called the 'iron wire line', a method that had a profound influence on Chinese painting during the T'ang dynasty from the seventh to the tenth century.

CHINESE ART

Because of the immense size of the country, which is separarated from India by huge mountain ranges and from northern Asia by the high Tibetan plateau, China was able to absorb various invaders and achieved the most continuous and the most uninterrupted development of any civilization. When invading peoples did enter China through the northern gateways of Mongolia and Turkestan, the Chinese rulers simply retreated farther south to safety; the invaders, who were generally nomads, soon settled down to farming and became absorbed into the Chinese population. Weak rulers adopted this policy of contraction or withdrawal when challenged by 'barbarian' invaders, but stronger rulers pursued an expansionist policy by extending Chinese territories. Under expansionist leaders the Chinese empire extended by sea to Japan and by land to Burma, Indo-China and as far as India.

Although the country was often divided into numerous states, China was united by a common language and method of writing, and by uniform religious creeds, mainly Taoism and Buddhism (which was introduced to China in the first century A.D.). These two religions, together with the philosophy of Confucianism, had a marked influence on the development of Chinese art and were responsible for its continuity over the centuries, for the Chinese worshipped their ancestors and revered the past. Very few art forms, once developed, were ever lost to succeeding generations, and much Chinese art consisted of repeating the masterpieces of the past. Westerners might say that such activities were not creative, but this is not the point, for as mentioned in the introduction to Indian art in the previous chapter, Eastern art is not 'art for art's sake'; instead it is a springboard to the world of the spirit, via the ecstasy achieved through the contemplation and appreciation of the purity of form of a work of art, whether it be a piece of pottery, a jade carving or a painting.

Architecture

When compared with the architectural achievements of other civilizations, the contribution of China is not very significant. It was not simply because Chinese buildings were constructed of very light and perishable materials, mainly wood, that ancient examples (those before the twelfth century) do not exist; it was rather because the Chinese concept of architecture differed from that of other nations. To the Chinese a building was conceived as a

[93] Nepalese pagoda: Bhadgaon Nyatapola temple, A.D. 1708

[94] Ritual vessel in the shape of an owl, bronze, Shang or early Chou dynasty, 1027 - c. 947 B.C. Height 21.5 cm. Cleveland Museum of Art. John L. Severance Fund

[95] Kuanyin, wood with colour and gold leaf, twelfth-thirteenth century A.D. Height 2.41 metres. Atkins Museum of Fine Arts, Kansas City. Nelson Fund

[96] Kuanyin guiding a soul, T'ang dynasty painting, seventh-tenth century A.D. British Museum, London

solitary object, bearing little relationship to similar objects or groups of objects in an organized architectural scheme.

One of the most characteristic architectural forms is the Chinese temple or pagoda, which is basically a wooden-walled, tiled-roofed tower made up of superimposed storeys, as in the early eighteenth century pagoda from Nepal shown in [93].

Sculpture

Three-dimensional sculpture was not common in China until the fifth and sixth centuries A.D. As was the case in India, it was only when Buddhism became a powerful force that there was a demand for such works. Prior to this period, sculpture consisted mainly of figurines such as T'ang horses, graceful dancers and servants which were placed in tombs to accompany the dead, and ritual vessels modelled in clay and cast in bronze that were used in religious rites, like the bronze ritual vessel in the shape of an owl, pictured in [94]. Note how the bird has been simplified to show only the essentials, and how appropriately the shape has been enriched and made dynamic by the geometric ornamentation.

Towards the end of the fifth century the Buddhist religion and the arts flourished, and by the tenth century Buddhism had become the foremost religion of China. From India came a new saint, the goddess of mercy Bodhisattva (known in China as Kuanyin), who could hear every cry of sorrow. In the Kuanyin sculpture illustrated in [95], there are indications of an Indian influence in the

scarves and necklaces, the general opulence and the expressive quality of the hands.

Painting

It was in the T'ang period from the seventh to the tenth centuries that Chinese painting come into its own. The T'ang period was also a time of great lyric poetry and these two art forms were closely interrelated; indeed, Chinese painters were usually philosophers and poets as well.

The main theme in Chinese painting was landscape. Chinese landscape painting is 'summarized': it always reflects the poetic contemplation of nature, and is an imaginative selection of its characteristic forms which are directly and spontaneously painted without reference to normal perspective as applied in Western art. Landforms are arranged across the surface in a two-dimensional way, and overlapped forms are separated by atmospheric space suggested by fluid washes of thin colour instead of the deliberate strokes used for the landscape features such as trees and mountains.

The painting in [96] is from the T'ang dynasty and depicts Kuanyin guiding a soul. The colour is rich and the

50

forms are outlined very precisely and definitely by rhythmically flowing lines. If you look back to the illustration of the Gupta fresco [92], you will see the influence that linear paintings such as this one had on works of the T'ang dynasty.

Pottery

A taste for pure form led the Chinese to love ceramics and they excelled over the ages in many varieties, the most famous being porcelain ware, the manufacture of which was not discovered by Western potters until the eighteenth century. In [97] is shown an example not of porcelain but of stoneware from the fifth and sixth centuries. The cock's head on the jug is decorative; it does not function as a spout. The crackled, light, bluish-green celadon glaze unevenly spread over the body of the jug is reminiscent of jade, and it is little wonder that Chinese emperors kept ceramic objects such as this in silken boxes, taking them out now and then to handle and contemplate their beautiful surfaces.

[97] Jug with cock's head added as ornament, stoneware, fifth-sixth century A.D. Museum of Far Eastern Art, Cologne

JAPANESE ART

Japanese art, like Chinese art, developed indirectly from Indian Buddhism. Beginning in the eighth century, religious teachers and artists from China travelled to the Japanese islands where both their religion and artistic innovations were readily adopted, for it was only in the sixth century that Japan emerged from its prehistoric state. It is therefore natural that early Japanese art echoes contemporary Chinese Buddhist sculpture and painting (although adapted somewhat), and that it took many centuries for the Japanese to evolve a style of their own.

Architecture

The earliest timber buildings that exist in the Far East are to be found in Japan, and one of the reasons for this is that at various intervals over the centuries, noteworthy buildings were dismantled and replaced by replicas. One such building is the famous monastery, the Horyuji temple near Nara, which dates back to the seventh century and illustrates the close relationship between Japan and China during the first Buddhist influence. [98] shows the five-storeyed pagoda of the temple.

The pagoda could be described as a typical example of Chinese architecture. Built — as were all temples and palaces — as a hall above a stone base or terrace, its curving tiled roofs with widely projecting eaves rest on wooden beams supported by wooden columns. (See also Nagoya castle [99].) The proportions of the pagoda are in delicate balance and it displays the features characteristic of all Japanese architecture — simplicity, refinement and lightness. Architecture in the Far East is the most conservative of all the arts, and this accounts for the fact that many contemporary domestic buildings in Japan bear a striking resemblance to the Horyuji temple, although it was founded over 1300 years ago.

Japanese buildings, simple and functional, are designed to blend with the environment, and sliding screens provide flowing space in the interior and link it with exterior gardens. These concepts, together with the employment of natural materials, are in accord with the aims of many modern Western architects, for example Frank Lloyd Wright (see page 152).

Sculpture

Early Japanese sculpture, like architecture, was based on that of China, but most Japanese sculpture was generally of wood or bronze because of the lack of stone. One of these early Japanese sculptures is illustrated in [100], which shows Gakko Bosatsu, one of the attendants of the Yakushi Buddha from the early eighth century. The elaborate head-dress, long ears and poised hands resemble similar elements in Indian sculpture, and the delicate, sweeping drapery which practically dominates the form can be compared to the Chinese Kuanyin figure in [95].

During the ninth century Japanese sculpture still drew its inspiration from Chinese sources. The terrifying figure of Shukongojin in the Hokkedo [101], carved in wood and intended to frighten away the forces of evil, closely resembles guardian figures used by Chinese Buddhists for a similar purpose.

Painting

At the end of the ninth century the power to rule Japan came into the hands of a single family, the Fujiwara, who gave their name to the art of the time. However, the Fujiwara, weakened by their love of luxury, were eventually

[98] Pagoda of the Horyuji temple, Nara, founded A.D. 607

[99] Nagoya castle, Nagoya, 1610-12

[100] Gakko Bosatsu, one of the attendants of the Yakushi Buddha, bronze, c. A.D. 720. Height 3.12 metres. Yakushiji, Nara

overthrown in 1185 by the Minamoto, a military family which established its court at Kamakura, near present-day Tokyo.

The Minamoto were austere and disciplined warriors, and their realistic vision of the world affected the artists who worked for them. This period marked the beginning of a semi-naturalistic genre (ordinary life) style of painting which existed side by side with the traditional, formal style. This semi-naturalism, however, is not to be identified with naturalism or realism as we understand the terms when referring to Western European styles of painting. The semi-naturalism is illustrated in the severely simple portrait of Minamoto no Yoritomo [102], shown wearing a dark blue garment with angular contours. This large blue area contrasts dramatically with the pale but expressive face of the warrior chieftain.

The heightened sense of realism which marked the birth of a semi-naturalistic style of painting, as illustrated in the Yoritomo portrait, is probably more apparent in the coloured woodblock prints produced from the seventeenth to the nineteenth century. The technique of woodblock printing requires a different block for each colour, and this suited the Japanese penchant for the hard diagrammatic use of line and for bright, clearly defined colours.

One of the most famous woodblock artists was Kitagawa Utamaro, best known for his genre scenes such as 'The Love Letter' [103]. When Japanese prints like this were seen in France in the nineteenth century, they were received with great enthusiasm and excitement by artists, particularly the Impressionists and Post-Impressionists who copied their large, flat, muted areas of colour, decorative lines and compositional devices (see pages 107, 113 and 115).

[101] Shukongojin, in the Hokkedo, wood, late Nara period. Height 1.7 metres. Todaiji, Nara

[102] Portrait of Minamoto no Yoritomo, by Fujiwara Takanobu, c. A.D. 1200

[103] Kitagawa Utamaro (1753-1806): 'The Love Letter', woodcut, British Museum, London

PRE-COLUMBIAN ART

There were two dominant areas in Pre-Columbian American culture, one in Central America and the other on the western side of South America; both these cultures developed in isolation, and despite being cut off from contact with both Europe and the Far East, Pre-Columbian art exhibits a high degree of development over the period from 200 B.C. to the Spanish conquest in the sixteenth century.

Central America comprises the present territories of Mexico, Guatemala and Honduras, and over the centuries several cultures flourished in these regions. These cultures had many features in common: they all used a terraced pyramid to raise the temple sanctuary high in the air, and their religions had rituals that included human sacrifice; they recorded calendars, time scales and the precise observation of the movements of planets, and even had a common ball game, a sacred ritual called *pelota* which appears to have combined the elements of basketball and soccer.

The earliest centre of Pre-Columbian civilization in Central America was located at Teotihuacan ('the place of the gods') where monuments like the Pyramid of the Sun [104] were constructed. The volcanic stones of which the pyramid was made were as carefully and as accurately cut as those of the Great Pyramid of Cheops in Egypt. This was a remarkable feat, for the early Americans had neither metal tools to work stone nor beasts of burden to carry it; however, in South America the Incas of Peru learned how to work bronze and employed the llama as a beast of burden.

One of the most influential cultures of Central America was that of the energetic Toltecs, a creative and aggressive people who greatly influenced the Maya civilization of Yucatan. The Maya-Toltec culture produced remarkable architectural complexes and sculptural decoration. Illustrated in [105] is a detail of the Temple of the Tigers, with its fearful serpent columns, at Chichen Itza in Yucatan. This temple flanked one side of the court where the sacred ball game was played, in which the flight of the ball symbolized the passage of the sun across the sky. The 'Tigers', incidentally, were warriors who belonged to a military clan.

The Mayas, besides being masters in the craft of working stone, were highly skilled in ceramics; the little painted clay figure in [106] shows superb artistic quality and great character. This tiny human figure, actually a whistle, was made from a mould and small pieces of clay were added later. The left hand holds a hat and a small vessel lies in the palm of the right hand.

The Aztecs, who dominated the Valley of Mexico from A.D. 1300 until the Spaniards arrived in the early sixteenth century, made human sacrifice the principle of their religious system, for their gods appeared to need blood to keep them strong. One of their deities, the ancient god of fire, took the form of a coyote. In the basalt sculpture in [107], the god is wearing a disguise of precious feathers, but the decorative, geometric plumage does not entirely conceal his ferocious expression.

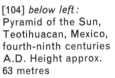

[104] *below left:* Pyramid of the Sun, Teotihuacan, Mexico, fourth-ninth centuries A.D. Height approx. 63 metres

[105] The Temple of the Tigers, Chichen Itza, Yucatan state, c. A.D. 987-1204

[106] Painted clay figure, Maya culture, height 18 cm. Jaina, Campeche state

[107] Olivine basalt sculpture of plumed coyote, Aztec culture, fifteenth century A.D. Height 40 cm. National Museum of Anthropology, Mexico City

PRIMITIVE (AFRICAN) ART

Before European colonization, the sculptors of Africa were among the most intense and imaginative artists of the world. However, their art can be better appreciated if their religious beliefs are understood. The religion is animistic; that is, all objects are endowed with souls. The primitive African Negroes also believe in a world of mysterious powers that can only be conceived through the imagination, and their art attempts to project the spiritual essence of those forces in symbolic form.

The representations in sculpture of the mysterious power that resides in animals, enemies, fire and ghosts are not only projections of the abstract ideas, but are the ideas themselves. The primitive artist makes no distinction between reality and unreality, and in creating sculpture he is creating the life force itself. His twofold objective, to represent and paradoxically not to represent, is apparent in the Bakota funerary figure [108], where human features are highly stylized.

The Bakuba kneeling figure [109] is confidently carved and has a marked four-sidedness; the sculptor squared the tree trunk into a solid rectangular box shape and carved out the figure from four separate sides.

Masks of many varieties and materials were used by the chief participants in practically all African Negro ceremonies, and the Bacham mask [110] is a marvellous example of decorative carving. An exciting sense of texture is achieved by the flat fields of fine, graceful reeding contrasted with the smoothly rounded forms between.

The heightened naturalism of the Benin plaque [111] would indicate a greater sense of security in relation to the forces of nature, for Benin was the largest, wealthiest and most developed African kingdom of the past. In the later nineteenth century when British colonists sacked Benin, thousands of similar bronze plaques were found, but as little artistic importance was attached to them they were melted down and only a few were kept as curiosities.

The African Negroes' abstraction of natural form provided exactly the sort of pure aesthetic idea sought by European artists, particularly Picasso, in the early twentieth century; carvings like the Bakuba kneeling figure greatly influenced the Cubists, who similarly reduced shapes to simplified forms with sharply divided planes in an endeavor to get beyond the mere physical appearance of things to their essential qualities (see page 123).

[108] Bakota funerary figure from Gabon, brass-plated, height 68 cm. British Museum, London

[109] Bakuba figure from the Congo, wood. British Museum, London

[110] Bacham mask from the Cameroon Highlands, wood, height 66 cm. Rietberg Museum, Zurich

[111] Benin plaque from Nigeria, bronze, height of central figure 43 cm. British Museum, London

OCEANIC ART

The term Oceania embraces Australia, Melanesia, Micronesia and Polynesia. Although each of these cultural areas shows certain similarities with at least one of the others, there are few stylistic features common to the whole group. We will restrict our survey to the art forms of the Australian Aborigines, the New Guineans, and the New Zealand Maoris.

NEW GUINEAN AND AUSTRALIAN ABORIGINAL ART

The present peoples of Oceania are descendants of several waves of mainland Asian immigrants, who had different racial origins and belonged to different levels of cultural evolution. The New Guineans, who derive their livelihood from agriculture and fishing, are largely settled and could be termed Neolithic people. Their architecture, sculpture and painting are of wood or in some cases stone, and often these three art forms are combined, as in the men's ceremonial Great House illustrated in [112]. The roof of this gigantic hut is turned up at the front to form a delicate canopy with a carved spire, and the frontispiece is decorated with painted bark.

The Australian Aborigines were among the least developed of primitive peoples, and when Europeans came to Australia the indigenous tribes had no houses (in the conventional sense), no crops, no metal, no pottery and practically no clothing: they roamed in small groups over a vast territory in a constant search for game and water.

Although the Aborigines had no concept of material wealth, they had developed a richly elaborated religious and ceremonial life which profoundly affected their art.

Rather than an act of self-expression, the Aborigine considered art a gift of supernatural power handed down from the great ones of the Dream Time. Realism was not necessarily a criterion, and a great deal of Aboriginal art was abstract, consisting of circles, spirals and parallel straight or wavy lines. Thus simple painted or incised decorations on portable objects such as woven baskets, spear throwers and spears were imbued with magical values. The more complex designs incised on the most sacred objects, *tjuringa* (oval or circular slabs of wood or stone), served as memory aids for the elders in initiation ceremonies. Generally, however, each tribe attributed its own significance to the various patterns, which related to its local mythology.

Aboriginal motifs based on reality referred to local animals and natural objects that had particular relevance. The artist represented life forms, known as totems, from which his group traced its descent — for example, the diver bird, spider or caterpillar. Ancestral beings connected with the Dream Time were often represented. This was the case with the Wandjina, who were believed to have come out of the sea with their families and companions and travelled throughout the northern Kimberley area of Western Australia, creating the tribal world, the people and their customs; when their travels ended they died, and became sacred paintings in a rock shelter.

The Australian Aborigine was primarily an outdoor artist, and much work painted on rocks, trees and stone wall faces suffered the effects of weathering. However, the rock paintings in [113] have been protected from the elements, and their boldly contrasting ochre colours are still vivid.

The largest sculptural forms created by the Aborigines are grave posts, found only on Bathurst and Melville

[112] Haus tambaran ('spirit house') at Maprik in the Sepik district, New Guinea

[113] Aboriginal rock paintings, North Queensland

[114] Pukamani grave posts, Northern Terr

Islands in northern Australia. Pictured in [114] is a group of Pukamani grave posts, some over 2 metres high. Carved from hardwood with stone implements, each post is decoratively painted with striking patterns. The number of posts carved depends on the status of the dead warrior, and after elaborate burial and mourning rites the posts are abandoned to the elements.

One of the most outstanding forms of primitive art is the bark painting of the Australian Aborigine. Bark paintings are done with red, brown and yellow ochre, white pipeclay and charcoal. Animal fats and blood are mixed with the pigments so that they adhere to the stringybark surface. The bark painting illustrated in [115] was painted by Narritjin Maymuru and relates the legend of two men who travelled by canoe from Groote Eylandt to the mainland on a hunting expedition. When they came to the Koolatong River (the middle strip of the painting) their canoe was capsized by the big crocodile and one man was drowned. A manta ray (right-hand side), escorted by a number of fish, took him up into the sky where he changed them into stars. He was so impressed by his efforts that he sent word down to his friend that he would turn all the things caught during hunting into stars. These subsequently became a river of stars (the Milky Way). Finally he caught the big crocodile and it was changed into the Southern Cross. The hunter then said to his friend, 'You've got a river of stars and plenty of food in the river, so take me up with you.' He was accordingly carried up into the sky by a whale (left-hand side). Both men were then changed into stars, so that we now have the Milky Way, the Southern Cross at the end of it, and the two men have become the 'pointers', which are just below the Milky Way and the Southern Cross.

MAORI ART   *Dr S. M. Mead*

Through many centuries of isolation and cultural selection the Maori of New Zealand developed an art tradition which, while related in a general way to the arts of Polynesia and Oceania, was distinctly different in many respects. The immediate cultural affinities of the Maori are with central and eastern Polynesia, and yet Maori art is more like that of Lake Sentani and the Massim area in New Guinea than the art of any other region of Polynesia. This is because the Maori's curvilinear style is not found developed to the same high level elsewhere in Polynesia, with the possible exception of the Marquesas. Despite the apparent similarities to Melanesian art, Maori art has a look of its own: its inventory of art elements and motifs is not quite like any other, and the forms created by artists constitute a distinctive style which is easily recognizable as Maori.

The human figure, portrayed either in naturalistic or in conventionalized form, was the most important art motif, and the artists used it in three-dimensional shapes, in single or multi-relief carving, or simply as surface decoration. Next in importance was the *manaia* motif which is interpreted as representing a bird man. Animal motifs included the lizard, whale, dog, and various birds and fish. Surface decoration consisted of many different types of spirals, notches, scrolls, crescents and parallel V-shaped grooves. Art objects were made mainly from wood, but bone and stone were also used, particularly the green nephrite for small objects.

Maori artists regarded the human body as a form subject to artistic modification. Facial tattoos differentiated the men from the women. Spirals and scrolls tattooed in indelible black were chiselled on to the faces, buttocks and thighs of warriors and chiefs. The hair was carefully combed into a top-knot and then further decorated by the addition of feathers and an ornamental comb of either wood or bone. The body was made to appear larger and given angular stress by the wearing of prestige cloaks made from the native flax plant and decorated with dog skin and hair, feathers and *taaniko* — woven patterns in black, red and white. Costume objects such as cloaks, kilts, belts, combs, and ear and neck ornaments were inspired by a desire to build and maintain personal or group prestige (*mana*).

[117] Interior view of the house Te Tokanga-nui-a-noho built at Te Kuiti in 1873 and still in use. This shows how the back of the house is decorated

[118] A carved slab representing the ancestor called Tuariki whose name is painted on the neck. The slab is typical of the ancestor slabs which are placed on the side walls of a meeting house in the Maataatua canoe area. From the house Ruataupare at Te Teko, 1882

[119] A *kumara* god whose function was to protect the crop of sweet potatoes from malignant influences. From Mokoia Island, Rotorua, and now in the Auckland War Memorial Museum

In warfare it was particularly important to distinguish the leading chiefs, as the main object was to kill them. This was achieved through differences in tattooing, costume and hairstyle. But in many cases the chiefs also carried a distinctive weapon known as *toki-pou-tangata* ('adze to despatch men'); this weapon was usually an art object decorated with an ancestor figure biting the tail of a lizard. Practically all of the objects associated with warfare, such as weapons, canoes and fortifications, were constructed

with care and decorated with great skill. Much art, therefore, was motivated by the beliefs and concerns associated with warfare.

Ancestor worship and the customs connected with death were equally important in inspiring the production of fine art. Bone chests, monuments and mausoleums of varying degrees of complexity, posts marking a burial site and house posts commemorating particular ancestors are examples. Although its classic Maori origin is in doubt, the meeting house which became quite common during the second half of the nineteenth century is, perhaps, the grandest result of ancestor worship (see [116]). The meeting house is named after an ancestor and the structure symbolizes his body. The ridge-pole represents his backbone, the bargeboards his arms, the porch his chest, and the inside his body. Large slabs of wood carved to represent ancestors are spaced out evenly along the side walls and the vertical poles supporting the ridge-pole usually also represent ancestors (see [117] and [118]). Thus, the whole structure with its complex of carved figures, painted scroll patterns and decorative lattice-work is a memorial to the dead.

In the early 1800s, especially in the North Auckland, Taupo and Rotorua areas, the focus of village pride was the decorated storehouse constructed on posts. Early storehouses were built especially to store the sweet potato (*kumara*), a root crop which made sedentary village life possible for the Maori. The storehouse was more elaborately decorated than the residences of chiefs at this time, but after the introduction of the ordinary potato by Europeans, storehouses were gradually phased out and the fine arts formerly lavished upon them were transferred to chiefs' houses and later to meeting houses.

Many personal possessions were objects of art. Treasure boxes (*waka huia*), in which the chiefs stored their sacred hair ornaments, provide an example. These boxes are well represented in museum collections all over the world. A few food bowls were carved in the form of a very fat dog and intricately decorated with surface patterning. Neck ornaments, such as the *rei-puta* and the *hei-tiki*, were often beautifully shaped and qualify as art objects. Agricultural implements, especially the *ko* (digging stick with footrest), received the attention of artists; in fact, there are some art motifs which appear to have been restricted to the handles of digging sticks. Sweet potato gods carved in stone, such as the one illustrated in [119], were associated with plantations. Thus there were some aesthetic activities prompted by the importance attached to the sweet potato.

Art was to be found in every aspect of Maori life — much of it inspired by a preoccupation with warfare, ancestor worship, death, prestige, and the propagation of the sweet potato. However, the range of objects decorated by Maori artists suggests that some art activity was motivated simply by a desire to exercise creative ability.

THE RENAISSANCE

The term Renaissance means 'rebirth', and following on from the Middle Ages it implies a rebirth of interest in classical antiquity and the philosophies and mythologies that formed part of a way of life for the ancient Greeks and Romans. This new era saw the gradual disappearance of many of the Medieval superstitious beliefs, and in their place the emergence of man as an individual, directing his energies into unexplored or forgotten fields of human endeavour. It is impossible to put an exact date on the beginning of the Renaissance period, as the seeds were certainly sown with the advent of Giotto; however, for our purposes the Renaissance period occupies the fifteenth century, known to the Italians as the *Quattrocento*.

During the Middle Ages the main theme of artistic expression had been religious, but with the emergence of secular rulers and wealthy merchants and bankers, artists depicted citizens of the day attired in contemporary fashions and participating in current events. Although ecclesiastical art was still dominant, a distinct worldly quality, reflecting the new social circumstances, was increasingly evident in works painted on church walls.

New subject matter reflected man's new-found freedom and expressed a new spirit; artists were no longer anonymous, and conscious of their individual skills they proudly signed their works. Painters, sculptors and architects found their talents in great demand, and wealthy noblemen and princes competed for their services. The prosperous commercial city of Florence, with its lucrative wool industry and trade relations, its powerful guilds, and above all, the highly influential Medici family, became the centre of this new-found humanistic learning and expression. To their court Cosimo and later Lorenzo dei Medici gathered some of the greatest artists, philosophers and writers of the day.

Filippo Brunelleschi (1377-1446)

Much impetus was given to the Renaissance period by the young Florentine architect Brunelleschi. After being apprenticed to a goldsmith, he took up sculpture and in 1401 submitted a design for the bronze north doors of the baptistry of San Giovanni in Florence; eventually the judges narrowed the prize down to two sculptors, Brunelleschi and Lorenzo Ghiberti. After much deliberation the prize eventually went to Ghiberti. Brunelleschi then turned his back on sculpture and journeyed to Rome, where he

[120] Brunelleschi: Pazzi chapel, Santa Croce, Florence. 1430-43

[121] Brunelleschi: Pazzi chapel interior

[122] Cathedral of Florence — dome designed by Brunelleschi. 1420-36

[123] Michelozzo: Medici-Riccardi palace, Florence. 1444-59

[124] Alberti: Rucellai palace, Florence. 1446-51

and the sculptor Donatello together studied the ruins of classical antiquity, which were to have a subsequent influence on his designs.

One of Brunelleschi's earliest architectural designs was for a chapel within the cloisters of the church of Santa Croce [120]; this small private chapel was commissioned by the powerful and influential Pazzi family. The plan of the Pazzi chapel is basically square, with a conical dome placed centrally over the main body of the church. The dome is in the form of an inverted cone supported on a circular drum, the thrust of which is taken by pendentives. The façade of the building is an open portico that recalls the Roman triumphal arch, with a large semicircular arch as the main entrance. Behind this we see further evidence of elements derived from antiquity, for example the triangular pediment over the central doorway, and the round-headed windows flanking this. Inside the building [121], Brunelleschi's contribution to architectural development in this period is evident. The stark white walls are relieved by the use of grey pilasters which break up and divide the wall surface, giving the interior a light, fresh appearance. We have only to compare Brunelleschi's design with [52], a Romanesque interior, or [62], a Gothic interior, to see how little the Pazzi chapel has in common with either of these two previous periods.

One of Brunelleschi's greatest feats was the construction of a dome for the cathedral of Florence [122]. Here he has married a dome designed in the new Renaissance style with a Gothic cathedral; the dome itself is 42·2 metres in diameter (compared to the 18 metres of the Pazzi chapel); it is eight-sided, ribbed, and pointed in form, and demonstrates Brunelleschi's mastery of Gothic principles of construction.

From Brunelleschi's interest in organizing space and creating a three-dimensional effect, he was able to pass on to other artists of the time mathematical laws governing perspective and the art of suggesting depth on a flat two-dimensional surface. The techniques he devised to render objects diminishing with distance came to be increasingly used by Renaissance artists, and can be seen repeatedly employed during this and subsequent periods.

Michelozzo di Bartolommeo (1396-1472)

Michelozzo was a pupil of Brunelleschi, and undoubtedly his most famous building is the palace that he designed for the elder Cosimo dei Medici, which was later sold to the Riccardi family in 1659 [123].

Perhaps the first thing that strikes us about the Medici palace is the symmetrical way in which the elements have been arranged. The building gives the impression that it could be extended almost indefinitely without upsetting the balance or harmony, as we find it is composed of a repetition of forms. In strong contrast to the light, airy buildings of the Gothic period, there is a tremendous feeling of strength and solidity which calls to mind the fortress-like buildings of the Romanesque period (cf. [51]). The palace virtually turns its back to the street, and is indeed an almost impregnable fortress of rectangular design, opening up on to an internal courtyard. This feeling of strength and permanence, largely achieved by the rusticated ground storey, is heightened by the heavy cornice which projects a distance of 2·4 metres over the street.

[126] Masaccio: *The Tribute Money*, fresco, *c.* 1427. 255 x 598 cm. Brancacci chapel, Santa Maria del Carmine, Florence

[125] Masaccio: Upper section of *The Holy Trinity with Virgin, St John and Donors*, fresco, 1427. Full size 667 x 317 cm. Santa Maria Novella, Florence

Leon Battista Alberti (1404-1472)

Alberti was a keen scholar of classical literature, and actually published the first book on architecture after the introduction of printing.

He studied the ruins of ancient Rome, the influence of which may be seen in his Rucellai palace in Florence [124]. If we compare Alberti's building with Michelozzo's Medici palace [123], we become aware of certain similarities in the overall appearance of the façade, the projecting cornice, and the number of storeys. Generally, however, the building lacks the feeling of strength that Michelozzo's derived from its rusticated walls and heavier cornice, although it gains in unity as a result.

When we look closely at the treatment of the Rucellai palace walls, we notice that Alberti subdivides the space of an otherwise flat surface by a series of incised lines, giving the impression of a building from classical antiquity.

Masaccio (1401-1428)

This artist was born Tommaso di Giovanni di Simone Guidi and was nicknamed Masaccio, which means 'Clumsy Thomas'. Although he died at the age of 27 he nevertheless established, in the few works that he executed, a concept and approach that was to remain basically unaltered for nearly 500 years.

In *Holy Trinity with Virgin, St John and Donors* [125], his achievement is obvious in the way he has created an illusion of depth, space and volume on a flat two-dimensional surface. This was partly attributable to Giotto (cf. [74]), and also to a thorough understanding of the laws of scientific perspective as formulated by the architect Brunelleschi. Indeed, the crucifixion scene, with its flat half-columns flanking either side of a Roman barrel-vaulted ceiling, could have been set inside one of Brunelleschi's chapels. Masaccio arranged the figures of this fresco in the form of a triangle, with the crucified Christ at its apex. This was to become a common compositional device during the Renaissance period. If we run imaginary lines along the tops of the heads of the Virgin and the donor on the left, and St John and the donor on the right, we find that the intersecting point is the wound made by the spear in Christ's side. The figures of St John, the Virgin and Christ are just under life size, while the figures of the donors are full life size; this further assists in creating the illusion of depth and perspective. Compared to the light, graceful figures of the late Gothic period, Masaccio's seem relatively solid and realistic, and at times static to the point of monumentality. The only movement in *The Holy Trinity* is introduced by the Virgin, who is looking directly at us and holding up her hand to indicate Christ. A subject performing this type of action is known as a 'witness figure'; the pose was used frequently by later artists as a means of focusing the spectator's attention on the centre of interest.

Masaccio's figures do not have the elegance of the International Gothic period, but they more than compensate with their great feeling of solid form; figures and buildings alike occupy space and stand firmly upon the ground. These qualities Masaccio achieved through his invention of chiaroscuro (the light-and-shade method of making forms appear solid), his understanding of perspective, and also the realization that colours lose their intensity with distance and become cooler and greyer as they recede (known as

61

[127] Masaccio: *The Expulsion from Paradise*, fresco, *c*. 1427. 208 x 88 cm. Brancacci chapel, Santa Maria del Carmine, Florence

[128] Uccello: *The Rout of San Romano*, tempera on wood, 1465. 182 x 330 cm. National Gallery, London

[129] Ghiberti: *Solomon Meeting the Queen of Sheba*, gilded bronze panel from the Porta del Paradiso, 1425-52. Baptistry of San Giovanni, Florence

[130] Donatello: *David*, bronze, 1440-3. Height 158 cm. Bargello, Florence

atmospheric perspective). This innovation can be seen in *The Tribute Money* [126] where the figures of Christ and his disciples are bathed in light and surrounded by atmosphere. This fresco in the Brancacci chapel of the Carmine church in Florence illustrates three stories or happenings in the one picture. In the middle is the tax collector demanding his dues of Christ, who in turn requests St Peter to fetch the money from the mouth of the large fish by the side of the lake; finally, St Peter thrusts the money into the tax collector's hand.

Even more important than the reality of space, weight and volume is the way in which Masaccio for the first time painted portraits of real people — the disciples in *The Tribute Money* are individuals with strongly modelled features. In another fresco from the Brancacci chapel, *The Expulsion from Paradise* [127], his portrayal of Adam and Eve banished from the Garden of Eden conveys a powerful expression of grief. In this as in other works, Masaccio gave conviction to his figures by embodying in them human emotions such as love, anger, compassion and guilt, that broke completely with the traditions of Medieval painting.

Paolo Uccello (1397-1475)

Uccello was a Florentine artist and a friend of the sculptor Donatello. In his paintings he experimented with a most difficult problem — the grafting of new knowledges involving solid forms, interpreted with foreshortening and perspective, on to the Medieval tradition of the picture as a flat pattern of colour. We have only to compare his *Rout of San Romano* [128], painted in 1465, with Masaccio's *Tribute Money* of almost forty years earlier to see how

obsessed Uccello became with one aspect of creating the illusion of depth on the two-dimensional picture plane. Masaccio's figures move in atmosphere; those of Uccello do not.

Uccello's battle scene gives the impression of a stage setting, rather than the gory reality of the actual event. The figures seem almost 'snap-frozen' in their positions, and the horses appear like those bobbing up and down on a merry-go-round rather than sweating, flesh-and-blood creatures. If we look closely at the picture we observe many pieces of broken and discarded armour — a surprising amount, as we can discern only one corpse — arranged so that the eye is led towards the soldier on the white horse just to the left of centre. The dead body is a fascinating study in foreshortening, and represents one of the earliest attempts to solve this problem of the illusion of three dimensions. The 'stage setting' effect that Uccello has created is further heightened by the fact that the figures in the rather strange landscape behind the hedge appear as part of a painted scenery backdrop, quite oblivious to the battle raging in the foreground.

Lorenzo Ghiberti (1378-1455)

Ghiberti received his early training as a goldsmith and painter, but it is for his sculpture that he is best remembered. In 1401, like Brunelleschi, he submitted a design for the second pair of bronze doors of the baptistry in Florence; he won the competition, and their execution was begun in 1403.

These doors, completed in 1424, display a Gothic influence, but in the third pair executed between 1425 and 1452 we see the results of Brunelleschi's rediscovery of the

scientific laws pertaining to perspective and an obvious influence by Donatello, together with Ghiberti's understanding of the problems of light and shade and the rendering of form. These qualities help to make them one of the finest examples of bronze sculpture in the world today.

Each wing contains five rectangular reliefs illustrating scenes from the Old Testament. Ghiberti's complete mastery of his medium is displayed in the panel showing the meeting of Solomon and the Queen of Sheba [129]. At first glance this relief sculpture could be mistaken for a painting, so convincing is the treatment of form and space. We can observe that the foreground figures are much more rounded than those to the rear, which also helps the feeling of perspective. Compositionally, Ghiberti has organized his figures into two parallel horizontal planes with the background figures smaller, except for the slightly hierarchical figures of Solomon and the Queen of Sheba.

It is perhaps interesting to note what the sculptor recorded of his own work: 'In some of these ten reliefs I introduced more than a hundred figures, in others fewer. . . . observing the laws of optics I succeeded in giving them an appearance of such reality that when seen from a distance the figures seem to be round. The nearer figures are largest, while those in the further planes diminish with size as occurs in nature.' Vasari described them thus — 'the most beautiful work that has appeared in ancient or modern time'; but the greatest compliment of all was when the mighty Michelangelo, upon seeing them for the first time, exclaimed: 'They are so fine that they might fittingly stand at the gates of Paradise.'

Donatello (1386-1466)

Donatello was a native of Florence but spent several years studying in Rome, where he came under the influence of the works of classical antiquity. His bronze statue of David [130] bears witness to this, and recalls the style of the Greek Hellenistic period; in fact, this is the first example of sculpture since classical times in which a feeling of real identity with youth is established — youth with its litheness and corporeal substance, with the bone structure evident at elbow, wrist and shoulderblade.

Donatello has impregnated the sculpture with both grace and awkwardness, simplicity and ornateness, symbolism and naturalism. The figure is lithe, sensuous and full of movement (as opposed to his *St George* [131] of 1416, sculpted for the Guild of Armourers, which is rather static and monumental in comparison). The dynamic quality of *David* is attributable to Donatello's interest in the Greek device of *contraposta*, the chest and shoulders being turned at an angle to the trunk. With his deep understanding of the human body's structure, and his fine interpretation of character and emotion, Donatello paralleled in sculpture the painting achievements of his contemporary, Masaccio.

Further evidence of his genius may be found in the moving figure of Mary Magdalene [132], which seems far removed from his classically Renaissance *David*. The 'Impressionistic' approach of this work seems to anticipate the style of Auguste Rodin, and indeed, in its intensity of feeling and portrayal of human suffering, is perhaps even closer in spirit to the works of the German Expressionists over four centuries later.

[131] Donatello: *St George*, marble, *c.* 1416. Height 195.5 cm. Bargello, Florence

[132] Donatello: *Mary Magdalene*, wood, *c.* 1454. Height 188 cm. Baptistry of San Giovanni, Florence

[133] Fra Angelico: *The Annunciation*, fresco, 1440-7. 256 x 334 cm. San Marco, Florence

[134] Fra Filippo Lippi: *The Coronation of the Virgin*, altarpiece panel, 1447. 200 x 287 cm. Uffizi, Florence

Fra Angelico (1387/1400-1455)

It is probable that Fra Angelico received early training in making illuminated manuscripts in the Gothic tradition; this influence may be seen in several of his paintings, and was a style that reached fulfilment in the works of Sandro Botticelli (see [136]).

The Annunciation [133], at the head of the stairway of the monastery of San Marco in Florence, owes much to the works of Masaccio, and to a certain extent those of Brunelleschi (in the architectural background). While many of the artists of the same era were concerned with experimentation and innovation, Fra Angelico was more interested in depicting the angel appearing before the Virgin with sincerity and simplicity. His figures have a feeling of calmness and dignity which is reminiscent of Masaccio (cf. [125]); though they lack the weight and power of Masaccio's figures, they have a decorative charm and serenity that is the dominant characteristic of Fra Angelico's work.

Fra Filippo Lippi (1406-1469)

In 1421 Fra Filippo Lippi became a monk in the Carmelite monastery of Santa Maria del Carmine in Florence, and it was during his ten-year sojourn there that he fell under the influence of Masaccio, who was at the time working on murals in the Brancacci chapel. Lippi's early paintings won him considerable acclaim and the powerful Cosimo dei Medici became his patron. While Fra Filippo's paintings retained a strong religious content and character, they were more contemporary in spirit than were Fra Angelico's, and they reveal a worldliness which reflects his own human relationships, for he ultimately married and the painter Filippino Lippi was his son.

The Coronation of the Virgin [134] is a typically Renaissance composition, the figures having something of Masaccio's sculptural quality. In this as in other paintings by Fra Filippo Lippi we are conscious of a more decorative use of colour than is the case with Masaccio, a quality which Lippi bequeathed to his best pupil, Sandro Botticelli.

Piero della Francesca (1420-1492)

After training in Florence, Piero returned to his native town of Borgo San Sepolcro in Umbria. Here he began to formulate a style that recalls Giotto and Masaccio, but which in its turn was to influence Perugino and Raphael. Piero's figures possess a rather statuesque quality somewhat reminiscent of Greek sculpture (cf. [23]).

In *The Resurrection* [135] we are aware of his command

[135] Della Francesca: *The Resurrection*, fresco, c. 1460. 225 x 200 cm. Palazzo Comunale, Borgo San Sepolcro

[136] Botticelli: *Primavera* (detail from right-hand side), tempera on wood, 1587. Full size 203 x 314 cm. Uffizi, Florence

[137] Botticelli: *Judith with the Head of Holofernes*, oil on wood, c. 1470. 27 x 21 cm. Uffizi, Florence

of light and colour. The figure of the risen Christ conveys a feeling of tremendous power, which is perhaps further emphasized by the lifeless attitudes of the sleeping soldiers. All the figures give the impression that they inhabit a silent, sombre world, depicted in the early morning light.

Piero della Francesca is considered one of the greatest mural painters of the Renaissance. The serene forms and subtle harmonies of colour that were carefully organised to retain the two-dimensional quality of the wall can only be seen today in his fresco series *The Search for the True Cross* in Arezzo. His frescoes in the Vatican were destroyed in order that Raphael could paint his three-dimensionally inclined works.

Sandro Botticelli (1444-1510)

Sandro Botticelli was a Florentine painter whose highly individual style had little influence outside his native city. He often infused pagan and mythological scenes with an almost religious interpretation, this aspect of his work largely resulting from the influence of his patrons. He was a favourite painter of the Medici family and many of his subjects were described to him in detail by influential members of this circle, which included philosophers and scholars of note.

At times Botticelli's figures appear quite weightless and his backgrounds seem more like a backdrop for a play, but the appeal of his work lies in the grace, charm and movement of his figures, qualities that are often missing in the works of other innovators of the Renaissance. The *Primavera* is one of the most treasured possessions of the great Uffizi gallery in Florence. Botticelli's paintings, while seemingly gay, often have a strange melancholy quality, and this can be seen in the detail reproduced in [136] showing Flora, the herald of spring: with her far-off dreaming eyes and the flowers in her hair, she could indeed be one of the 'flower people' of the 1970s; the artist depicts her with attendants, in a richly flowered woodland setting. The faces in this composition, as in many of Botticelli's works, are those of Florentine women of the Medici circle. Undoubtedly much of the charm of the painting lies in its richly flowing linear pattern.

Another of Botticelli's paintings that displays this wistful grace is *Judith with the Head of Holofernes* [137], based on the biblical tale of the Israelite woman who inspires her countrymen to victory over the besieging Assyrians by beguiling their general into a drunken slumber and then hacking off his head. In the painting, the battle raging below appears in strange contrast to the calm, pensive mood of Judith returning home in company with her maid, who bears the head of Holofernes and the empty wine jars; the painting has the cool, diffused light of early morning and recalls the general mood of the work of his teacher, Fra Filippo Lippi.

65

RENAISSANCE PAINTING OUTSIDE ITALY

Rogier van der Weyden (1400-1464)

Rogier van der Weyden studied under Robert Campin, the Master of Flémalle, and was to become one of the great masters of early Flemish painting.

His work is obviously influenced by both Campin and van Eyck, but whereas the latter was interested in creating the illusion of reality through the use of detail, Rogier is more interested in the depiction of human emotions. This can best be seen by studying *The Deposition* [138]. His figures are arranged on a shallow stage, and while there is still a marked Gothic influence, especially in the rhythm and colour, they give the impression of having weight and volume, almost to the point of being sculpturesque. The most significant aspect, however, is the feeling of grief and dejection portrayed in the faces of Christ's followers as the body is gently lowered from the cross.

Hieronymus Bosch (*c.* 1450-1516)

We know little of Bosch and much of his life and work is likely to remain a mystery. His real name was apparently van Aken, but he evidently preferred to take his name from the place of his birth, Hertogenbosch.

It is impossible to fully appreciate the meaning behind his enigmatic works, but when we remember the traditions of Medieval culture with their various superstitious beliefs, we can perhaps come closer to an understanding of them. He seems to use many of the new Renaissance techniques to lend conviction to his weird compositions, which at times are peopled by Surrealistic figures and nightmarish creatures. One definition of twentieth century Surrealism is 'the painting of dream-like scenes or sequences', and we can see that the modernity of Bosch's style may well have provided inspiration for the contemporary Surrealist. On the other hand, it is probably true to say that it anticipates the Mannerist period in its strange visionary qualities.

In his *Christ Carrying the Cross* [139] we are strongly reminded of Leonardo's *Grotesque Faces* [151]. The figure of Christ is almost completely obscured amongst one of the most repulsive and hideous collections of humanity ever assembled. To really appreciate Bosch's strange mixture of the sacred and the profane, we have only to look at such examples as his *Hay Wain*, *Ship of Fools* and *The Garden of Delights*, part of which is reproduced in [140]. This is the right-hand wing of a triptych now in the Prado, Madrid.

In this painting, Bosch's original intention was probably to relate a moral sermon: the left-hand panel depicts God introducing Adam and Eve into a weird landscape in which strange, fantastic animals or creatures graze; the central panel is peopled by men and women in grotesque and sensual poses, and the final panel (see [140]) represents Satan's hell, with terrifying creatures assisting him in diabolical forms of torture that give a persuasive power to the artist's visual sermon.

[138] *above left* Van der Weyden: *The Deposition*, oil on wood, *c.* 1435. 220 x 262 cm. Prado, Madrid
[139] *left* Bosch: *Christ Carrying the Cross*, oil on wood, date unknown. 74 x 81 cm. Museum of Fine Arts, Ghent
[140] *above* Bosch: *Hell* (right-hand wing of triptych *The Garden of Delights*), oil and tempera on wood, *c.* 1500. 220 x 97 cm. Prado, Madrid

[141] Dürer: *Portrait of the Artist's Father*, oil on wood, 1490.
138 x 112 cm. Uffizi, Florence
[142] Dürer: *Italian Mountains*, watercolour and gouache on
paper, 1495. 21.6 x 30.5 cm. Ashmolean Museum, Oxford
[143] Holbein: *Portrait of Nicolas Kratzer*, oil on wood, 1528.
83 x 67 cm. Louvre, Paris

Albrecht Dürer (1471-1528)

Dürer, born at Nuremberg in Germany, ranks as one of the great Renaissance artists. His father, a goldsmith, had him apprenticed to Nuremberg's leading artist who trained him in the crafts of painting, engraving and the woodcut. After the completion of his apprenticeship he travelled widely, visiting engraving workshops and embarking on a series of sketching expeditions; finally he visited Italy, where he saw the work of his Renaissance contemporaries and was particularly impressed with that of Mantegna.

On his return to Nuremberg Dürer opened his own workshop; in the ensuing years he produced many paintings, drawings and etchings that were to raise the status of artists throughout the northern countries and give him prestige equal to that of a nobleman. Dürer is particularly noted for his etchings and engravings such as *Knight, Death and the Devil* and *The Nativity*, and paintings such as his *Four Apostles*. Some of his most moving and sensitive work is to be found in drawings and watercolours such as *The Artist's Mother* and *Italian Mountains*.

In Dürer's portrait of his father [141], we see evidence of his obvious devotion to his parents. In writing of his father, Dürer described him as a man who 'passed his life in great toil and stern hard labour . . . but won praise from all who knew him, for he lived an honourable Christian life, was a man patient of spirit, mild and peaceable to all'. We have only to look at the portrait to see how successful Dürer was in capturing these qualities. Painted when the artist was 19 years of age, it clearly displays his sympathy with the subject, together with his superb draughtsmanship, and mastery of form through the use of chiaroscuro.

Evidence of Dürer's innate curiosity and his rare powers of observation when directed to nature may be found in many of his paintings. In *Italian Mountains* [142], we see a delightful watercolour executed during his travels as a journeyman. In the foreground, particularly, it has a wonderfully free plastic quality that anticipates the approach adopted by Paul Cézanne some 400 years later.

Hans Holbein (1497-1543)

Holbein was twenty-six years younger than Dürer; his paintings show none of the conflict between Gothic and Renaissance influences that is evidenced in Dürer's work, because of his exposure to contemporary commercial life in Augsburg, the city of his birth, and the humanistic cultural climate that prevailed in Switzerland, where he lived for many years. He went to England several times and became court painter to King Henry VIII.

Compared to portraits by his southern contemporaries, Holbein's works appear 'plain' or perhaps even austere. However, he is a painter of great skill and has no need of frills or gimmicks to make his work interesting; there is a feeling of authenticity by which the personality of the sitter comes through to us with conviction. Such is the case in the portrait of Nicolas Kratzer [143]. In depicting the earnest court astronomer to Henry VIII at work with a polyhedron and various other pieces of ancillary equipment, Holbein has recorded a real person without flattery. Despite the simplicity of statement, he has created an effect of nobility and monumentality comparable with the achievements of his High Renaissance contemporaries.

RENAISSANCE PAINTING IN NORTHERN ITALY

Giovanni Bellini (1430-1516)

Giovanni Bellini and his brother Gentile trained in the workshop founded by their father Jacopo. Mantegna, a relative by marriage, had a strong influence on the young artists who were instrumental in establishing the traditions of Venetian painting.

Giovanni was by far the more successful of the two brothers and enjoyed a great deal of popularity. Masaccio's *Holy Trinity* [125] is a probable source of inspiration for such paintings as Giovanni's San Giobbe altarpiece of 1487 [144]; we observe that both employ the Renaissance pyramidal composition and have the same symmetrical balancing of figures; further, they both place the eye at or near ground level and rely heavily on an architectural setting. It is difficult to discern subtle differences in prints of this size, but if we look closely, we may observe in Bellini's altarpiece a softer rendering of forms, a greater interest in the use of light and atmosphere, and an ex-ultation in colour that was to typify this artist's later work and become one of the most dominant factors in Venetian painting.

Andrea Mantegna (1431-1506)

Andrea Mantegna trained in Padua and gave great impetus to the Renaissance movement in northern Italy. His early works were executed in the chapel of the church of the Eremitani in Padua (which was almost totally destroyed by bombing in 1944), and show the influence of the sculptor Donatello who had spent ten years in northern Italy.

Looking at Mantegna's *St Sebastian* [145], we are perhaps reminded of *The Rout of San Romano* [128] and Uccello's interest in perspective and the rendering of objects that diminish with distance. This, however, is where the similarity ends, as Uccello's figures appear toy-like when compared with Mantegna's St Sebastian; the figure is full of movement in the classical *contraposta* position (strongly reminiscent of Donatello's *David* [130]), and gives the impression of being carved from stone, as it appears no softer than the classical column to which the saint is bound. It is reported that Mantegna had an interest in the ruins of classical antiquity equal to that of an archaeologist, and this is manifest in the skill with which he has depicted the broken marble and crumbling masonry.

[144] Bellini: San Giobbe altarpiece, oil on wood, 1487. 471 x 258 cm. Accademia, Venice

[145] Mantegna: *St Sebastian*, oil on canvas, *c.* 1455-9. 260 x 147 cm. Louvre, Paris

THE HIGH RENAISSANCE

Donato Bramante (1444-1514)

Bramante was born at Monte Asdrualdo near Urbino, one of the great centres of the period, and his birth preceded the death of Brunelleschi by two years. He was trained for a time by the painter Andrea Mantegna, and in addition to this there is evidence of an undoubted influence by Leonardo late in the fifteenth century.

From Leonardo he probably derived his interest in the centralized plan, evidence of which we may see in several of his designs. He often had grandiose schemes, many of which never came to fruition; among these were his proposed plan for the Law Courts and his design for St Peter's in Rome. He is considered an important figure in architecture because he perpetuated the style and traditions established by Brunelleschi and Alberti, and had a subsequent influence on the architecture of Italy and Europe in general.

The Tempietto [146] is a delightful little chapel (4·6 metres internal diameter) in the cloisters of San Pietro in Montorio, Rome. Its design recalls a Roman temple and is considered to be a yardstick of architectural perfection. In it Bramante has achieved a sculptural quality heightened by the effect of light striking the Doric peristyle and recessed window openings of the drum.

[146] Bramante: The Tempietto, San Pietro in Montorio, Rome. 1502

[147] Leonardo: *The Virgin of the Rocks*, oil on wood, *c.* 1483-1506. 189.5 x 120 cm. National Gallery, London

Leonardo da Vinci (1452-1519)

Leonardo is the epitome of the High Renaissance ideal of the universal man. His brilliant inquiring mind led him to investigate previously unexplored areas of scientific endeavour, resulting in valuable contributions in the fields of anatomy, defence, astronomy, architecture, aeronautics, physics, geology and physiology. Unfortunately, the genius of his mind was such that he rarely developed fully any one investigation before he began to explore some new project.

Leonardo, born at the town of Vinci near Florence, was the illegitimate son of a noted Florentine lawyer. He was raised in his father's house and at the age of 17 was apprenticed to one of the leading artists of the day, Andrea del Verrocchio. His formal training was in the traditional Florentine style, and his painting of the left-hand angel in his master's *Baptism* in the Uffizi, Florence, is said to be the reason for Verrocchio giving up painting in preference to sculpture; he reputedly considered the young da Vinci better equipped to handle the painting commissions in his workshop.

[148] Leonardo: *The Last Supper*, fresco, 1497. 420 x 910 cm. Santa Maria delle Grazie, Milan

[149] Leonardo: *Mona Lisa*, oil on canvas, 1507. 97 x 51.5 cm. Louvre, Paris

[150] Leonardo: *Self-portrait*, red chalk, 1512. 33.3 x 21.4 cm. Palazzo Reale, Turin

[151] Leonardo: *Grotesque Faces*, pen drawing, c. 1490. 26 x 20.5 cm. Royal Collection, Windsor Castle

Although much earlier than the works of either Michelangelo or Raphael, his painting of *The Virgin of the Rocks* [147] has been considered by some authorities to herald the beginning of the High Renaissance period, as it introduces Leonardo's technique of *sfumato*, the softening of forms using light and shade. Objects appear to dissolve slightly and merge, and so are more closely related. This invention, while lending weight and volume to the forms, gave a greater sense of vitality to the composition and was a technique that was later developed by Caravaggio and Rembrandt.

Leonardo's *Last Supper* [148] is generally acknowledged as the first painting of the High Renaissance; although in a very poor state of repair it clearly indicates da Vinci's mastery of rendering three-dimensional forms in space. Painted for the monastery of Santa Maria delle Grazie in Milan, it depicts the poignant moment after Christ makes the prophecy of betrayal. For the purposes of compositional harmony Leonardo has crowded all the disciples on one side of the table, where they are arranged symmetrically in four groups of three, and contrary to previous practice he has not segregated the figure of Judas, although he is still obvious because of his truculent attitude. The architectural lines of the walls and ceiling lead directly to the central figure of Christ, who appears as a quietly passive figure in the drama that is being enacted. The disciples are a study of human emotions, for in each face we see reflected their close personal relationship with Christ and their differing reactions to his pronouncement.

The *Mona Lisa* [149] is the embodiment of Leonardo's ideals of painting; he has represented not only the physical features of the sitter but also her personality and character. The mood is difficult to define, and for years art historians, poets and songwriters have puzzled over the subject's enigmatic quality and timeless charm. Leonardo has again used his invention of *sfumato* to soften the expression and create 'lost and found' areas where parts of the figure appear to merge into the background; this, coupled with the masterly painting of the drapery and hands, is further evidence of Leonardo's expertise. The background displays a strange, almost Surrealistic quality with snaking roads and waterways and moon-like rock forms. The left-hand landscape appears lower than that on the right and the rather nebulous rock forms by the lake in the top right disappear in an atmospheric haze, further strengthening the timeless quality of the portrait.

Just as important as his paintings are Leonardo's drawings, which cover a tremendous range of subject matter from notations on his scientific experiments to those of his figure studies represented here. It is interesting to compare the delightful self-portrait draw in red chalk [150] with the portrait Raphael painted of Leonardo as Plato in *The School of Athens* [152]. This portrait gives us an insight into the inquiring mind of this titan of the Renaissance, and even in old age it displays the handsome features for which he was noted as a young man.

While other artists of the day often sought inspiration in classical antiquity and its idealized beauty, Leonardo in his search for truth was not afraid to depict old age and ugliness, as in his *Grotesque Faces* [151].

In both these drawings we see Leonardo's mastery of technique, together with a variation of outline that gives the drawing a sense of 'open form'; this, coupled with an economy of line and emphasis on essential aspects only, has strengthened Leonardo's place amongst the world's greatest draughtsmen.

[152] Raphael: *The School of Athens*, fresco, 1510-1. Stanza della Segnatura, Vatican, Rome

Raphael Sanzio (1483-1520)

Raphael was born in Urbino, and received his early training from his father, who was a mediocre artist. However, his important formal training was received in the workshop of Pietro Perugino, an Umbrian painter of considerable note, and Raphael's early works display a strong influence by his master. It was not long before Raphael's work had eclipsed that of Perugino and in 1504 he journeyed to Florence, where he came under the spell of the Florentine painters and in particular Leonardo da Vinci, who was thirty-one years his senior.

Having assimilated the skills and techniques of the Florentines, he journeyed to Rome where his famous architect uncle, Donato Bramante, was instrumental in obtaining commissions for him with the powerful Pope Julius II. Because of his obvious skill and easy relaxed manner, Raphael's services were in great demand. One of his most important commissions was the decoration of the rooms of the pope's apartment (known as the Stanze); among the famous frescoes that he painted here is *The School of Athens* [152]. We have previously seen architectural settings used for figure compositions, and in this we recall Masaccio's achievements [125], but never had architecture been used in such a grand manner before; *The School of Athens* is considered one of the greatest spatial compositions of all time. The vast coffered and vaulted

ceiling, together with the general feeling of richness and splendour, is a fitting backdrop to the two great philosophers, Plato and Aristotle. The philosophers are clearly indicated by the lines of perspective in the marble flooring and the architectural lines of the walls, which lead us directly to the dominant figures as they do in da Vinci's *Last Supper* [148]. Raphael has arranged the disciples of each school of philosophy on either side, and they are depicted busily engaged in discussion, argument, or the solving of mathematical problems. For the Christ-like figure of Plato, Raphael has used a portrait of Leonardo, while the figure of Pythagoras is a portrait of the architect Bramante; the figure of Heraclitus sitting on the lowest step is a portrait of Michelangelo, and at the right we see what may be a self-portrait of the artist. This painting expresses the ideals of the High Renaissance, with its association of Neo-Platonic thought and the cross-fertilization of religious beliefs, as well as the humanistic belief in the importance and dignity of man.

After *The School of Athens*, Raphael relied less on architectural setting and more on the figures and their movement for compositional harmony; in his *Triumph of Galatea* [153] we see illustrated a theme from Greek mythology which bears witness to this. The centrally placed figure of the nymph is being drawn across the sea in her shell chariot by two dolphins, and she turns smiling as she is pursued by Polyphemus. The composition is a

71

[153] Raphael: *The Triumph of Galatea*, fresco, 1511-2. 295 x 225 cm. Villa Farnesina, Rome

[154] Raphael: *Madonna del Granduca*, oil on wood, 1504-5. 84.5 x 65.9 cm. Palazzo Pitti, Florence

[155] Michelangelo: *David*, marble, 1501-4. Height 505 cm. Accademia, Florence

masterpiece of harmony and balance, with each figure relating to and complementing the others. The flat triangular format of the main figures is repeated by the cupids, who hover above the nymph and further direct our attention to her.

It is interesting to compare Raphael's *Madonna del Granduca* [154] with da Vinci's *Mona Lisa* [149]. Raphael has assimilated Leonardo's invention of *sfumato*, as evidenced by the softness of the features of his Madonna, and this, together with his mastery of chiaroscuro, has enabled him to create a Madonna that in its charm and grace has never been surpassed.

Raphael is considered by many to be an eclectic, borrowing from both Leonardo and Michelangelo; while his work lacks the range and depth of knowledge of da Vinci and the power and vitality of Michelangelo, he is still esteemed the key figure in the development of the 'grand manner' of the High Renaissance period. His work, more than that of any other artist, combines the classical ideals of the Renaissance, its compositional order and humanism, with the scientific discoveries relating to form and space; thus, with his great draughtsmanship and colour sense, he produced paintings that charmed and were appreciated by all levels of society.

Michelangelo Buonarroti (1475-1564)

Michelangelo is considered by many to be the greatest artist of the sixteenth century, and both the power and the range of his work do much to support this claim. He was a sculptor, painter and architect, and his displays of expertise in each of these fields confirmed for artists an equality of status with the philosophers and writers of the powerful Medici court.

Michelangelo's father was a magistrate at Caprese, the place of his son's birth, and shortly after that event he moved his family to the thriving commercial city of Florence, where the young Michelangelo was apprenticed to the leading fresco painter of the day, Domenico Ghirlandaio. His brief apprenticeship to this artist was sufficient for him to gain a thorough knowledge of the art of fresco painting. Thence he entered the garden workshop of Lorenzo dei Medici, where under *Il Magnifico's* patronage he received a thorough grounding in the skills of sculpture from Bertoldo, who had been a pupil of Donatello.

Much of Michelangelo's security was shattered by the death of Lorenzo, who had taken the young artist into his household; shortly after this Michelangelo went to Bologna and then to Rome, where he did much to establish his reputation with the completion of his first *Pietà* in 1500. Returning to Florence he was commissioned to carve *David* [155] by the city fathers. It is understandable that this huge figure should owe allegiance to the works of the ancient Hellenic sculptors, for while in Rome Michelangelo studied at length sculptural finds from the Classic period. As Donatello's *David* was the first free-standing monumental nude since classical antiquity, so Michelangelo's is the first work of this kind in the High Renaissance and typifies the spirit of this short-lived period — man confident in his own abilities. The sculpture makes evident a pride in intellect, youth and freedom. We may observe that Michelangelo's *David* is more static than Donatello's [130], with its sinuous movement, or Bernini's [172], with its explosive, dynamic quality, but it must be remembered that it represents a different moment in time. Whereas Donatello has depicted David after the defeat of Goliath, and Bernini's David is engaged in the conflict, Michelangelo has portrayed David, slingshot in hand, as he looks off into the distance towards his adversary. He appears as a youth, caught between adolescence and manhood, with fully developed hands and head that look out of keeping with his youthful but powerful body. Rather

[156] Michelangelo: *The Last Judgment*, fresco, 1536-41. Altar wall, Sistine chapel, Rome

[157] Michelangelo: Vestibule of the Laurentian library, Florence. 1524-6

[158] Michelangelo: *Madonna and Child*, marble, 1524-7 (unfinished). Height 223 cm. Medici chapel, Florence

than detracting from the work, however, this lends conviction and power to a figure which exhibits a combination of both relaxation and tension.

Michelangelo, who outlived the High Renaissance, was responsible for a great deal of the impetus for the Mannerist period, and in his later work, particularly architecture, he anticipated the Baroque.

Michelangelo never considered himself a painter, and indeed he was reluctant to disclose that he had trained as such, but it is undoubtedly his Sistine ceiling, executed between 1508 and 1512 on the order of Pope Julius II, for which he is best remembered. Twenty-two years later he was recalled to Rome by Pope Paul III to decorate the end wall of the Sistine chapel, and it is in his *Last Judgment* [156] that we see depicted with religious fervour the feelings of the Counter-Reformation. The quiet relaxed harmonies of the High Renaissance are replaced by this seething mass of humanity on Judgment Day — there is not one smiling or tranquil face in the vast composition, and the saved and condemned are overpowered by the titanic figure of God, who is pronouncing his judgment on the damned. Just below this powerful figure we see St Bartholomew holding his tattered skin (indicating his martyrdom in which he had been flayed alive), and on the grisly remains is Michelangelo's self-portrait.

In this painting, as in all of the frescoes by Michelangelo, we see figures conceived by a sculptor and envisaged in the round — this, together with his vast knowledge of human anatomy gained from his dissection of many corpses, lends a weight and power to his figures that has rarely been equalled.

Michelangelo's contribution to architecture in the Mannerist period is seen in his vestibule for the Laurentian library [157]. Here in stone and mortar are the feelings of tension and unrest evident in the paintings of the period. All the natural orders seem to be reversed: a feeling of compression is achieved by a variety of caprices, such as the blank marble where we would expect to see light issuing from what appear as window openings; columns that appear locked within the walls and give the impression of being neither supported nor supporting; and finally a staircase that appears to flow downwards at us, and in its overpowering movement almost prohibits our ascent. As though that were not sufficient, Michelangelo has further added to the apparent tension by introducing stairs, on either side of the main flight, that appear to lead to a blank wall. All of this combines to produce a feeling of excitement in space which is so often a characteristic of Mannerism.

In quieter mood, but still in keeping with the Mannerist tendencies, is the *Madonna and Child* [158] from the Medici mortuary chapel. This piece is one of a group of seven, and as in all of his mature work there is a retention of the quality of the marble from which it is carved; this 'organic' quality becomes more and more pronounced in the artist's later sculpture, for example the unfinished slaves with their forms under extreme tension as they seem to struggle and miraculously materialize from the block.

Michelangelo worked with an almost religious fervour even in his old age, and the last years of his life were largely devoted to his designs for the great church of Christendom, St Peter's in Rome.

THE HIGH RENAISSANCE
IN NORTHERN ITALY

Giorgione (c. 1478-1510)

Giorgio Barbarelli, known as Giorgione, was born at Castelfranco, a small village near Venice. According to Vasari, at an early age he was sent to study in the workshop of Giovanni Bellini, and it is possible that here he acquired some of the lyrical charm that is evident in the handful of paintings attributed to him.

Giorgione's work is, in a way, as revolutionary as that of the innovators of the early Renaissance, for he uses light and colour as vehicles for emotional expression and in so doing liberates Venetian art from the artistic traditions of Florence and Rome. Vasari reported that Giorgione did not draw compositions on the canvas but built his forms with patches of colour. This resulted in his paintings possessing the delightfully fresh paint quality that was to become the heritage of Venetian art.

The lyrical quality of Giorgione's work is evident in his painting *The Tempest* [159], which probably represents a scene from ancient mythology. The subject matter of the painting is intriguing. We can only speculate on the reason why the young mother feeding her child has been banished from the city, and also on the presence of the shepherd. The unreality of the situation is heightened by Giorgione's dramatic use of light in contrasting the dark, forbidding cloud masses with the high-keyed city buildings and foreground figures.

Giorgione knew how to invest his paintings with an air of mystery — to have them pose questions that seem to require logical answers but that defy reasoning: thus he continues to enchant and mystify with both the world he created and the manner of its creation.

Titian (1477/85-1576)

Tiziano Vecelli, whom we call Titian, was born at Pieve di Cadore in the Dolomites; while there is an old document which puts his birth at 1477, it is thought most unlikely that he was born prior to 1485. His early training was in the workshop of the Venetian painters Gentile and Giovanni Bellini, and later that of Giorgione, from whom he derived the more significant inspiration.

After the latter's death in his early thirties, Titian carried on the traditions formulated by the Bellini and Giorgione, and in so doing was the motivating force in Venetian painting for the next fifty years. He spent most of his painting life within the Mannerist period, but while his

[159] Giorgione: *The Tempest*, oil on canvas, c. 1505. 82 x 73 cm. Accademia, Venice

work often showed Mannerist tendencies he largely remained classical in approach, and his breadth of vision coupled with his grandness of style made him essentially an artist of the High Renaissance. He earns a place of greatness alongside Michelangelo, Leonardo and Raphael for his exciting compositions and noble, character-probing portraits.

Man with a Glove [160] illustrates the rich paint quality and compositional strength of his creations. There is nothing to distract attention from the sitter — there are no props or compositional 'gimmicks'. The background is quite abstract with just a suggestion of gradation of tone, and lends a soft, dark, velvety quality to the painting; it also complements the pensive, nostalgic appearance of the subject.

It is not only on paint quality and directness of approach that Titian's reputation is built, for we find in his *Entombment* [161] that he is also a master of pictorial organization in the classical sense. In studying *The Entombment* we become aware of the ease of the figure placement and the way our attention is attracted to the figure of

[160] Titian: *Man with a Glove*, oil on canvas, 1522. 100 x 89 cm. Louvre, Paris

Christ, both by the semi-elliptic forms of the disciples who support his legs and body, and by the directional gaze of the Virgin and Mary Magdalene to the left. We also become aware of the way in which the semicircular form of the dead Christ answers the rhythm of the disciples who support him; they in turn lead to the third disciple, who supports his arm and forms the apex of a shallow triangular composition. In this as in all Titian's compositions, we see the unifying light which relates every figure and results in a balanced, harmonious composition.

[161] Titian: *The Entombment*, oil on canvas, c. 1525. 148 x 205 cm. Louvre, Paris

[162] Veronese: *The Feast in the House of Levi*, oil on canvas, 1573. 550 x 1278 cm. Accademia, Venice

MANNERISM (*c.*1520-*c.*1580)

Mannerism forms a link or bridge between High Renaissance art and that of the Baroque period. The great art historian Vasari described the term as meaning 'in the manner of' Michelangelo and Raphael. It was a time of political unrest and bloodshed, with the Inquisition's reign of terror in Spain, the sack of Rome in 1527, and the challenge to the authority of the Roman Catholic Church by Martin Luther. 1520 was the year of Raphael's death and marked the decline of the High Renaissance ideals of harmony, balance and beauty; even Michelangelo was abandoning many of the idealized attitudes of the High Renaissance period.

As a result of this, we find at times overcrowded canvases, ill-defined and rather dramatic lighting effects, figures that appear to hover in space or move out of the canvas, harsh metallic surface treatment, and the use of strong diagonal recession to create a nightmarish feeling of depth. The period has been described as 'a time out of joint', and evidence of this can be seen in Michelangelo's design for the Laurentian library [157] and Palladio's Villa Rotunda [169].

Paolo Veronese (1528-1588)

Chronologically Paolo Cagliari, called Veronese, belongs to the Mannerist period, but his work is not as turbulent as the paintings of the other Mannerists. Until 1553 he lived in Verona where he came under the influence of Mantegna and Bellini, but it was Raphael who probably had most influence on his compositions. In his early years in Venice he received many commissions for large mural decorations, and in these he created an exciting illusionistic art form, for he was a brilliant decorator, inheriting the Venetian love of colour and anecdote.

One such painting is *The Feast in the House of Levi* [162], a colossal canvas 12·8 metres in length, commissioned by the Venetian monastery of SS Giovanni e Paolo as a *Last Supper*. It is interesting to compare Veronese's interpretation, with its great crowd of figures and gay feeling of pageantry, with Leonardo's treatment of the same subject [148]. The main architectural lines formed by the staircase lead the eye not to Christ, but rather to a 'master of ceremonies' on the right and a self-portrait on the left, and it is of interest that Veronese included, seated centrally under the left-hand archway, a portrait of Titian, and under the right, one of Michelangelo. This gala banquet caused Veronese to be called before the Inquisition — the transcript of his examination makes very interesting reading — and the eventual

verdict was that he should repaint certain parts of the picture; instead, he chose to merely change the title to its present *Feast in the House of Levi*.

Pieter Breughel the Elder (*c.* 1525-1569)

Little is known about Breughel's origins; the date and place of his birth, as well as the social position of his parents, are matters of conjecture. It is interesting to speculate on his background as it could well provide the key to an understanding of his favourite subject, peasant life. Breughel's early training as an engraver in Antwerp preceded his admission to the Guild of Painters in 1551. This was followed by a trip to Italy, during which one of his main interests appears to have been depicting panoramic views observed in his travels.

His *Hunters in the Snow* [163] displays this interest in landscape and is in fact a landscape with figures rather than a figure composition. It owes ancestry to the Gothic tradition (cf. Limbourg's prayer-book illumination for the month of February, [76]) and there is a fairly obvious influence from the work of Hieronymus Bosch. Breughel has made his figures appear as faceless nonentities, trudging wearily homewards after a day's hunting. The cold starkness of the colours is in keeping with the mood of winter, and this is relieved only by the warmth of the brickwork of the inn to the left of the composition, and the coats of some of the dogs accompanying the hunters. The figures are overpowered by the landscape, particularly those skating on the frozen ponds; the people, dogs and trees do not cast shadows, although they are all carefully modelled. Breughel has based his composition on a series of receding diagonals to lead the eye from the bottom right-hand corner to the inn, thence down the snowdrift to the skating figures, and on into the marvellous snow-covered landscape stretching away into the distance.

Typical of Breughel's peasant paintings is his *Country Wedding* [164]. The diagonal placement of the guests' table reminds us of Tintoretto's *Last Supper* [165]. The bride is seated in front of the cloth hanging on the wall; her hands are folded and on her face there is a rather smug, stupid expression. It is more difficult to ascertain the whereabouts of the groom, but it is possible that he is the figure sitting on the bride's right, greedily shovelling food into his mouth. To the right of the red-coated attendant carrying food on a tray improvised from a door we see the priest, who has obviously officiated at the ceremony, engaged in conversation with the only person of noble

[163] Breughel: *Hunters in the Snow*, oil on wood, 1565. 117 x 162 cm. Kunsthistorisches Museum, Vienna

[164] Breughel: *Country Wedding*, oil on wood, *c.* 1568. 114 x 163 cm. Kunsthistorisches Museum, Vienna

[165] Tintoretto: *The Last Supper*, oil on canvas, 1592-4. 365.5 x 569 cm. San Giorgio Maggiore, Venice

bearing in the entire assembly. The satirical observation in this and other similar pictures indicates that Breughel was probably an interested outsider looking on, rather than himself a member of this peasant way of life.

In many of his paintings we find Mannerist tendencies, for example the nightmarish depiction of space and the strong use of diagonal recession, and while his works do not appear explicitly religious they are often parables on such worldly sins as the gluttony evident in *Country Wedding*.

Tintoretto (1518-1594)

Jacopo Robusti, a pupil of Titian in Venice, was nicknamed Tintoretto. His painting is perhaps the complete embodiment of the Mannerist period, and its anticlassical tendencies form the bridge between the High Renaissance and Baroque periods. Tintoretto allegedly wanted to design in the manner of Michelangelo and paint like Titian, and indeed, the influence of both is evident in his work.

In keeping with Mannerist tendencies he developed a style in which at times we see strange, harsh lighting effects highlighting vibrant colours, the elongation of forms (such as *Christ Walking on the Waves*), rapid nervous brushwork, and compositions which appear strangely Surrealistic, with a feeling of space that often screams off into the distance.

The drama with which Tintoretto imbued his work is seen when we compare his *Last Supper* [165] with that of Leonardo [148] or Veronese [162], both of which appear static beside Tintoretto's violent movement and strong diagonal recession. In addition to differences in spatial composition, the feature of da Vinci's picture is Christ's declaration that 'one of you shall betray me', an announcement that has a marked effect on the disciples. Judas Iscariot played an important role in Leonardo's painting, but Tintoretto's Judas is a relatively unimportant figure; he is isolated and on the opposite side of the table to Christ, who is performing the sacrament. It is interesting to note that the figure of Christ, while centrally placed, would be comparatively insignificant were it not for the blinding light emanating from his body. From the serving maid kneeling on the floor in the foreground, the eye is led to the servant with his back to us, thence around the room via the group of figures and back along the trestle table. Tintoretto makes a theatrical statement of flickering light and smoke which become angels in various positions of violent foreshortening.

One of Tintoretto's most daring examples of foreshortening is the descending saint in *St Mark Rescuing a Slave* [166]. The brilliance of this work is perhaps best summed up in the words of the leading contemporary Venetian art critic Aretino, writing to Tintoretto: '. . . so there is no man so little instructed in the virtues of drawing, that he is not amazed at the relief of the figure, where it lies all naked on the ground, offered up to the cruelty of martyrdom. The colours are flesh, the lines are rounded, the body is alive. And I swear to you by the goodwill I bear you, that the complexion, the expression and the aspect of the crowd that surrounds him are befitting to the part they play, that the scene appears more real than feigned.' This evaluation suggests the stature which Tintoretto enjoyed in his lifetime, and certainly time has proved that his work represents one of the peaks in the tradition of Western art.

El Greco (1541-1614)

Domenicos Theotocopoulos was born in Crete (then under Venetian domination) and became known as El Greco, meaning 'The Greek'. In about 1564-5 he travelled to Venice where he entered the workshop of Titian and was greatly influenced by this master, as well as by Tintoretto and Veronese, both of whom were working in Venice at the time. In 1570 he moved to Rome where the composition and manner of both Michelangelo and Raphael had an impact on him, as did the Roman Mannerist painters with their, at times, spaceless qualities. In 1576 he journeyed to Toledo, Spain, which was subsequently to become his home.

He enjoyed popularity in his lifetime and painted numerous portraits of the nobility of Toledo. In these portraits his sitters are often endowed with an ethereal look and a feeling of intensity approaching that of religious fervour. This quality was heightened by the elongated and distorted appearance of his figures, which seem to reach heavenward with a flickering flame-like quality.

In his *View of Toledo* [167] painted *c.* 1600, we see perhaps not the first example of landscape painting in the Western world, but certainly the most expressive up to this point of time. The painting is far removed from a purely topographical recording of landscape elements, and appears to take on an almost religious quality. We can sense the affection that El Greco had for this city, and this is further borne out by the fact that a similar view appears time and again as the backdrop to other compositions. Unlike many of his figure paintings, which are noted for their 'Titianesque' colouring, *Toledo* is by comparison very quiet and subdued, with its yellowy greens and silvery greys which reflect the colours of the Spanish countryside. To really appreciate the tonal composition of an El Greco painting we should view it through half-closed eyes. In doing this we discover the strong darks and lights leading the eye up and through the picture surface, which now appears to have flattened out considerably, taking on a rather two-dimensional abstract quality.

In his *Espolio* (the disrobing of Christ) [168] we see figures crowding around the central figure of Christ, and at variance with the harmonious Renaissance ideal we find

[166] Tintoretto: *St Mark Rescuing a Slave*, oil on canvas, 1548. 415 x 543.5 cm. Accademia, Venice

[167] El Greco: *View of Toledo*, oil on canvas, *c.* 1600. 121 x 107.8 cm. Metropolitan Museum of Art, New York. Bequest of Mrs H. O. Havermeyer, 1929; The H. O. Havermeyer Collection

79

[168] El Greco: *El Espolio*, oil on canvas, 1577-9. 285 x 173 cm. Cathedral sacristy, Toledo

an almost chaotic, jostling mob, contrasting strongly with the calm central figure whose compositional dominance is accentuated by the brilliance of his robe.

Andrea Palladio (1508-1580)

Palladio is considered one of the greatest architects of the second half of the sixteenth century. Like Alberti he published a treatise on the theory of architecture, and this, together with his obvious ability as a practical architect, resulted in his widespread reputation. In addition to his study of the ruins of classical antiquity in Rome, Palladio was obviously influenced by the works of both Bramante and Michelangelo.

The Villa Rotunda [169], one of his most famous buildings, shows the inspiration of classical architecture in its use of the temple front in the Ionic order, imposed on an otherwise square edifice. So successful was Palladio in creating the feeling of a classical building that we are reminded strongly of the Roman Pantheon erected some 1400 years earlier. An interesting facet of Palladio's villa is that there are four identical sides; this may at first appear confusing, but it certainly lends a sense of charm and grace to the structure, and after all, it follows an axiom of modern architecture which states that a building has neither front, back, nor sides, but four elevations.

Palladio's influence on subsequent periods was considerable, and in the first half of the eighteenth century English architects in particular set about carefully following his doctrines; in so doing they created what is known today as the Palladian style.

[169] Palladio: Villa Rotunda, Vicenza. Begun *c.* 1550

[170] Borromini: Façade of San Carlo alle Quattro Fontane, Rome. 1665-7

THE SEVENTEENTH CENTURY

Baroque Architecture

The Baroque style marks the time of the Counter-Reformation. Its confident lavishness sought to win people back to Catholicism, not by the sword as in the Reformation, but with displays of opulence and heavenly splendour.

To achieve these effects architects employed classical forms, but used them in such a way that the buildings took on a sculptural or plastic quality; designs frequently involved curved wall surfaces which led the eye to a central focal point, as opposed to the straight-line repetition of forms that was common in Renaissance architecture. Interiors also shared in the change, and we find ceilings blazing forth with colourful hosts of angels and the promise of life hereafter; these figures are often placed in a painted architectural environment in which it is difficult to distinguish between actual and illusionistic detail.

In the history of art, names or labels have frequently been given to periods as a term of derision (for example, 'Gothic' meaning grotesque); 'Baroque' may have originally been derived from the Portuguese *barroco*, meaning an irregularly shaped pearl, the intended reference being to the over-extravagant and dramatic forms used in both building and decoration alike.

Francesco Borromini (1599-1667)

Borromini was to a certain extent overshadowed by the personality of his great contemporary Bernini, but while his buildings at times may not be as grand in scale as those of his colleague, they are no less important architecturally.

Borromini's skill is evidenced in the diminutive church of San Carlo alle Quattro Fontane in Rome [170], which is typically Baroque in the sculptural quality of its façade that appears to flow from both sides to the centrally placed doorway. This sense of climax is further emphasized in the flowing sculptural effect leading up to the central medallion, which together with the high statues of angels and saints indicates the function of the building. The overall effect is far removed from the static, relaxed mood of Brunelleschi's Pazzi chapel [120], and rather suggests a writhing restless tension, as though it had life and was capable of movement. This same feeling of movement and sculptural form is present in his famous church of Sant' Agnese in the Piazza Navona, Rome, but in this the treatment is far more restrained.

[171] Bernini: *The Ecstasy of St Theresa*, marble, 1645-52. Life size. Cornaro chapel, Santa Maria della Vittoria, Rome

Giovanni Lorenzo Bernini (1598-1680)

Bernini was undoubtedly the greatest sculptor-architect of his century and in the power and range of his work he reminds us of Michelangelo, who had died thirty-four years before Bernini's birth. He was the son of the sculptor Pietro Bernini, and served his apprenticeship under his father.

As an architect, most of his time was spent on St Peter's cathedral in Rome, designing the massive bronze baldachin, a combination of architectural and sculptural forms with its strange twisted and richly decorated columns. This canopy covers the tomb of St Peter and rises to a height of 30 metres directly under Michelangelo's dome. His other architectural works for St Peter's include the bronze throne of the patron saint and the gigantic piazza, with its Doric colonnades.

In the field of portraiture Bernini displayed his consummate skill. His powerful figures are reminiscent of the Hellenistic Greek period, and his dramatic sculptural style ideally suited the requirements of the Jesuit Order. His life-size group of Saint Theresa [171] in the Cornaro chapel of Santa Maria della Vittoria at Rome is evidence of the way Bernini's sculpture expressed the ideals of the Counter-Reformation. At first glance it may appear theatrical and sentimental, but its function was to win back to Catholicism those whose faith was in doubt by displays of heavenly splendour. Saint Theresa, who was canonized

[172] Bernini: *David*,
marble, 1623. Height 170
cm. Borghese Gallery,
Rome

[173] Caravaggio: *The
Calling of St Matthew*, oil
on canvas, 1600. 338 x
348 cm. San Luigi dei
Francesi, Rome

[174] Caravaggio: *The
Supper at Emmaus*, oil on
canvas, *c.* 1598. 139 x 195
cm. National Gallery,
London

during the seventeenth century, described how an angel of
the Lord had pierced her heart with a flaming arrow — in
Bernini's representation the closed eyes and slightly parted
lips all contribute to the ecstasy of the divine moment.
Gilded bronze rays of light lit by a concealed window
impart a further dramatic if somewhat theatrical impact to
the work.

It is interesting to compare the different concepts behind
the *Davids* of Donatello [130], Michelangelo [155] and
Bernini [172]. All three owe a debt to classical antiquity
and all three employ *contraposta* in the rendering of the
figure. Donatello's is a rather sensuous youth, obviously
conscious of his own physical beauty but possessing a
lyrical charm and grace. Michelangelo's gigantic youth
appears confident in his own ability and is the most static
of the three, but nevertheless symbolizes the ideals of the
High Renaissance. Bernini's, full of movement and power,
appears as a fierce determined fighter and perhaps the most
suitable opponent for the mighty Goliath. So convincing is
the energy and power of Bernini's *David* that we are made
conscious of Goliath, invisible though he is. We may well
have a preference for a particular *David*, but we cannot say
that one is better than the other because all three are in
accord with the differing requirements and ideals of their
respective periods.

Michelangelo da Caravaggio (1573-1610)

Michelangelo Merisi was born in the small town of
Caravaggio which lies in the foothills of the alps between
Brescia and Milan. He finished his apprenticeship at the age
of 15 and probably arrived in Rome two years later,
where he quickly established a reputation for having a
violent temper; he was frequently wanted by the authorities
for offences ranging from common assault to murder, and
as a result he seemed to spend a great deal of his life as a
fugitive.

Caravaggio's painting displays a radical break with both
the High Renaissance and Mannerist traditions, and he was
not particularly popular with the public, who expected
views of heavenly splendour in the Baroque style. Instead
they were shocked by a realism in which Christ and his
followers were seen as hard-working fishermen or tradesmen. Compared with the previous styles, Caravaggio's
paintings in another way give the impression of an almost
'super-realism'; the figures are so strongly modelled in
light and shade that they appear to be standing out from
the background in high relief.

The Calling of St Matthew [173] is obviously set in an
inn where Matthew has been busily engaged counting out
the tax money that he and his associates have collected.
The sword at the thigh of the figure with his back to us
indicates that he and the other figure in similar attire are
bodyguards to the collectors; further, their cavalier dress

is in strong contrast to the simple peasant garb of Christ and his disciple. Light plays a significant part in all of Caravaggio's compositions, for it is used not only to model form but also to lend poignancy to the dramatic moment.

The Supper at Emmaus [174], of which Caravaggio painted two versions, depicts the dramatic moment when Christ, through the breaking of the bread, reveals his identity to his two disciples Peter Simon and Cleophas. The use of chiaroscuro in this and other works by Caravaggio was an undoubted source of inspiration to many artists of the later Baroque period (cf. Velázquez' *Old Woman Cooking Eggs* [184]), and in particular to the man who was to become the undisputed master of chiaroscuro, Rembrandt van Rijn.

Frans Hals (*c.* 1580-1666)

There is very little documented evidence on the life of Hals; he was apparently born in Antwerp, and his parents moved to the prosperous trading city of Haarlem where he was enrolled in an art school between 1601 and 1604.

His early paintings were influenced by Rubens, but it was not long before Hals developed his own personal style which displayed brilliant technical dexterity and verve. It is often said that Hals was in the habit of frequenting the beer halls and taverns of Haarlem, and that he was just as much at home with a tankard of ale as he was with a brush, but it now seems that this reputation was largely undeserved. In his painting *The Lute Player* [175], his mastery of the fleeting impression — an almost snapshot-like quality — is apparent, and there is obvious rapport between subject and artist. If his early paintings at times appear to lack a deep emotional content, this is more than compensated for by their spontaneous freshness, sparkle and feeling of comradeship. The model for *The Lute Player* was a pupil of Hals who wagered that he could serenade a gracious lady and in so doing gain her attention. Hals has captured his pupil as he glances up and an infectious smile spreads across his face. To appreciate the life and vitality that Hals brought to portraiture we have only to compare *The Lute Player* with Holbein's *Portrait of Nicolas Kratzer* [143] or Dürer's *Portrait of the Artist's Father* [141].

Another painting which has this same spontaneity is *Malle Babbe, Sorceress of Haarlem* [176]. Here we see depicted this half-madwoman, half-witch (signified by the owl on her shoulder). As in Bernini's *David* [172], we are conscious of an implied person or persons; in this case they are the other occupants of the tavern who are obviously mocking the wretched creature, and we can almost hear the maniacal laugh as she hurls profanities back at her tormentors. Hals' last years were spent in a poorhouse, and his *Women Governors of the Old Men's Almshouse* of 1664 displays a profound understanding of human tragedy and suffering.

[175] Hals: *The Lute Player*, oil on canvas, date unknown. 66 x 58.4 cm. Rijksmuseum, Amsterdam

[176] Hals: *Malle Babbe, Sorceress of Haarlem*, oil on canvas, 1640. 75 x 64 cm. Gemäldegalerie, Berlin-Dahlem

Rembrandt van Rijn (1606-1669)

Rembrandt was born of reasonably affluent middle-class parents in Leiden. He studied at the University of Leiden where he acquired an interest in mythology. His studies were short-lived, however, as his love of drawing prevailed; his father first apprenticed him to a landscape painter, and later he trained in Amsterdam with Pieter Lastman, an artist of some note, whose love of chiaroscuro was to have a profound effect on him.

Returning to Leiden, Rembrandt received many portrait commissions. In 1631 he considered it expedient to move to the prosperous merchant city of Amsterdam, where he met and eventually married Saskia van Uylenburch, the daughter of a successful art dealer. Then followed one of the happiest and most prosperous periods of his life; he executed a splendid succession of paintings, drawings and etchings which reflect his state of well-being. Although Rembrandt himself was a Protestant, his style during this period was in keeping with the rather theatrical Baroque of the Roman Catholic Church, with its dramatic lighting reminiscent of Caravaggio and general feeling of richness.

In 1642 he painted the famous *Night Watch*, and in the same year Saskia died, a few months after the birth of their son Titus. His popularity as a painter now began to wane as a result of his stylistic development contrary to public taste; unwise expenditures contributed to his increasing financial difficulties, and eventually, in 1656, he was declared bankrupt. After the sale of his possessions and house, Hendrickje Stoffels, a faithful housekeeper, and his son Titus formed a business partnership to relieve him of financial worry by handling the sale of his works; this arrangement enabled him to paint in peace, unmolested by his creditors. More tragedy marked the last years of Rembrandt's life with the deaths of Hendrickje in 1664 and Titus in 1668.

Rembrandt's personal life is recorded forever in his paintings. Nowhere do we find a series of self-portraits as searching and as full of human understanding as those he executed: we can follow his life from the self-confidence of youth to the tragic loneliness of old age.

In all his pictures we see a very painterly approach, and we have only to look at *Woman Bathing* [177] to appreciate his tremendous technical dexterity. As in many of Rembrandt's paintings, we find a marvellous combination of 'lost and found' areas; the strong diagonal line of the right shoulder of the model (probably Hendrickje) contrasts with the rich dark background. Ignoring the verticality of the figure, we notice that Rembrandt has a diagonal of light running from the bottom left to the top right-hand corner of the composition, separating the two roughly triangular dark areas forming the foreground and background. Even where the loose-fitting garment covers the body, there is still a marvellous suggestion of the form

[177] Rembrandt: *Woman Bathing*, oil on canvas, 1655. 61.8 x 47 cm. National Gallery, London

[178] Rembrandt: *The Syndics of the Cloth Guild*, oil on canvas, 1662. 191 x 279 cm. Rijksmuseum, Amsterdam

beneath. The figure, with its solid, earthy quality, is a far cry from Botticelli's graceful goddesses, but Rembrandt's is no less delightful with its sparkle of freshness and directness of approach.

One of Rembrandt's last group portraits is also one of his greatest — *The Syndics of the Cloth Guild* of 1662 [178]. The various guilds of this time were powerful organizations, and the importance of the guild leaders in this portrait is suggested by the way in which the spectator's eye level is set slightly lower than the table at which the figures are seated. It is a remarkable group portrait: they all retain a feeling of individuality, and yet each in turn is related to the whole.

In addition to being one of the world's greatest painters, Rembrandt also left behind a series of etchings and drawings that in themselves would have earned him a place in the history of art.

Jan Vermeer (1632-1675)

We know very little about Vermeer's background except that he was born in Delft and is often known as Jan Vermeer van Delft; it is possible that he trained under one of Rembrandt's most brilliant pupils, but if not, his work certainly shows a strong influence from Rembrandt.

His paintings are almost as enigmatic as the life of the artist himself, for he manages to impart an air of timelessness to even the most mundane of domestic genre scenes. Vermeer explored, as a vehicle for his expression, a very limited field; time and again we see the same female type whose expression varies little from pose to pose, and yet he has imbued each composition with dignity and each object with an almost gem-like quality.

In *The Letter* [179] we see objects and figures alike arranged as in a still-life, bathed in a cool light that enters through a window to our left; Vermeer's observation of detail here recalls van Eyck's *Arnolfini*, even perhaps to the shoes in the foreground of both pictures; certainly the figures themselves are motionless.

The same soft, cool lighting effect evident in *The Letter* pervades most of Vermeer's works; the walls of his interiors reflect the subtle nuances of colour that are our one link with reality in these quiet compositions that seem to suggest a moment in time that is eternal.

Peter Paul Rubens (1577-1640)

Rubens was born at Siegen in Westphalia, and later moved to Antwerp where he received his training in both the social graces and intellectual studies that fitted him for his later activities as a diplomatic courier. The most important period of his artistic training was the eight years after 1600 that he spent in Italy, where he studied and copied works of

[179] Vermeer: *The Letter*, oil on canvas, *c.* 1662. 46.5 x 39 cm. Rijksmuseum, Amsterdam

the great Italian masters including his favourite, Titian; it was from this artist that he developed his marvellous colour sense and his method of spontaneous paint application. Born a Protestant he was converted to Catholicism, and his style of painting suited the requirements of the Counter-Reformation. In 1620 he was commissioned to paint forty pictures for the Jesuit church of Antwerp, and in order to carry out this and many other commissions he employed a large workshop of assistants. Usually Rubens would make small sketches in oils in which the overall composition would be designed and the colour scheme orchestrated; this would then be turned over to the assistants to paint on the large canvas. It is remarkable that the great bulk of work produced in Rubens' studio was so uniform in standard and unmistakably bore the master's stamp; it seems that often, with just a few deft strokes of the brush, he was able to give vitality and spontaneity to an assistant's work.

It is probable that part of the reason for Rubens' success was his business acumen: coupled with his pleasing personality, this enabled him to employ artists and craftsmen of the calibre of his best pupil, Anthony van Dyck.

Rubens tackled huge religious paintings and scenes from mythology with equal gusto, and we are able to get some idea of the vitality of his work from his painting *The Rape of the Daughters of Leucippus* [180]. This illustrates the legendary rape of the Sabine women, when Romulus, unable to procure wives for his soldiers, devised a plot to carry off women from the neighbouring town of Sabina. In the painting we see Romulus and Remus, the founders of ancient Rome, abducting two of the beautiful Sabines. Rubens has achieved a marvellous sense of movement through the twisting, turning figures; the two female forms balance one another perfectly, as do the figures of Romulus and Remus. Obviously the violent movement helps give the painting its sense of vitality, but it is the spontaneous application of paint that lends sparkle to the composition; in this work in which assistants participated, especially van

[180] Rubens: *The Rape of the Daughters of Leucippus*, oil on canvas, *c*. 1618. 222 x 209 cm. Alte Pinakothek, Munich

[181] Rubens: *Head of a Child*, oil on wood, 1616. 37 x 27 cm. Liechtenstein Gallery, Vaduz

[182] Van Dyck: *Self-portrait*, oil on canvas, 1621. 80 x 68 cm. Alte Pinakothek, Munich

Dyck, and in all of Rubens' paintings, we are never conscious of a 'tired' overworked appearance.

In addition to his mastery in landscape painting, Rubens displays consummate skill in portraiture, as evidenced in the delightfully sensitive *Head of a Child* [181], which comes to life through his wonderful handling of paint and use of chiaroscuro.

Anthony van Dyck (1599-1641)

Van Dyck was undoubtedly the best pupil to emerge from the workshop of Peter Paul Rubens. He completely absorbed Rubens' style and his painting has the same dramatic and at times theatrical lighting effects, but his work does not encompass the range or achieve the power of his master. However, he had the ability to portray human emotions in a most convincing manner, and in all of his portraits we are conscious of the bearing and personality of the sitter.

In 1620 he visited England and a year later journeyed throughout Italy, where he fell under the spell of Titian; in 1632 he settled in London and became court painter to Charles I. With the death of Rubens in 1640 he journeyed to Antwerp seeking success once more in his homeland; he failed to achieve this and so he returned to England where he died the following year.

In his *Self-portrait* of 1621 [182], we see depicted an aristocratic good-looking young man with reddish brown hair and the rather delicate colouring of a sensitive face. In the tradition of the Baroque period, there is a strong use of chiaroscuro with the hair and shoulders melting into the soft, warm tones of the background. The otherwise subdued colour scheme is relieved by the flash of white of the artist's cravat. This portrait, typical of van Dyck, was to set the trend of English portraiture for the next century.

Georges de la Tour (1593-1652)

The French Baroque was rather modified relative to its Italian counterpart in that it retained some classical qualities of painting. One of the greatest exponents of this fusion of the Baroque style and Classicism was the artist La Tour, whose important contribution to art has been reassessed in recent years.

The influence of Caravaggio on his work is strong, and we have only to compare *Joseph the Carpenter* [183] with Caravaggio's *The Calling of St Matthew* [173] to see how derivative La Tour sometimes was. His use of chiaroscuro in *Joseph the Carpenter* gives the simple composition a richness and dignity typical of his work. The candle that the Christ child holds for the aged Joseph is a common element in La Tour's paintings, and is used as a source of illumination in *The Magdalene*, *The Nativity* and *The Newborn Child* to achieve the same soft modelling of forms that is a characteristic of these quietly moving works of art.

Diego Velázquez (1599-1660)

Velázquez, one of the greatest Spanish painters, began his career as a painter of still-life and genre scenes in the manner of Caravaggio. In 1623 he moved to Madrid where he was appointed court painter to Philip IV. Two trips to Italy — the first of which was on the advice of Rubens — did much to enlarge his artistic horizons. His work shows the influence of Titian as well as his friend Rubens, and it is possible that on one of his sojourns in Italy he came into contact with the work of Frans Hals.

Velázquez was a master with a wide range of subject matter, from his early still-life and genre scenes to group portraits and massed figure studies. Unlike most Italian Renaissance painters he depicted physical deformities (as in his paintings of court dwarfs), but he never laboured the point; they are treated as easily and naturally as his sympathetic and dignified rendering of the *Old Woman Cooking Eggs* [184]. There are elements reminiscent of Caravaggio in the style of this painting, and despite his youth there is a subtlety, power and keen observation that is characteristic of his later work. The picture also demonstrates the interest in reflected light and shadow that was to play such an important part in his later paintings.

Around 1627 Velázquez abandoned his chiaroscuro style for a type of Impressionism that involved very direct brushwork, appearing to anticipate the work of Monet. This is particularly evident in his painting *The Spinners* [185], which depicts the female workers in the royal tapestry factory at Madrid. There is something of a social comment in the contrast between the women working at their looms in the foreground and the ladies who have come to inspect the tapestries hanging in the adjoining room. It is first and foremost, however, a painting of light and

[183] La Tour: *Joseph the Carpenter*, oil on canvas, 1645. 132 x 98 cm. Louvre, Paris

[184] Velazquez: *Old Woman Cooking Eggs*, oil on canvas, 1618. 99 x 116.9 cm. National Gallery of Scotland, Edinburgh

[185] Velázquez: *The Spinners*, oil on canvas, c. 1644-8. 220 x 289 cm. Prado, Madrid

[186] Velázquez: *Pope Innocent X*, oil on canvas, 1650. 140 x 120 cm. Galleria Doria, Rome

colour, soft shadows and marvellous textured effects that lend weight and volume to the delightfully relaxed and natural figures of the spinners.

At the request of Philip IV Velázquez journeyed to Italy in 1649 to purchase works of art to establish an academy of art in Spain. In addition to purchasing works by Tintoretto and Titian he acquired some 300 pieces of sculpture; it was in 1650, while engaged upon this mission, that he painted the portrait of Pope Innocent X [186]. This powerful portrait displays Velázquez' technical dexterity in the skilful, direct rendering of the textures of flesh, satin, lace and metal, and in the rich orchestration of colour. However, it is not mere technical competence that makes this painting great: it is the insightful depiction of the sitter's personality — his piercing intelligent eyes and the determined, thin-lipped mouth. This portrait of Innocent X moved Sir Joshua Reynolds to state it to be 'the best picture in Rome'.

Nicolas Poussin (1594-1665)

Poussin, together with another French artist, Claude Lorrain, sought inspiration in Rome, and through a desire to break with the flamboyancy of the Baroque he formulated a style of painting that was quiet, intellectual, and usually based on themes from ancient mythology and

[187] Poussin: *The Holy Family on the Steps*, oil on canvas, 1648. 69 x 97 cm. National Gallery of Art, Washington D.C.

religion. This style, far more linear in approach than the Baroque, became known as Classicism.

Poussin developed a love of classical sculpture and a profound admiration for the works of Raphael, as they reflected his own interest and admiration for the classical spirit. These influences can be seen in both his figure compositions and quietly ordered landscapes.

In his *Holy Family on the Steps* [187] the actual application of paint is more closely related to the works of Raphael than to Baroque contemporaries such as Rubens, Velázquez or Rembrandt. The composition, too, is Renaissance in concept, with the figures arranged parallel to the picture plane and in the classical pyramidal composition, one figure answering the movements of another. Naturally enough, Poussin has absorbed the Baroque tendencies, for we find that colour and tone are used to dramatize the group and that the feeling of space is far more apparent, with a flight of steps leading the eye up to and into the sky, suggesting that this particular scene is only one small portion of a wider world beyond. To fully appreciate this we have only to compare it with Masaccio's *Holy Trinity* [125], in which the whole action is depicted in a very tight shallow space and is complete in itself. As in most of Poussin's paintings the figures have a calm and dignity that is strongly reminiscent of classical antiquity.

Claude Lorrain (1600-1682)

Claude Gellée, also known as Claude Lorrain (or briefly, Claude), was born at Chamagne, near Toul, in the French province of Lorraine. At an early age he left France for Italy, and spent most of his life in Rome. He and Poussin are the two most important figures in the development of the art style known as Classicism.

Claude arrived at much the same result in his interpretation of classical landscape themes as did Poussin, but in the case of Claude it was through his sensitive response to the stimulus of an actual landscape rather than a direct study of the statuary and ruins of antiquity. As with Poussin, Claude's paintings are 'figures in a landscape' in which relatively unimportant figures are set in lyrical natural surroundings that reflect the lighting and tonal values of the south. In his *Flight into Egypt* [188], we see a beautifully ordered landscape bathed in a soft golden light that lends an air of timelessness to the painting. In typical Claude manner the light source is within the picture area — this proved to be the undoing of his imitators and the focus of Turner's rivalry.

Claude had a profound influence on subsequent landscape artists, but perhaps the closest link may be observed in the work of Watteau (see [191]); here prevails the same feeling of melancholy, induced by the soft gold and silvery lighting effects.

[188] Claude: *The Flight into Egypt*, oil on canvas, 1647. 102 x 134 cm. Gemäldegalerie, Dresden

The Palace of Versailles (1661-1756)

Versailles, a town outside Paris, is the site of one of the world's great palaces. It was originally built for Louis XIV by the architect Louis Levau, and after the completion of the central block, Jules Hardouin Mansart was commissioned to extend the building north and south.

The palace has three main groupings. While belonging to the Baroque period, it reminds us of a Renaissance building with its repetition of forms. As the garden façade in the aerial photograph [190] shows, this similarity is particularly evident in the ground floor, which recalls the Medici palace [123]. The second storey with its delicate Ionic columns and the third with its balustrade and rows of statuary both contribute to the elegant repetitive effect. From the aerial view we are able to see the grouping of the elements, and the importance of the vast formal gardens with their 'vistas' and wooded areas that occupy square miles of countryside.

The interior of Versailles, with its lavish mirrors, inlaid marble, tapestry, porcelain and furnishing, was to lead the world in all fields of décor and domestic accoutrements, through the successive styles of Louis XIV, Louis XV and Louis XVI. The palace was the setting for the fall of the decadent Bourbon monarchy, and since then has witnessed significant events in the history of both France and the world — it was here that the peace treaty was signed in the famous Hall of Mirrors at the end of World War I.

[189] Palace of Versailles, from the east

[190] Aerial view of the Palace of Versailles

THE EIGHTEENTH CENTURY

Antoine Watteau (1684-1721)

Watteau was born in Flanders, and the early influence of Flemish painters (particularly Rubens) was strong. In 1702 he arrived in Paris, but did not win official recognition of his work until in 1709 he was awarded a prize in the Prix de Rome. However, it was not until 1717 that his painting *The Embarkation for Cythera* [191] won him admittance to the French Academy.

In this painting we see the attitudes and superficialities of the French court combined with those of the theatre, from which Watteau drew much inspiration. It is now generally considered that *The Embarkation for Cythera* could in fact be a reluctant departure from this 'isle of love' (symbolized by the garlanded Venus statue on the right). Watteau has arranged his couples in a serpentine line moving from the lower right-hand side and culminating in the group on the opposite side of the composition. His figures appear as actors on a stage, playing a part in a make-believe world where grace and elegance reign supreme. The underlying mood of the painting is set by the lighting, which recalls the work of Giorgione (see [159]) and suggests that the lovers' happiness is a transient thing as they prepare to leave their fantasy world in the warm glow of twilight.

[191] Watteau: *The Embarkation for Cythera*, oil on canvas, 1717. 128 x 193 cm. Louvre, Paris

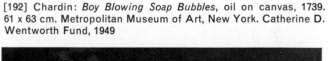

[192] Chardin: *Boy Blowing Soap Bubbles*, oil on canvas, 1739. 61 x 63 cm. Metropolitan Museum of Art, New York. Catherine D. Wentworth Fund, 1949

Jean Baptiste Siméon Chardin (1699-1779)

Chardin belongs to the Rococo period, but his work has more in common with Flemish painting than with his French or Italian contemporaries; this fact is attributable to Chardin's studies under an artist-collector who had trained in Amsterdam.

Chardin is a painter of genre and still-life subjects, and his work derives its charm from its quiet statement and well-structured arrangements of everyday objects and people from middle-class walks of life. His work recalls that of Vermeer (see [179]) in its orderly composition, and he manages to bestow, even on simple still-life objects, a sense of significance and quiet dignity.

In *Boy Blowing Soap Bubbles* [192], Chardin achieves a 'relaxed', classical, triangular composition in which marvellous subtleties of light and dark shades give the figure a wonderful feeling of form.

Jean Honoré Fragonard (1732-1806)

There is a happy eclecticism about the work of Fragonard. His paintings reflect the influence of his early studies with both Chardin and Boucher. Further, there is a charm that recalls the work of Watteau, and there are qualities in the interpretation of subject matter that are reminiscent of Tiepolo, whom he greatly admired.

In *The Swing* [193] we see a softness of lighting and a treatment of figures that are typical of the Rococo period (see [191]), yet the composition is the traditional Renaissance pyramid, with the lover lounging in the bottom left-hand corner, balancing the right-hand figure who is busily engaged working the ropes of the swing, on which the noble lady in all her finery forms the apex of the group.

[193] Fragonard: *The Swing*, oil on canvas, c. 1766. 83 x 66 cm. The Wallace Collection, London

Francois Boucher (1703-1770)

Boucher studied in Paris, won the Prix de Rome, and while on his travels in Italy came under the spell of the great illusionistic painter, Tiepolo. He returned to Paris where he eventually became president of the Academy as well as the favoured painter of Madame de Pompadour.

Boucher's style of painting carried on the traditions of Watteau, but his works were frivolous and extravagant decoration for elegant boudoirs. In some cases, Boucher's paintings ostensibly depict scenes from mythology or classical antiquity, but in essence abound with rich nudes, often arranged in erotic poses — such works pandered to the tastes of the influential patrons of the decadent French court.

In his *Diana Bathing* [194] we see Boucher's mastery of sensuous form, and the ease and grace with which he has depicted the beautiful female figures that are reminiscent of the work of Peter Paul Rubens.

[194] Boucher: *Diana Bathing*, oil on canvas, 1742. 57 x 75 cm. Louvre, Paris

Giovanni Battista Tiepolo (1696-1770)

Tiepolo was a Venetian by birth, and like Titian and Veronese was a master of light and colour. At the age of 19 he was receiving commissions, and these eventually took him to Spain and Germany where he created some of the greatest illusionistic ceiling paintings ever executed.

His *Banquet of Cleopatra* [195], a huge oil painting on canvas, is a *tour de force* in the play of light on the figures and their drapery. The painting reminds us of a stage setting and the figures appear as though 'frozen' in a particular moment of time. This can perhaps be better appreciated when we understand the action depicted. In an endeavour to woo the beautiful Cleopatra, the Roman general, Mark Antony, has given a series of sumptuous banquets in her honour. The queen, unimpressed, wagers that she can

[195] Tiepolo: *The Banquet of Cleopatra*, oil on canvas, 1743. 249 x 346 cm. National Gallery of Victoria, Melbourne

produce a dish far more costly than those provided by her host; removing one of her pearl ear-rings she dissolves it in wine. Tiepolo has centred our attention on the action of Cleopatra about to drop the priceless gem into the wine, and it is difficult for the eye to wander from the highlighted queen to the spellbound spectators of the drama.

Tiepolo's popularity waned in his own lifetime with the advent of Neoclassicism and its desire for less flamboyant subject matter, but his reputation endures today as a brilliant decorator and one of the great exponents of the Baroque style.

Francisco de Goya (1746-1828)

Goya was born near the Spanish town of Saragossa, where he received his early training, and in 1766 he moved to Madrid. This was followed by a short visit to Rome where he came under the influence of Tiepolo. Returning to Madrid he produced a series of design cartoons for the royal tapestry factory, and this marked the beginning of his successful career. He was appointed deputy director of painting at the Royal Academy of San Fernando in Madrid, and subsequently became principal painter to the Spanish court, where he painted his extraordinary series of royal portraits. At first glance, these portraits appear to follow the accepted traditions of Velázquez, but in point of fact

they are so analytical and so heavily laden with satire that one marvels that Goya was not imprisoned or banished for his audacity. However, he not only retained favour in royal circles but also found himself inundated with commissions.

Goya's career as an artist encompassed a turbulent period in European history: he was on hand to record a crumbling empire, to depict events prior to and during Spain's war of independence, and his drawings and etchings are a reflection of the horrors of the Napoleonic invasion of his country.

In 1792 he suffered an illness that invalided him for months and left him completely deaf. After this he was a changed man, and the deep brooding of his silent world is reflected in a far more penetrating form of expression.

In 1814 he painted two pictures, identical in size, of the people's uprising: one is entitled *The Citizens of Madrid Fighting Murat's Cavalry in Puerta del Sol, 2 May 1808*; the second is *The Third of May* [196]. In the latter painting we see depicted the reprisals which began at daybreak after the unsuccessful uprising and continued long into the night. It is interesting that Goya has not shown us the face of a single executioner, and so has succeeded in creating the impression that the soldiers' actions are almost machine-like: they are dehumanized. This, of course, helps to centre our attention on the faces of those about to die, where we see on the one hand defiance, and on the other sheer blinding terror at the thought of impending massacre. The feeling of anguish and hopelessness is heightened by the attitude of

93

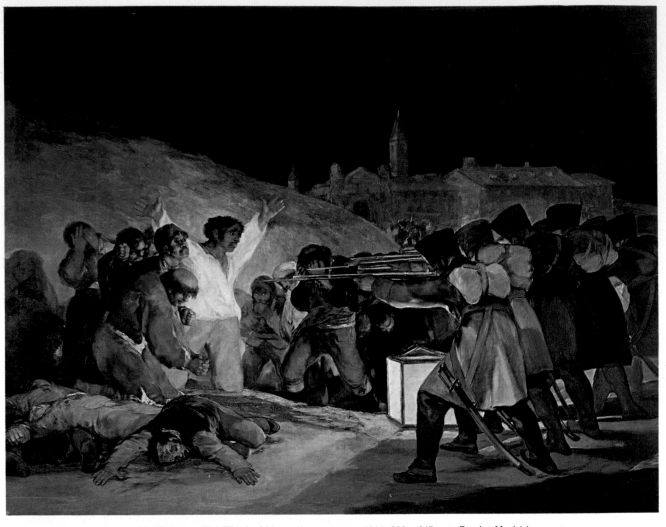

[196] Goya: *The Third of May*, oil on canvas, 1814. 266'x 345 cm. Prado, Madrid

the woman in the background clutching her hands to her head; this gesture is repeated by the leading figure awaiting his turn for execution. In *The Third of May*, Goya has created a moving and dramatic painting which not only records an actual event, but embodies the full horror of man's inhumanity to man.

To appreciate Goya's ability as a portrait painter we have only to look at the delightful *Doña Isabel Cobos de Porcel* of 1806 [197], which typifies the contemporary Spanish ideal of beauty. The sitter was an acquaintance of the artist, and the work makes obvious his sympathetic appreciation of her personality. Goya has imparted a warm luminous glow to both the flesh tones and drapery, and it is this quality, coupled with the expressiveness of the portraiture, that gives the painting its alluring charm.

Goya's influence on subsequent artists and movements was considerable. The paintings of both Delacroix and Manet reflect their profound admiration for his work, and his series of etchings on the disasters of war and his fantasy horror paintings were to be a source of inspiration to twentieth century Surrealists and Expressionists.

[197] Goya: *Doña Isabel Cobos de Porcel*, oil on canvas, 1806. 82 x 54.5 cm. National Gallery, London

ENGLISH ART

Sir Christopher Wren (1632-1723)

Christopher Wren was a scholar of considerable note; he was an astronomer, scientist and mathematician before he began to practise architecture. A trip to France afforded him the opportunity to be associated with the architects Bernini and Mansart, both of whom were attached to the court of Louis XIV, and this resulted in the French Baroque style having a strong influence on his subsequent designs.

The Great Fire of London in 1666 presented Wren with the opportunity to design and erect a large number of new buildings, ranging from cathedrals, hospitals and houses of commerce to domestic dwellings. Undoubtedly the grandest of these structures is the magnificent St Paul's cathedral. Although small by comparison with the mighty St Peter's in Rome, it is still some 157 metres long and 110 metres tall at its highest point (the equivalent of a modern skyscraper of approximately 33 storeys).

The façade of St Paul's [198] is reminiscent of several previous styles; the central façade with its temple front shows the influence of classical antiquity [26], the drum and dome recall Bramante's Tempietto [146], and the treatment of the towers reminds us strongly of Borromini's church of San Carlo alle Quattro Fontane [170]. The grouping of the elements and the articulation of space give the building a feeling of 'restrained Baroque' and a sense of calm and dignity. This feeling is further emphasized in the interior [199], for there are no hosts of angels or visions of heavenly splendour to distract the attention, and it looks, as it was intended, a place for quiet contemplation and worship.

William Hogarth (1697-1764)

Hogarth was a London artist who was appalled by the failure of the collectors and connoisseurs of his day to commission and purchase works by English painters. He was a man of unpretentious taste who aspired to bring about the acceptance of local talent. His training as a silversmith, and his contact with French art, explain his fondness for at times complex detail.

Deciding that straight portraiture was a precarious means of existence for an artist, he embarked on a series of paintings which satirized and exposed the follies of his time; it was the sale of engravings made from these paintings that was largely responsible for both his income and reputation. Hogarth wrote of his work: 'I have endeavoured to treat my subject as a dramatic writer; my picture is my

[198] Wren: St Paul's cathedral, west front, 1675-1712

[199] Wren: The choir and high altar, St Paul's

[200] Hogarth: *The Orgy*, oil on canvas, *c.* 1732. 62 x 75 cm. Trustees of Sir John Soane's Museum, London

stage, my men and women my actors.' An example of this moral and satirical message may be seen in his stage-like setting *The Orgy* [200], one of a series of eight paintings called 'A Rake's Progress'. He makes an incisive comment on the degradation of a life of vice. A rather amusing note has been introduced by the expression on the faces of the two servants to the left of the composition; they gaze with open-mouthed disbelief at the scene of abandon before their eyes.

More refreshing in its treatment is *The Shrimp Girl* [201], which displays a boldness and directness of application of paint that anticipates nineteenth century Impressionism.

[201] Hogarth: *The Shrimp Girl*, oil on canvas, date unknown. 63.5 x 52.5 cm. National Gallery, London

[202] Reynolds: *Lord Heathfield*, oil on canvas, 1787. 142 x 113.5 cm. National Gallery, London

[203] Gainsborough: *The Morning Walk*, oil on canvas, 1785. 236 x 179 cm. National Gallery, London

Sir Joshua Reynolds (1723-1792)

In 1749 Reynolds went to Italy and spent three years there, visiting Rome, Venice, Florence and other important cities. On his return to his native England he established himself as a fashionable portrait painter. Reynolds believed that his mission in life was to raise the status of English painters to that of their European counterparts. In order to do this, he set down what he considered to be teachable rules, although he was often guilty of preaching one thing and practising another.

Reynolds had as his idol Michelangelo, but his work is not of the calibre to really carry on the 'grand style' of either Michelangelo or the later Baroque masters whom he greatly admired. His easy manner and his friendship with such influential people as Doctor Johnson and Oliver Goldsmith assured his social and financial success. In 1769 he was honoured with a knighthood, after becoming the foundation president of the British Royal Academy in the previous year — a post he held for fourteen years. In this position he remained a powerful figure in eighteenth century British painting.

Reynolds' portrait of Lord Heathfield [202] is a well-constructed painting in the classical manner, and with its rich, warm tones vividly expresses the spirit of the English nobility at that time.

Thomas Gainsborough (1727-1788)

Gainsborough began his career as a landscape painter; it is in this field that we find some of his most lyrical statements, and it is in these sketches and paintings that he displays a delightfully fresh approach to the rendering of the English countryside.

It was in portraiture, however, that his reputation lay, and in this he is regarded as perhaps the only great exponent of the Rococo style in England. While some of his works appear to follow the aristocratic tradition of van Dyck, we can also see much of the charm of Watteau. In *The Morning Walk* [203] the attitudes of Squire Hallet and his wife possess something of the same wistful quality that is present in Watteau's *Embarkation for Cythera* [191]. This similarity is perhaps more easily appreciated when we compare the treatment of light and foliage in the backgrounds of both works. Gainsborough was a recorder of his times, and with his wonderful technical dexterity has left us a lively record of contemporary society and their elegant dress.

97

[205] Constable: Sketch for *Dedham Mill*, oil on canvas, 1819. 53.5 x 76 cm. Tate Gallery, London

[204] Blake: *Satan Arousing the Rebel Angels*, watercolour, 1808. 51.4 x 38.4 cm. Victoria and Albert Museum, London

William Blake (1757-1827)

The English artist Blake is almost impossible to categorize; he has achieved recognition for his lyric and symbolic poetry as well as for his paintings and etchings, which illustrate ·the works of Dante, biblical stories, his own poems, and his mystical and metaphysical systems of belief.

While his early paintings displayed a Neoclassical tendency, he soon developed a highly personal style which sometimes lacked the traditional academic technique, but which carried the power of his personality and lent conviction to his strange visionary interpretations. His medium was usually watercolour with a strong linear technique, and his religious paintings such as *Satan Arousing the Rebel Angels* [204] combine an obvious influence of Michelangelo with both a Medieval and Mannerist flavour that anticipates the work of the Surrealists with their dream-like sequences.

John Constable (1776-1837)

John Constable and William Turner were the two leading British Romantic painters and together made the greatest contributions to nineteenth century painting in England. Constable's father was a prosperous miller in Suffolk, and when not in London Constable spent his time there, never leaving England.

He was an admirer of Claude Lorrain (see [188]), but he never strove for the beautifully ordered compositions of that artist and said of his own work that he wanted it 'to

have dew and sparkle of trees and bushes and grass in the real, light-drenched world'; this is exactly what his paintings are about. He painted out of doors and recorded the changing effects of light, wind-driven clouds, and the freshness and sparkle of the English countryside. From these vivid, spontaneous sketches he carefully constructed the finished paintings. It is these directly recorded preliminary sketches of nature that are prized today.

In 1824 he won much acclaim (and a gold medal) at the Paris Salon for his paintings *The Hay Wain* and *A View on Stour*, and his style was to have considerable effect on both the Barbizon and Impressionist schools. From the sketch *Dedham Mill* [205] we can obtain some idea of the freshness of his approach; this delightfully serene landscape, like all of his compositions, bears witness to the importance he placed on the orchestration of colour and movement in the sky and cloud formations. Further evidence of this may be found in a letter he wrote to a friend, in which he stated that the 'landscape painter who does not make his skies a very material part of his composition neglects to avail himself of one of his greatest aids'.

Joseph Mallord William Turner (1775-1851)

Born the son of an English barber, Turner was admitted to the Royal Academy at the age of 14 and first exhibited there in the following year. In 1808 he was made Professor of Perspective and for a while he worked with the famous English watercolourist, Thomas Girtin; most of Turner's early paintings were watercolours which were difficult to distinguish from those of Girtin. Turner frequently went on sketching trips and recorded scenes of nature in

[207] Turner: *Steamer in a Snowstorm*, oil on canvas, 1842. 91.5 x 122 cm. National Gallery, London

[206] Turner: *The Burning of the Houses of Parliament*, oil on canvas, 1835. 92.5 x 123 cm. Cleveland Museum of Art. Bequest of John L. Severance

Romantic fashion, often depicting the vastness and tremendous forces of nature. In his trips to Italy he was influenced by the works of both Claude Lorrain and Nicolas Poussin, but it was the magical effects of the light in Venice which had the most profound effect on his work.

Light became the central theme of Turner's art, and the translucent qualities of his watercolours were carried over into his oils. It was this obsession with light that brought down on him a tremendous weight of criticism — for example, Constable's comment that he painted in 'tinted steam'. Bitter attacks by some of the leading art authorities caused Turner to lose popularity, but his cause was enthusiastically championed by Ruskin, the noted critic and historian.

In *The Burning of the Houses of Parliament* [206] we see a ready-made subject which displays the qualities for which he is now famous. The whole painting is composed of nebulous forms that appear to melt into, or rather never fully materialize out of the atmosphere of light and vaporous smoke that pervades the work. We are just able to make out the thousands of spectators who jammed the banks of the Thames to view the tremendous conflagration of 1834. The towers of Westminster Abbey in the background were rendered in a vague suggestion of form that was to become almost the trademark of Turner's painting.

Further evidence of the dissolving of solid form into a hazy atmospheric suggestion can be seen in his *Steamer in a Snowstorm* [207]. In this Romantic interpretation of man pitted against the elements, we are given the impression of a swirling, violent vortex with the steamer (represented mainly by the funnel and mast with its flag) struggling for survival. It was paintings such as this that greatly impressed Pissarro and Monet and became a significant influence in the development of French Impressionism.

The Pre-Raphaelites (*c.* 1850)

The Pre-Raphaelites were a group of artists who rebelled at the lack of form in the paintings of their contemporaries in both France and England; indeed, they were even of the opinion that such masters as Titian, Rubens and Rembrandt, with their free use of paint, had done much to destroy the art of painting. They decided that in order to fulfil their aspirations they would revert to the period and style before Raphael, as this had been the point at which painters had begun to idealize and so, in their opinion, lose much of the 'down-to-earth' craftsmanship of the Medieval artist. In addition to this, the movement was a revolt against the machine age of the Industrial Revolution, which partly explains the seeking of subject matter from a past era — historical or religious topics, and expressions of noble principles — all of which were at times treated with heavy sentiment; this, coupled with the artificiality that often resulted from their attempts to achieve a primitive naïveté, led them to the inevitable dead end.

This sentiment can be seen in the work of Sir Edward Burne-Jones (1833-1898). In *King Cophetua and the Beggar Maid* [208] we observe the powerful king, crown in hand, sitting at the feet of the low-born girl who is the object of his love; she, clad in the poor clothing indicative of her station in life, is obviously unable to believe the materialization of her dream. The whole picture, with its rich use of golds and forcefully decorative quality, reminds us of a Byzantine painting in reverse, with the king or the most powerful figure at the bottom, the maiden and the two relatively unimportant witnesses to the scene at the top of the picture.

William Holman Hunt (1827-1910) chose religious scenes for most of his paintings, which seem obsessed with

detail. To further his knowledge of the scriptures he journeyed to Egypt, and from these travels he made the simple, delightful *Study of an Arab Girl* [209]; the figure is rendered with a grace and economy of line that makes it particularly appealing.

The style of Dante Gabriel Rossetti (1828-1882) is intensely· personal. His paintings are at times highly emotional, and like the other Pre-Raphaelites he sought to recapture the spirit of the Medieval world; it makes an interesting comparison to view his *Annunciation* [210] together with that of Fra Angelico [133]. Certainly his work is sincere, and when compared with the Baroque period it appears simple in its interpretation; but simplicity and sincerity alone do not necessarily constitute a great work of art, and we realize that Fra Angelico's *Annunciation* with its stark austerity is the more successful interpretation, despite the obvious charm of the Rossetti painting.

[208] Burne-Jones: *King Cophetua and the Beggar Maid*, oil on canvas, 1884. 290 x 136 cm. Tate Gallery, London

[209] Holman Hunt: *Study of an Arab Girl*, pencil heightened with white, 1854. 22.8 x 14 cm. National Gallery of Victoria, Melbourne. Felton Bequest, 1907

[210] Rossetti: *The Annunciation*, oil on canvas, 1850. 72.4 x 43.2 cm. Tate Gallery, London

[211] David: *The Oath of the Horatii*, oil on canvas, 1785. 330 x 427 cm. Louvre, Paris

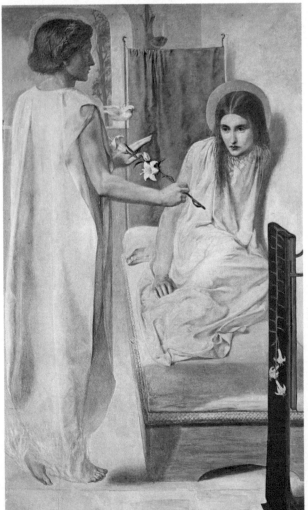

NINETEENTH CENTURY FRENCH PAINTING PRIOR TO IMPRESSIONISM

NEOCLASSICISM

Jacques Louis David (1748-1825)

David, of French birth, ushered in a new style known as Neoclassicism which was at variance with the frequent excesses of the Baroque and Rococo in France. Early in the French Revolution he was a friend and follower of Robespierre and narrowly escaped the guillotine. With the rise of Napoleon he became one of the most powerful figures in French art, but after the latter's final defeat in 1815 David also fell from favour and was eventually exiled to Brussels.

In 1774, at his third attempt to win the Prix de Rome, David was successful — his winning work *Antiochus and Stratonice* was a display of virtuosity in chiaroscuro and the treatment of figures and drapery.

On David's return from Rome he painted *The Oath of the Horatii* [211], which is considered to be one of the most important paintings of the Neoclassic period. David hated the work of Rubens, and if we compare *The Oath of the Horatii* with *The Rape of the Daughters of Leucippus* [180] we are aware of the tremendous difference in interpretation of these two scenes from ancient Roman history. *The Oath* appears very static in composition when compared with the flowing movement of the Rubens work, and this static quality is further emphasized by the hard, metallic surface treatment (as opposed to the fluid painterly quality of Rubens). In *The Oath* we are made very conscious of the number three — the three Roman arches in the background, the three groups of figures, the three sons swearing an oath on the three swords. The painting portrays the Horatii swearing an oath to their father that they will fight to the death with three brothers from the city of Alba. The battle to take place before the armies of both cities is to determine which city shall rule the other. An added tragedy lies in the fact that the Alban Curiatii and the Roman Horatii are linked by marriage. In this as in most of David's works we are conscious of a cold serenity in the composition that imparts a timeless quality; its influence can be observed in other paintings of the time, and in contemporary décor arrangements, women's fashions and hairstyles.

Jean Auguste Dominique Ingres (1780-1867)

Ingres was born at Montauban in France, and his father was a painter who was quick to appreciate his son's talent; he was enrolled at the academy in Toulouse and then went to Paris to study under David. He was 21 years of age when he won the Prix de Rome with his painting *The Envoys of Agamemnon*, and between this time and his departure for Italy in 1806 he earned a reputation as a portrait painter. The prize entitled him to three years' study in Rome; however, he remained in Italy for eighteen years, at times having to resort to pencil sketches for a livelihood. After he returned in 1824, his work was accepted by the Paris Salon and suddenly he found himself acclaimed as the leader of the Neoclassic movement in direct opposition to Delacroix, who had exhibited his 'Massacre' series earlier that year and was already celebrated as the leading figure of the Romantic movement.

While Ingres professed a liking for historical paintings, he never achieved any real degree of proficiency in this field and was never happier than when painting the female form, where he was free to compose using the softly rounded flesh of the nude either singly or crowded together in harem scenes. This, incidentally, is a further indication that Neoclassicism was not as far removed from Romanticism as was thought at the time. A typical example is *The Odalisque with the Slave* [212], in which we see the beautifully rounded forms of the odalisque (harem girl), her pose and grace recalling Titian's *Venus of Urbino*. A certain 'relaxed sensuality' is apparent, just as in the artist's other works on similar subjects.

[212] Ingres: *The Odalisque with the Slave*, oil on canvas, 1840. 76 x 105.5 cm. Walters Art Gallery, Baltimore

[213] Ingres: *Portrait of Louis Bertin*, oil on canvas, 1832. 116 x 95 cm. Louvre, Paris

[214] Géricault: *The Raft of the Medusa*, oil on canvas, 1818. 491 x 717 cm. Louvre, Paris

Ingres claimed a dislike for portraiture, but this, together with his figure studies, is the basis for his greatness as an artist. Evidence of this ability is to be found in his portrait of Louis Bertin [213], which not only conveys a physical likeness of the sitter but also projects an impression of tremendous energy and vitality of personality. Although the harsh contours of the work make it appear almost photographic, it bears striking witness to the artist's powers of intellectual penetration.

ROMANTICISM

Théodore Géricault (1791-1824)

Géricault came under the influence of both David and his pupil Antoine Gros, and had it not been for his untimely death he may well have attained an even higher place in the history of art than he now holds. Géricault headed a new Romantic movement, and undoubtedly much of the vitality and vast physical energy of his work can be attributed to his admiration for Michelangelo, whose works he studied while in Rome in 1816.

We can gauge the calibre of his artistic expression from *The Raft of the Medusa* [214]. The story of the foundering of the *Medusa* captured the imagination of the public, resulting in a scandal and subsequent trial (James Michener in his *Tales of the Sea* relates the full story). Apparently through a series of bunglings on the part of the captain, the *Medusa* was lost off the west coast of Africa at the cost of hundreds of lives, and the handful that we see on the raft were the only survivors. Géricault went to great lengths to achieve authenticity in this huge canvas, visiting the morgue so that he might sketch actual corpses. He arranged his figures in a surging triangular composition, starting with the naked figure to the bottom left of the painting and reaching to the dramatic figure of the negro waving desperately at a ship that is a speck on the horizon. The sky space is divided into three sections by means of the negro and the makeshift mast, and the placement of the dead figure in the bottom right-hand corner echoes the dying figure on the opposite side. The theme of man against the elements was popular with the Romantic painters and Géricault's *Raft of the Medusa* enjoyed a great deal of success.

This artist's sensitivity and directness of approach are displayed in *The Mad Assassin* [215]. Géricault frequented the insane asylum as well as the morgue, and there he made numerous sketches of the inmates; we are reminded in this searching portrait of the work of Frans Hals, but whereas Hals may give the impression of laughing at his madwoman [176], Géricault seems to delve into this tormented mind to record and understand its sufferings.

102

Géricault: *The Mad Assassin*, oil on [canvas], 1822-3. 60 x 50 cm. Museum of Fine [Arts], Ghent

[216] Delacroix: *The Tiger Hunt*, oil on canvas, 1854. 74 x 93 cm. Louvre, Paris

[217] Delacroix: *Portrait of Frédéric Chopin*, oil on canvas, 1838. 45.5 x 38 cm. Louvre, Paris

Eugène Delacroix (1798-1863)

Delacroix was born on the outskirts of Paris and his father was a minister under the Directoire. In 1815 he entered the École des Beaux-Arts where he first came into contact with Géricault, whose work undoubtedly had a strong influence on his subsequent painting. He was impressed at an early stage by Reynolds and Constable (after seeing the latter's landscapes he completely repainted the background for *The Massacre at Chios*); he made copies of works by the Venetians, Rembrandt, Rubens and Watteau, all of whom he admired greatly, and his Romantic inclinations led him to a close study of Shakespeare, Sir Walter Scott and Lord Byron as well as the Polish composer, Frédéric Chopin.

Evidence of this Romantic spirit may be seen in *The Tiger Hunt* [216]. Here we have a recurring Romantic theme of man versus nature, and one of which Delacroix was particularly fond, an Arabian hunting scene. This picture contains all the trappings of the 'Romantic image' — the writhing, turbulent forms of the centrally placed man, precariously balanced on the wounded and terrified stallion, and the slashing, tearing tiger. While there is a certain classical logic and order in the pyramidal grouping of the figures and the diagonal movement of the road, we are aware that these qualities are subservient to the wonderful plasticity of form and the bold, direct application of paint.

The portrait of Frédéric Chopin [217] was conceived as a double portrait to include the novelist George Sand; however, the original scheme did not come to fruition, and the painting we see is a complete work in itself. In its delightfully free brushwork and directness of approach we are somewhat reminded of Frans Hals' *Malle Babbe* [176], and also Géricault's *Mad Assassin* [215]; certainly, Delacroix has succeeded in capturing the feeling and emotional depth of this creative genius just as convincingly as Géricault depicts the disturbed and troubled mind of his assassin.

PRE-IMPRESSIONISTS

Jean Baptiste Camille Corot (1796-1875)

In one way Corot was more fortunate than many of his contemporaries as his father was a reasonably well-to-do draper who set his son up with an allowance, so that his failure to sell a painting in thirty years was not of financial significance.

He worked for some time in Italy, particularly in and around Rome, but he retained a home near Barbizon in France and so came into close contact with the Barbizon school of painters. His paintings owed much to Poussin, but unlike that master of landscape he did not reorganize the elements but rather presented an atmospheric view of an actual scene in which we see existing buildings and landscape forms. It is through the subtle arrangements of tonal values to strengthen or diminish important or unimportant objects that Corot created a marvellous plastic quality.

Usually his landscapes depict either the early morning light or twilight, and in them he achieved a soft silvery colouring for which he is perhaps best remembered. *The Bridge at Mantes* [218] is a painting that recalls the work of Poussin in its formal composition and order, but the rendering of the actual scene is characterized by

[218] Corot: *The Bridge at Mantes*, oil on canvas, 1868-70. 38.4 x 55.6 cm. Louvre, Paris

[219] Millet: *The Gleaners*, oil on canvas, 1848. 54 x 66 cm. Louvre, Paris

[220] Courbet: *The Stone Breakers*, oil on canvas, 1850. 159.4 x 259.1 cm. Formerly in the Gemäldegalerie, Dresden

Corot's unique quality. For his own pleasure, he also painted figure studies that are delightful lyrical harmonies of tone and colour — these are now considered to be among his finest works. He was made a member of the Legion of Honour at the age of 50, and in his later life enjoyed a great deal of popularity; his influence on subsequent movements in France, particularly Impressionism, was considerable.

Jean François Millet (1814-1875)

Millet, born of Normandy farming stock, worked with other artists of similar outlook in the small picturesque village of Barbizon close to Paris. In addition to landscapes of this delightful village, they depicted the commonplace working people carrying out their gruelling daily tasks.

Millet's *Gleaners* [219] is one of these fine studies of peasants engaged in their unglamorous labours. Because of familiarity, we are perhaps inclined to dismiss this work as 'sentimental', but upon closer observation we become conscious of the feeling of form, a certain nobility, and an affinity with the earth. Millet was often accused of being a socialist, but his chief aim was to invest such paintings as *Man with a Hoe*, *The Sower* and *The Gleaners* with a dignity he associated with people who work the soil.

Gustave Courbet (1819-1877)

Born the son of a vine grower at Ornans, a French town which lies close to the Swiss border, Courbet was largely self taught. He made copies of the great masters in the Louvre, his most important influence being the Italian master Caravaggio.

Courbet's style of painting has at times been described as 'tonal Impressionism', and certainly he was considered the leader of the Realist movement in nineteenth century French art. His painting was based generally on a down-to-earth observation of nature; he was strongly opposed to both Romanticism and Classicism and is alleged to have stated: 'Show me an angel and I will paint one.' He was an anti-intellectual and an anti-academic, and became involved in the politics of the Revolution of 1848 and the later Paris Commune of 1871 with unfortunate personal consequences; as chairman of the Commune's art committee he was involved in the destruction of the Column of Napoleon in the Place Vendôme. He was imprisoned for six months, and on his release fled to Switzerland where for the last seven years of his life he painted landscapes in an endeavour to pay off the enormous fine imposed by the French government.

Courbet's paintings caused a scandal as they were considered earthy and vulgar; he did win a gold medal from the Paris Salon on one occasion, but more often than not his paintings were rejected for exhibition. In *The Stone Breakers* [220], we see much of Caravaggio's influence in the strong tonal contrast of the dark background against the light shirts of both figures. The painting makes evident Courbet's compassion for the old man breaking rock and the young boy struggling with the heavy basket of stone—attired in their tattered labourers' clothes, they are the antitheses of Delacroix's Romantic *Tiger Hunt* [216]. There is, however, the same truth and nobility that we find in Millet's *Gleaners* [219], and the fact that we can see neither face indicates that Courbet wanted nothing to distract our attention from either the position or the attitude of the toiling figures.

In similar vein, and just as shocking in its time, was *Bonjour, Monsieur Courbet* [221], in which he has depicted himself in the situation of a labourer; coatless, with his painting gear on his back, he is being greeted by his patron. Compared to the well-ordered compositions of the Romantics it must certainly have given many of his contemporaries the impression of an artless 'snapshot', but again it has a dignity and simplicity far more realistic than the lion hunts and exotic Arabian scenes that were characteristically artificial in the work of the French Romantics.

[221] Courbet: *Bonjour, Monsieur Courbet*, oil on canvas, 1854. 129 x 149 cm. Musée Fabre, Montpellier

[222] Daumier: *Don Quixote*, oil on canvas, c. 1868. 52 x 32 cm. Neue Pinakothek, Munich

Honoré Daumier (1808-1879)

Daumier, born at Marseilles, worked for a time with a lithographer in Paris and in 1830 joined the staff of the journal *La Caricature* as a cartoonist; over the next forty years he produced no fewer than 4000 lithographs for various periodicals. It was not until 1848 that Daumier actually began to paint, and most of his oils were executed between about 1855 and 1870.

He is primarily a draughtsman, portraying people from all walks of life with an economy of line and detail that accentuates the sharpness of his observation. He made scathing attacks on the corruption and callous inhumanity of the judicial system, and on the other social evils of his time; he depicted with compassion the hunger, toil and privation of people from lowly walks of life, and showed peasant women bathing, or washing clothes in the river.

Even in his canvases it is obvious that Daumier is a draughtsman, drawing in paint with a judicious elimination of detail that simplifies and yet amplifies, at times bordering on the abstract. In his *Don Quixote* [222], we see evidence of this economy of means, and are able to appreciate the marvellous feeling of fluidity that he achieves by applying the paint so that it follows the direction of the forms, a technique that was to become an important aspect of the work of the German Expressionist painter Kokoschka, and the Australian artist William Dobell.

IMPRESSIONISM

The second half of the nineteenth century brought fundamental changes in the social, economic, scientific and political life of Europe. The growth of commerce and industry caused city populations to increase rapidly, and city dwellers rented accommodation in the newly-built city apartments and terraces. Leisure time from factories and offices was soon catered for by a growing number of music halls, restaurants and theatres, as well as by such pastimes as boating, seaside bathing, horse racing and picnicking. Newspapers, periodicals and books increased their circulations, and, with improved educational facilities, the people of Europe were learning much more about the rest of the world. In addition to this, economic expansion brought Europeans into contact with the ancient civilizations of the East, whose cultures were largely unknown or had been forgotten.

At the same time as industrialized city life provided new amenities for many people, it brought social distress to others: conditions in many factories and workshops were poor and unemployment was frequent. As a result, discontent with the old political scheme was widespread and social reform was sought by vigorous parliamentary action or revolutionary agitation.

Scientific research offered new explanations for natural phenomena and traditional concepts of religion were being re-examined in the light of Darwin's theory of evolution; a mechanical contrivance called the camera had begun to record the life of man with pleasing economy and accuracy. Against this background of change, the writers and painters of the period were creating works of art which related to the widespread interest in science, the growing social concern for the common man, the more tolerant moral climate and the awareness of non-European culture.

In recording this pattern of change, the young artists found themselves in conflict with the art academies and the official exhibition centres like the Paris Salon. Here the art authorities rigidly controlled subject matter and methods of applying oil paint; the depiction of Greek and Roman mythology, sentimental and heroic stories and portraits of distinguished people or noble animals was acceptable to the official Salon, provided the artist applied his paints carefully and mixed his colours according to the academy formulae. Such attitudes towards content and technique could not accommodate the smoke of railway stations, the pattern of movement in dance halls, the colour of the race-track or the sweat of the factory worker. Collision between the artists and the academies followed,

and from the conflict emerged Impressionism — the most revolutionary change in the visual arts since the Renaissance.

Édouard Manet (1832-1883)

Although strictly never an Impressionist himself, Manet gave the lead to many aspects of Impressionism. He was certainly the leader in revolutionary attitudes towards the subject matter of paintings, and for this he attracted the

[223] Manet: *The Old Musician*, oil on canvas, 1862. 186 x 247 cm. National Gallery of Art, Washington D.C. Chester Dale Collection

[224] Manet: Detail from *Claude Monet and his Wife in his Floating Studio*, oil on canvas, 1874. Full size 80 x 97.8 cm. Neue Pinakothek, Munich

106

antagonism of the official Salon and the critics, but was accorded the adulation of the young artists. In the early 1860s Manet exhibited two now-famous works, *Lunch on the Grass* and *Olympia*. These paintings attacked the hypocritical 'rules' for works depicting the female nude. These 'rules' permitted the painting of the nude female and even the semi-nude male if suitably antique accessories and a background of Greek or Roman columns were included in the composition. However, Manet's paintings portrayed nude women against a background of contemporary Paris, and he was charged with causing a public scandal and had to flee the country. Further, the critics attacked his methods of painting because of their 'foreign' flavour. Manet's delight in coloured Japanese prints — seen in Paris for the first time about 1860 — was largely responsible for simple figure compositions like the *Fifer*, with its marvellous sense of space and lightness, and for his use of broad flat areas of colour.

The three Manet pictures reproduced here give us some idea of the wide range of his work. *The Old Musician* [223] was painted before *Lunch on the Grass* and *Olympia*. It reveals Manet's great love of humanity and has the quality of a Goya painting in this respect. In its composition we see the powerful contrast of tone which was characteristic of much of his work.

Although Manet hung none of his paintings in the various Impressionist exhibitions of the 1870s, his influence on Renoir, Monet, Pissarro and Sisley was immense. He, in turn, was fascinated by the colour and spontaneous brushwork of the young Impressionists; the detail from *Claude Monet and his Wife in his Floating Studio* [224] demonstrates the vitality of Monet's painting and his ability to record the sitters' personalities with freshness and charm, using a minimum of rapidly applied strokes of colour.

Argenteuil [225], painted in the same year, is often considered to be Manet's finest outdoors painting. The solid, patterned figures are bathed in and surrounded by vibrant sunlight, and Manet makes a powerful colour and pattern composition of river, banks, trees, houses, boats and people. He was concerned, however, at the loss of form and structure in some of the young Impressionists' works, and wanted his own paintings to retain the compositional strength of Velázquez. Perhaps *Argenteuil* does incorporate this strength, as well as the luminosity of the works of Monet — but whether this analysis is valid or not, it is certainly one of the nineteenth century's most exciting paintings.

[225] Manet: *Argenteuil*, oil on canvas, 1874. 149 x 131 cm. Museum of Fine Arts, Tournai

Claude Monet (1840-1926)

In the Paris of the 1860s, Claude Monet, then in his early twenties, met Sisley, Pissarro, Renoir and Manet. He began a series of experiments in open-air painting in which he attempted to record colour and light changes with spots and strokes of oil paint in the colours of the spectrum — all the colours visible in a rainbow. Monet, like many other people of his time, was fascinated by physical experiments which had revealed that light passing through a prism was broken into the spectral colour range. The art movement in Paris temporarily collapsed with the Franco-Prussian War in 1870 and Monet went to London. Here he exulted in the marvellous colour effects of J. M. W. Turner's paintings; the dazzling glow of Turner's pictures of sunsets, seascapes, fog, steam and water inspired him to experiment further. After the war he returned to France where he rejoined Renoir and Pissarro; they continued to paint pictures which attempted to represent the effects of light more realistically than ever before.

107

[226] Monet: *Impression — Sunrise*, oil on canvas, 1872. 50 x 62 cm. Musée Marmottan, Paris

In 1874 they mounted their first exhibition of works in the new manner. *Impression — Sunrise* [226], a small painting by Monet, typified for one critic the whole exhibition, which he scornfully dismissed as 'impressionist'. The public and most of the critics were outraged by these works which, to them, lacked definition and seemed unfinished or carelessly painted with obvious brushmarks. The idea of using the distance between the painting and the viewer to assist in the optical mixing of patches of pure colour and to achieve an illusion of shape was not understood.

Despite the general hostility to the Impressionist technique (as it was now called), Monet, more than any other member of the group, continued the study of light. The picture of Rouen cathedral [227] is one of many that he did of this subject; he painted the façade of the cathedral showing the different atmospheric effects caused by the changes in light between sunrise and sunset. He carried out similar series of paintings of haystacks and waterlilies, and there is no doubt that in some of these pictures his absorption in the changing light effects resulted in less concern for old rules of composition. Despite the excitement of his colour, his treatment of form and shape disturbed other painters like Cézanne and Gauguin. *The Douanier's Hut at Varengeville* [228], however, is an example of his stunning colour technique and beautifully ordered composition.

[227] Monet: *Rouen Cathedral, West Façade, Sunlight*, oil on canvas, 1894. 100.4 x 66 cm. National Gallery of Art, Washington D.C. Chester Dale Collection

[228] Monet: *The Douanier's Hut at Varengeville*, oil on canvas, 1882. 60 x 78 c Boymans-Van Beunin Museum, Rotterdam

[229] Renoir: *The Luncheon of the Boating Party*, oil on canvas, 1881. 128 x 172.5 cm. Phillips Memorial Gallery, Washington D.C.

Auguste Renoir (1841-1919)

Renoir came to Paris in the 1860s after a short career as a painter of designs on porcelain at Limoges, one of France's great ceramic centres. He spent two years in the company of Monet, experimenting with techniques of applying paint from a palette of pure colour. His work was interrupted by a period of military service during the Franco-Prussian War, but in the early 1870s he painted many charming landscapes, very similar in theme and treatment to those executed by Claude Monet at this time. He abandoned landscape to work on genre pictures, depicting groups of people in domestic situations or in relaxed moments in restaurants and theatres; his love of humanity and his sheer love of life resulted in his making

people the subject of his works for the remainder of his long career. In this respect he differs from Monet, Pissarro and Sisley, who were largely concerned with the play of light in landscapes, street scenes and similar situations.

Luncheon of the Boating Party [229] is a fine example of Renoir's painting: the gay informality and relaxed feeling of the boating party is achieved by the vitality and freshness of the paint, the fascinating pattern of light, and the solid charm of all the human figures. It seems reasonable to attribute the glowing flesh colour in all of his pictures to his early training as a painter of porcelain. The luminosity of Renoir's colour and his finely structured compositions have had considerable influence on the artists of the twentieth century, and the sheer joy expressed in his work was to give him wide public appeal.

[230] Degas: Study for a portrait of Edouard Manet, black chalk and estompe, 1865. Metropolitan Museum of Art, New York. Rogers Fund, 1918

[231] Degas: *Musicians*, oil on canvas, 1872. 69 x 49 cm. Städelsches Kunstinstitut, Frankfurt

[232] Degas: *Diego Martelli*, oil on canvas, 1879. 110 x 100 cm. National Gallery of Scotland, Edinburgh

Edgar Degas (1834-1917)

After an early training in the classical academy traditions, where he developed great powers of draughtsmanship, Degas joined the Impressionists in the 1870s. He was fascinated by their experiments in colour, and he proceeded to add the Impressionist colour palette to his pictures. He introduced a significant change to the Impressionist movement in his choice of pastel instead of oil paints as a medium for many of his major works. Like Renoir, Degas made people the main subject matter of his pictures; there are many reproductions of his ballet dancers at rehearsal on stage or waiting in the wings, his laundresses toiling at the ironing board, his jockeys parading their mounts at the race-track, and musicians performing in Parisian cabarets. In these pictures there is none of the loss of structure that sometimes occurred in Monet's work. Although light was the main subject of Monet's pictures, this was not the case with Degas; in fact, he only used what he wanted of the Impressionist theories and he created compositions in which the placement of the main subject was startlingly different. It was from early photographic experiments that Degas derived ideas for figure placement in space: the 'chopped-off' appearance of people and objects looks very much like the motion picture 'stills' of later generations.

Degas' subjects reveal an intense feeling for life and there is a basic quality in his depiction of human beings beyond mere physical beauty. Although the dancers, laundresses and even the female nudes are generally graceless people — often 'caught' by the artist in awkward stances — and are usually of commonplace appearance, there is a strong humanitarian quality in Degas' work.

The three works reproduced here reveal aspects of his achievements during his formative painting years. The drawing of Édouard Manet [230] shows Degas' skill as a draughtsman and projects his great admiration for the sitter: Degas was a master of recording the swift observation. The painting of the musicians [231] shows his compositional skill and the arresting quality of his colour. But it is the Martelli portrait [232], perhaps, which best displays the artist's capacity to create a work of intense feeling and compositional strength.

Degas' many exquisite wax sculptures (now cast in bronze) give added confirmation of his position as one of the most significant artists of the nineteenth century.

Camille Pissarro (1830-1903)

In Paris in the 1860s Pissarro joined Monet and Renoir in their painting experiments. He, like his young companions, was full of admiration for the courage of Manet in defying the restrictions imposed by the official Salon. Pissarro went to London with Monet in 1870, when Paris was occupied by the Prussian army. He, too, reacted to the colour excitement of the work of Constable and Turner and on his return to France he continued to experiment

with the Impressionist palette. He was a dominant figure in the staging of the first Impressionist exhibition in 1874. So strong indeed was his determination to further the principles of the Impressionist movement that he, alone of all the Impressionist painters, exhibited in every one of the eight exhibitions between 1874 and 1886. The derision of the critics and the general public failed to make any impact on Pissarro's work. He painted landscapes almost exclusively, and always succeeded in infusing them with a joyful, lyrical quality. As with his friend Monet, the main subject of his pictures was the study of light: he exulted in the shimmering effect of sunlight on the leaves and branches of trees, yet his paintings always retained a strong sense of form. Sometimes Pissarro sought the picturesque streets of Paris as subjects for his works; the painting of a street in Montmartre [233] is typical of his paintings of Parisian city life.

During the 1880s Pissarro came into contact with Seurat and Signac. He became interested in their theory of Pointillism and attempted pictures using this technique, but the rigid nature of the colour theory did not suit him entirely. However, when he returned to his earlier style of painting, his colour was greatly enriched and his composition became more relaxed; [233] belongs to this period, and exemplifies the work of his maturity.

Alfred Sisley (1839-1899)

Sisley is considered to be, along with Monet, the most 'orthodox' of the Impressionists, for he persisted almost entirely with painting atmospheric changes in landscape.

The colours he used were exclusively those of the spectrum, and with these he constantly conveyed the effects of light on the surfaces of hillsides, rivers, lakes and trees. His dedication to the colour theories of Impressionism was made manifest in pleasantly unified compositions that retained a distinct feeling for natural form and structure. Sisley rarely attempted to look for subjects beyond his landscape theme, and the reproduction [234] is a good example of his work.

111

AFTER IMPRESSIONISM

Georges Seurat (1859-1891)

In his brief life of thirty-two years, Georges Seurat made a considerable contribution to the era of painting immediately following the last Impressionist exhibition in 1886. From the Impressionist experiments in colour mixing, he developed a system of applying colour called Pointillism or Divisionism.

In 1884 Seurat and his friend Paul Signac began experimenting with the application of new scientific theories of colour and optical illusion. The two painters proceeded to apply complementary pure colours in tiny dots, so that the desired colour effect was achieved through simultaneous optical blending by the viewer; this colour mixing technique was achieved by precise mathematical methods. Seurat spent many years painting the most famous of his Pointillist compositions, *Sunday Afternoon on the Grande Jatte*: he not only made many sketches in black and white of the figures and the background, together with several major colour studies, but also completed a full canvas of all the natural forms in the picture, without any figures, before painting the final work. *The Circus* [235] was painted in the last year of Seurat's life. The ordered quality of his composition in line as well as colour and shape is intriguing. There is an excitement about the work and at the same time the fascination of arrested motion: whereas Renoir's men and women will chatter for ever over the luncheon of the boating party, the performers in Seurat's picture have been captured momentarily by the artist and frozen in space for all time.

Seurat wrote comprehensively about his theories. These documents, in conjunction with his paintings, awakened in the young artists of the twentieth century an interest in scientific analysis of all the elements of composition. His inspiration still actively influences works of art today.

Paul Signac (1863-1935)

It was Paul Signac who first encouraged Seurat to embark on the scientific study of the Impressionist colour theories, and eventually helped him establish a salon for the exhibition of their work in the Pointillist manner. Signac was passionate in his dedication to the principle of

[235] Seurat: *The Circus*, oil on canvas, 1891. 180 x 148 cm. Louvre, Paris

[236] Signac: *The Harbour*, oil on canvas, 1907. 88.9 x 116.8 cm. Boymans-Van Beuningen Museum, Rotterdam

[237] Toulouse-Lautrec: *At the Moulin Rouge*, oil on canvas, 1892. 122.9 x 140.3 cm. Art Institute of Chicago. Helen Birch Bartlett Memorial Collection

simultaneous colour contrast and the optical mixing of pure colour, and although the sudden death of Seurat in 1891 robbed the movement of its principal personality, Signac carried on with the movement alone and did considerable further study and experiment on theories of colour. He made a great contribution to early twentieth century painting in his capacity as the president of the Society of Independent Artists in Paris, and his encouragement of the young Fauves and Cubists is noteworthy.

Signac's picture *The Harbour* [236] gives us an understanding of both his accomplishment in the Pointillist technique and the lyrical charm of his work.

Henri de Toulouse-Lautrec (1864-1901)

Toulouse-Lautrec was a member of an aristocratic French family which could trace its ancestry from the Crusades. During his childhood on the family estate he suffered two horse-riding accidents which resulted in a deformity in both his legs; it was during the long periods of his convalescence that Toulouse-Lautrec began his life-long devotion to painting. He left his home in the 1880s to study in Paris, where he became interested in the fascinating design qualities of Japanese prints; in particular, he was attracted to the work of Edgar Degas because of the uncompromising honesty of the subject matter of his paintings. For the next fifteen years the city of Paris itself was to become the studio of Toulouse-Lautrec: his pictures depicted clowns and acrobats at circuses, dancers and jugglers in the cafés, diners in restaurants, the inmates of brothels and drinkers in bars. He painted these pictures of the night life of Paris without moralizing and without sentimentality. His work was honest and vigorous, with the glowing colours of the Impressionists laid on with spontaneous brushwork which achieved lightness and vibrancy. It is, however, undoubtedly the excitement of the pictorial compositions which gives the work of Toulouse-Lautrec its uniqueness and power, and his influence on artists like Picasso and Matisse was considerable.

In the last few years of his life Toulouse-Lautrec became interested in the graphic arts, particularly in colour lithography. In this medium he created advertising posters which were to have a significant influence in the field of commercial art in the twentieth century.

Although he is often grouped with the Impressionists, Toulouse-Lautrec refused to be bound by any theory of art: he had little affinity with the subject matter of Monet, although he certainly extended the subject areas pioneered by Manet and Degas. *At the Moulin Rouge* [237] is a fine example of his work. Its dramatic composition underlines the dominant concern in the paintings of Toulouse-Lautrec — humanity.

THE POST-IMPRESSIONISTS

The term Post-Impressionism was first applied to the works of van Gogh, Gauguin, Cézanne and certain others during the famous exhibition of their works at the Grafton Galleries in London in 1911, and since then it has designated the twenty-year period which followed the last Impressionist exhibition in 1886.

It is from the three dominant figures of this era — Paul Cézanne, Paul Gauguin and Vincent van Gogh — that the mainstreams of twentieth century art can be traced.

[238] Cézanne: *The Card Players*, oil on canvas, *c*. 1893. 59.5 x 73 cm. Courtauld Institute Galleries, University of London

Paul Cézanne (1839-1906)

Paul Cézanne belonged to a comfortable, middle-class family. He had first to overcome his family's determination for him to follow a career in banking, before he could dedicate his life to painting.

After a short period of painting in the town of Aix-en-Provence, Cézanne went to Paris where he continued his schoolboy friendship with the writer Émile Zola, and proceeded to meet the young intellectual group, including the Impressionist painters Monet, Degas and Renoir. Cézanne struggled to achieve a personal style, and after a decade of painting with somewhat heavy colour, he finally lightened his palette. In 1874 he contributed works to the

[239] Cézanne: *Mont Sainte Victoire*, oil on canvas, *c*. 1886-8. 66 x 89.5 cm. Courtauld Institute Galleries, University of London

[240] Cézanne: *The Gardener*, oil on canvas, *c*. 1906. 65.5 x 55 cm. Tate Gallery, London

first Impressionist exhibition. However, Cézanne was sceptical of much of the Impressionists' experimental work and he began to evolve a new style in which there was a quality of strong volume. He painted many still-lifes and portraits and a series of 'Bathers', in which he made a personal statement of compositional unity achieved by his unique use of colour and tone. Cézanne's work was not acceptable to either the Impressionists or the official Salon. In 1882 he did achieve a small success with the exhibition of one of his pictures by the Salon, but this was not sufficient to overcome his embittered attitude to the art world of Paris, and he abandoned the city and devoted himself to painting in Provence. Apart from a very occasional trip to Paris, he continued thus for the rest of his life, becoming increasingly withdrawn from normal society: he broke his long friendship with Zola, quarrelled with Monet, and eventually was estranged from his own family. He persisted with his theories of painting, and during the period 1885-95 he produced two of the works in this volume, [238] and [239], which demonstrate how Cézanne projected nature in a new way. His pictures were 'built' with small blockish planes of colour and plane-defining lines so that the forms, whether cylindrical, conical, block-like or irregular, were controlled by his technique, to achieve complete pictorial unity. The vagaries of light and atmosphere were not recorded, and only the enduring qualities or constants in nature were revealed, as we see in the monumental strength of the two card players, the rugged force of the mountain of Sainte Victoire, and the columnar dignity of the trees.

The Gardener [240] represents work done in the last year of Cézanne's life, when critics and artists were finally beginning to realize his genius. This work is typical of the humble subject he often sought for his paintings, and it embodies the grace and dignity with which he represented life.

Cézanne once said that he would make of 'Impressionism something as solid and durable as the paintings in the museums', and the method he used to achieve this has affected nearly every painter of the twentieth century in one way or another.

Paul Gauguin (1848-1903)

Unlike his Post-Impressionist contemporary Cézanne, whose life was physically bounded by the distance between Paris and Provence, Gauguin's life, which began in Paris, involved a childhood sojourn in Peru, and varying periods of residence in France, Copenhagen, Panama, Martinique, Tahiti and the Marquesas, where he died in 1903.

Gauguin began to paint in the early 1880s and he contributed to the Impressionist exhibitions in this period. Yet he was not entirely happy with the 'soft' compositions of many Impressionist painters, and thus remained on the fringe of the Impressionist movement. Eventually he decided that being a 'Sunday painter' was not enough: he abandoned his occupation as a stockbroker to devote himself entirely to art, and embarked on a series of pictures showing village life in Brittany. *Landscape in Brittany* [241] was painted about a year before Gauguin left France for Tahiti. It is of particular interest in that, while the application of colour is reminiscent of the Impressionists (and Cézanne), the foreground shapes demonstrate the simplification of form and colour which became a dominant characteristic of Gauguin's work.

Gauguin, like van Gogh, was impressed by the Japanese print and the unity of the pictorial elements in this art form; this interest was supplemented by his study of Javanese, Egyptian, Peruvian and Polynesian art. The search for compositional strength and unity motivated Gauguin's famous statement, 'We shall be rejuvenated through barbarism.' 'Barbarism' here meant direct contact with life, uncluttered by the tired sophistication of Europe — the kind of unspoiled life Gauguin hoped to find on his first visit to the tropical island of Martinique in 1887. His work achieved greater simplification of colour and shape, but he found Martinique physically trying and returned to France. Here he produced a series of paintings in a manner somewhat similar to stained glass, called Cloissonism, and after three years of artistic exchange with his contemporaries — notably Vincent van Gogh, for a few tense

[241] Gauguin: *Landscape in Brittany*, oil on canvas, 1889. 92.5 x 73.5 cm. Collection Rodolphe Staechelin, Basle (on loan to Kunstmuseum, Basle)

[242] Gauguin: *The Day of the God*, oil on canvas, 1894. 69.5 x 90.5 cm.
Art Institute of Chicago. Helen Birch Bartlett Memorial Collection

months—Gauguin 'freed' himself from Europe and went to Tahiti.

Although he did not find his unspoiled paradise — Europeans had already corrupted the people and their culture—Gauguin made some magnificent studies of the exotic environment and its people. These symphonic 'arrangements of lines and colours', as he called them, were acclaimed by his fellow artists in Paris in 1893. But Gauguin's pictures bewildered the public. It was during his sojourn in Paris (1893-5), when he returned with his first batch of Tahitian paintings, that Gauguin painted *The Day of the God* [242], a fantasy of life in Tahiti before the coming of the white man. The colour excitement and the striking organization of shapes in the composition are evident even in a reproduction of this size. Gauguin left France for the last time in 1895 and spent the remainder of his now-tormented life in Tahiti and finally the Marquesas.

The White Horse [243] is from this last period. Its mood is tranquil, but there is a full orchestration of shape and colour, and a striking unity of all the elements in nature: rocks, water, trees, vines, animals and men achieve a new statement of harmony on the canvas.

Gauguin combined the grand and the basic, the serene and the simple, and he gave the lead for the subsequent incorporation of primitive cultures throughout the world into the mainstream of Western art.

116

[243] Gauguin: *The White Horse*, oil on canvas, 1898. 141 x 91 cm. Louvre, Paris

[244] Van Gogh:
Cypresses with Two Figures, oil on canvas, 1889-90. 43 x 27 cm. V. W. van Gogh Collection (on loan to Stedelijk Museum, Amsterdam)

[245] Van Gogh:
Le Moulin de la Galette (new title: *The Mill 'Le Radet'*), oil on canvas, 1886. 38.5 x 46 cm. Rijksmuseum Kroller-Müller, Otterlo

[246] Van Gogh: *The Postman Roulin*, oil on canvas, 1889. 65 x 54 cm. Rijksmuseum Kroller-Müller, Otterlo

Vincent van Gogh (1853-1890)

Unlike the other two great Post-Impressionists, Vincent van Gogh was Dutch, although he did most of his painting in France. Cézanne and Gauguin were both obsessed with the need to paint, but, intense and fierce though their need was, in the case of van Gogh it was even more profound and passionate. Ironically, he was the only one of the great Impressionists and Post-Impressionists who achieved no public appreciation in his lifetime: the genius of all the others was accorded some recognition before death — slight though this was in several instances.

Van Gogh's early career as a preacher in a small mining village in Belgium provided the background for his dark, poignant paintings and drawings of peasant life. In these works he endowed the poverty of the peasants with dignity and courage, and indicated the intensity of his compassion for their miserable existence. He went to Paris in 1886 and met the Impressionists and Post-Impressionists Pissarro, Degas, Seurat and Gauguin. Changing his palette, he experimented with the pure colour range of the Impressionists, and did some paintings using the Pointillist technique. Then his own style began to evolve, and for four amazing years, in the south of France, van Gogh painted a series of landscapes, street scenes, still-lifes, interiors and portraits that has become part of the great tradition of Western art. During these years of intense activity, his mental health began to deteriorate and he had to spend periods of time in hospital; even here his work did not stop, and he made magnificent studies of his doctor, the other patients and the corridors and garden of the institution.

The affinity that van Gogh felt with man and nature is indicated in the three works [244], [245] and [246]. Whether

117

he was painting a building, some trees, the sky or a postman, he endowed each picture with a life force which was all-pervasive. His pictures acquired almost a relief surface, for he painted with pigment-loaded brush strokes that swept and swirled and jabbed — borne along by his emotional response to the subject, and creating an excitement in colour that was new in the history of art. The dramatic use that van Gogh made of colour and texture invokes sensations of movement in clouds and trees, and projects the life-giving quality of the earth itself. His depiction of bricks, mortar and timber in the walls and roof of the mill has the quality of human habitation; his figures, like that of his friend Roulin the postman, embody the dignity and glory of life that van Gogh felt so passionately.

Ironically, the intensity of van Gogh's feeling for life, recorded so eloquently in his letters to his brother Theo, resulted in the final shattering of his own being in a corn field in Provence. He died believing he had failed. Yet, within a generation, retrospective exhibitions of his work were seen in Paris, London and New York, and his paintings were linked with those of Cézanne and Gauguin as a collective source of inspiration to the painters of the new century.

HENRI ROUSSEAU (Le Douanier) (1844-1910)

Rousseau spent five years as a saxophone player in a French military band, before joining the customs service and becoming a toll officer (thus 'Le Douanier'). In 1885, after some years as an untrained 'Sunday painter', he devoted himself to a full-time painting career. He exhibited his pictures regularly at the Gallery of Independent Artists for the next twenty-five years, to the gradual acclaim of his fellow painters and the continued disdain of the general public, who could not understand the 'primitive' or 'naïve' quality of his draughtsmanship. This aspect of his work impeded general appreciation of his paintings until the early 1900s, when his intuitively balanced compositions and his luminous colour harmonies brought him wide recognition; his achievement led to great interest in untutored or 'innocent' painting in the twentieth century.

Much of the charm of Rousseau's work can be attributed not only to his painterly treatment of his subject matter, but to the subject matter itself: his scenes of the Parisian suburbs with citizens in their carriages and in the parks, his portraits of friends and family, and above all, his fantastic landscapes of jungles and deserts with wild animals and exotic gypsies or tribal warriors, have acquired widespread popularity. *The Tiger Hunt* [247] is typical of Rousseau's

[247] Rousseau le Douanier: *The Tiger Hunt*, oil on canvas, *c.* 1893. 38 x 46 cm. Columbus Gallery of Fine Arts. Howald Collection

imaginary landscapes: there is an ingenuous charm in his depiction of animals and men, while the arrangement of shapes and the colour relationships achieve a compositional balance of great distinction.

Rousseau belonged to no movement: his work spanned the period from Impressionism to Cubism and remained uniquely unconcerned with the fluctuations of contemporary art movements.

THE INTIME PAINTERS

Pierre Bonnard (1867-1947)

Bonnard, the French painter, book illustrator, lithographer and etcher, studied law before he came under the influence of Degas, Renoir and Toulouse-Lautrec. He studied art with Vuillard and together they became associated with the Nabis group (from the Hebrew *Nebiim*, meaning 'divinely inspired'). These artists were influenced by the Japanese print as had been the Impressionists, van Gogh and Gauguin, and they wanted to use its basic qualities to clarify the purposes of painting at the close of the nineteenth century. Bonnard and Vuillard developed their own range of subject matter and became known as Intimists or Intime painters; this name derived from their almost exclusive absorption with the 'intimacy' of the interior domestic situation.

Bonnard's work covers fifty years of pictorial statements of the bedroom, dining room, terrace and bathroom. *The Breakfast Room* [248] typifies the superb, glistening harmony of colours and forms which Bonnard integrated so completely: subject and background have an indivisibility which is characteristic of his genius. A remarkable feature of Bonnard's paintings was his ability to project youthful exuberance into the works of his maturity, even those of his eighth decade.

Édouard Vuillard (1868-1940)

Vuillard spent nearly all his life in the Montmartre district of Paris. He was associated with Bonnard and the Nabis and he demonstrated in this period attitudes to colour which anticipated the Fauve movement; his association with

Bonnard caused his colour to quieten and he proceeded to paint dimly-lit domestic interiors, characterized by subtle textural harmonies. He painted many portraits of his mother at her daily tasks — sewing, reading and cooking — and these works have a simplicity and repose which is enhanced by the gently muted colours of his palette. *The Dining Room* [249] is indicative of the placid charm and decorative harmony of Vuillard's Intimism.

[249] Vuillard: *The Dining Room*, oil on canvas, 1902. Neue Pinakothek, Munich

[248] Bonnard: *The Breakfast Room*, oil on canvas, c. 1930-1. 159.7 x 114 cm. Collection, The Museum of Modern Art, New York

FAUVISM

The Fauves and Henri Matisse (1869-1954)

After an early training in law, Henri Matisse enrolled in art classes in Paris in the 1890s and became friendly with some of the young artists — Dufy, Rouault, Marquet, Derain, Vlaminck, Braque and Friesz. He was deeply affected by the work of the Impressionists and the Post-Impressionists: the series of retrospective exhibitions of Cézanne, van Gogh and Gauguin at the turn of the century impelled his work towards new methods of painting and a new philosophy of art. It was in the area of colour — he had been fascinated by the colour theory of Seurat and Signac — that Matisse proceeded to initiate the most aggressively colourful movement in painting since the Middle Ages. He abandoned all the academy theories for making pictures, and in 1905 he exhibited his first paintings in which colour was used without reference to the subject: he placed colour on the canvas to create pictorial values and ignored the descriptive function it had performed for so long. The appearance of reality was reorganized so that the formal structure of the subject and perspective were both transformed into a colour statement. The exhibition in 1905 of works by Matisse and his friends was overwhelming, with purple water, orange skies, cerise tree trunks and portrait heads lined in vermilions and greens. In fact, a critic looking around the gallery containing these pictures pointed to a Donatello-type marble bust and commented on its being *au milieu des fauves* — 'in the midst of wild beasts'. Thus 'Fauves' became the name for Matisse, Braque, Derain, Dufy, Vlaminck and the others during their joint exhibitions in the years 1905-8.

The self-portrait illustrated in [250] is not as 'wild' in colour as some of his other portraits (for example the well-

[250] Matisse: *Portrait of the Artist*, oil on canvas, 1906. 55 x 46 cm. Royal Museum of Fine Arts, Copenhagen. Rump Collection

[251] Matisse: *Interior with a Violin*, oil on canvas, 1917-8. 121 x 89 cm. Royal Museum of Fine Arts, Copenhagen. Rump Collection

[253] Dufy: *Deauville: Drying the Sails*, oil on canvas, 1933. 46.4 x 110.2 cm. Tate Gallery, London

2] Matisse: *The Sorrows of the King*, gouache on cut and pasted ·er, 1952. 292 x 386 cm. Museum of Modern Art, Paris

known portrait of his wife called *Woman with the Green Stripe*), but it demonstrates the superb simplicity with which he achieved form, and the power of his colour statement.

After 1908, Braque joined Picasso in the analytical Cubist period, and Derain, Dufy, Vlaminck and the others proceeded to develop their own particular styles: Fauvism, despite the violence of its impact, was finished as a movement. The principles of the colour compositions of van Gogh and Gauguin had been carried into practice with such force and drive by the Fauves that almost immediately they were to influence the emergence of the Expressionist movement elsewhere in Europe.

Matisse after 1908

Following the Fauvist years Matisse travelled to Spain and Morocco, and incorporated the decorative excitement of these countries in a series of interior paintings such as *Interior with a Violin* [251]; this work reveals the decorative brilliance of his interiors and the manner in which he makes a statement of space through colour. Over the following forty years Matisse painted pictures which ranged from the relatively realistic, such as the wonderful *White Plumes*, to the gorgeously exotic series of odalisques — reclining female figures on a variety of settees and lounges.

In the 1940s Matisse began paper cut-out experiments, of which *The Sorrows of the King* [252] is a fine example. For this type of work Matisse used scissors to invent his compositions, and with the cut shapes of colour he achieved a delicate simplicity as well as a logical pictorial symbolism. The extension of this technique is seen in his wall decorations and stained glass for a chapel at Vence in France — a work which Matisse executed in his eighties.

Along with other painters like Degas, Renoir and Picasso, Matisse was also a brilliant sculptor; his work was significant because of its monumental quality and its powerful three-dimensional analysis of geometrical form. However, it is mainly for his painting that Matisse has been hailed as the greatest artist that France has produced in this century.

Raoul Dufy (1877-1953)

Dufy was a French painter who thrilled to the impact of the Matisse works in 1905: he abandoned his somewhat Impressionist style and proceeded to paint in the Fauve manner until 1908. Like Vlaminck he then experimented in the paint theories of Cézanne, but eventually he evolved his own style of landscape and still-life painting in which he superimposed line work, somewhat akin to a shorthand script, on deftly organized areas of colour. Dufy's technique had a remarkable vitality, with both decorative charm and pictorial strength. *Deauville: Drying the Sails* [253] is typical of both Dufy's technique and the festive subject matter of most of his pictures: his numerous works showing regattas, processions, beach crowds, picnics and orchestras are highlights in the painting of the first half of this century.

André Derain (1880-1954)

Derain, in his late youth, was a close associate of Vlaminck and was strongly influenced by Matisse, with whom he exhibited in the Fauve years, 1905-8. This was the period of Derain's best work: he painted a series of themes on the city of London, and *The Pool of London* [254], with its sweeping pattern of colour and powerful organization of shapes, typifies Derain's Fauve technique, which had a

121

[254] Derain: *The Pool of London*, oil on canvas, 1906.
81 x 99 cm. Leeds City Art Gallery

[255] Vlaminck: *Still-life with White Pottery*, oil on canvas, 1909.
89 x 111.5 cm. Collection Marlborough Fine Art Limited, London

considerable influence on his young contemporaries. After 1908 Derain became involved with Negroid art and dabbled in Cubism; within a few years he was absorbed in a study of the old masters, and although his landscapes and portraits retained strong painterly qualities, he gave no new lead to twentieth century art after his Fauve period.

Maurice de Vlaminck (1876-1958)

Vlaminck grew up in France with little formal education; he was a forceful, exuberant man, whose early friendship with André Derain resulted in a period of painting in which they concentrated on colour experiments. The retrospective exhibition of van Gogh's works in 1901 captivated Vlaminck: the intensity of the colour and the forceful patterns of the paint were features which he attempted to incorporate in his own work, and in association with Matisse and Derain he made a major contribution to the first Fauve exhibition in 1905. For the next four years Vlaminck painted still-lifes and landscapes which were notable for the exciting violence of their colour composition.

In 1908-9 Vlaminck began to experiment in the manner of Cézanne and he proceeded to abandon the Fauve technique: *Still-life with White Pottery* [255] was painted in this period of transition. Fierce colour and wild spontaneous brush strokes have been replaced by a more detached and less emotional approach to painting; the influence of Cézanne is seen in the organization of the still-life shapes as well as in the manner in which the colour and tone are realized. The structural strength of the composition gives an indication of the powerful landscape technique which was to be characteristic of Vlaminck's work in his mature years; the Expressionist realism with which he painted village houses, trees and snow was achieved with strong dark colours, dramatically contrasted with slashes of red, green or blue. Vlaminck's work in these landscapes presents a fascinating combination of the emotionalism of his Fauve period and the controlled quality shown in the 1909 still-life reproduced here.

CUBISM

Pablo Picasso (*b.* 1881)

In 1900 Pablo Picasso left Spain, the country of his birth, and went to Paris. He was already an accomplished painter, and in the following five years he painted a series of pictures in which his style was dominantly linear and in which he used firstly blue, and later pink, as his main colour. The 'blue' period was concerned with the impressions of a young and sensitive man looking intently at the basic drama of everyday life. There is a gentle melancholy in his work which is typified by the picture *Maternity* [256]. The blue colour helps to evoke a tender mood, but the quality of line carries this tenderness into something akin to desolation. Many of the 'blue' period works are starkly tragic — paintings of emaciated beggars and bereft families. They achieve an intensity of emotion, resulting from the deliberate elongation of figure, which owes a great deal to the work of El Greco (see page 79), whose painting achievement was being reassessed at this time by art and literary circles in Paris.

The Family of Saltimbanques [257] is a good example of the 'pink' or 'rose' period, which encompasses the predominantly pink pictures of jugglers, acrobats and animals that Picasso painted in the years 1904-5. The paintings of this period show greater compositional strength; the figures have more solidity, yet they retain both charm and simplicity.

In the following year Picasso's adherence to traditional practice in the depiction of the human form was overwhelmed by the impact of African Negro sculpture. He exulted in the primitive representation of the human form in carvings and ritual masks. *Les Demoiselles d'Avignon*, painted in 1907, was a dramatic statement of deliberate distortion of the human figure in the Negro and ancient Iberian tradition. This initial experimental work was followed in the next decade by a series of works by Picasso and the French artist Georges Braque, in which the elements of Negro art were allied to some of the artistic achievements of Paul Cézanne. The representation of natural forms by coloured spheres, cones, cylinders and cubes was a basic part of what became known as Cubism. Picasso and Braque reorganized the 'geometrical' elements of their subjects (see *The Mandolin* [260]) without regard for their normal relationships. Cubism tried to state something of the existence of an object or a being which was not necessarily its physical exterior: it has been suggested that Cubism was concerned with the 'apple-ness' of the apple,

[256] Picasso: *Maternity*, pastel, 1903. 46.7 x 40.6 cm. Museum of Modern Art, Barcelona

and not just with the external appearance of the apple. Thus the concept of an object and not its visual identity was the aim of Cubism. The colours of the first Cubist paintings were mainly of the earth: brown and yellow ochres with some greys and greens. Some of the colour effects were almost monochromatic and the original colour of the subject matter was nearly lost. The early 'analytical' Cubism was succeeded by experiments which incorporated the full gamut of colour, the reorganization of the elements of the subject, and the introduction of materials like gravel, newspaper headlines, areas of printing and wallpaper. The works in this period of 'synthetic' Cubism, with a variety of materials pasted on to the surface of the canvas, created startling textural effects and new exciting picture patterns. Collage was to become a significant method of picture making later in the century. The two Picasso paintings, *Seated Woman* [258] and *Girl before a Mirror* [259], were painted before and after the collage period. The 1909 portrait is an interesting example of the low-keyed colour composition of analytical Cubism, while the 1932 work demonstrates the masterfully decorative assemblage which Picasso was able to achieve when painting people

[257] Picasso: *The Family of Saltimbanques*, oil on canvas, 1905. 102 x 220 cm.
National Gallery of Art, Washington D.C.

in their environment. The picture is a brilliant intellectual exposition of the elements of design.

Picasso's paintings range in style from the visually realistic to the geometrically symbolic, and in inspiration from classical Greek art to the paintings of Velázquez and beyond: his subject matter embraces such diverse themes as the lyrical beauty of young children and the stark horror of war. (*Guernica*, his huge mural of 1937, was inspired by the terroristic dive-bombing of unarmed civilians, an unprecedented outrage that shocked the world during the Spanish Civil War. This famous painting, with its black, white and grey colours symbolic of mourning, was a powerful protest against the threatened destruction of European civilization by Fascism.)

Picasso's versatility is also evident in his designs for costumes and backdrops for several Diaghilev ballets between 1917 and 1924, and in his many media experiments, particularly in etching and lithography. To sculpture he introduced new materials and techniques (one significant example is the bull's head assemblage that he created from push-bike parts). His period of ceramics at Vallauris in southern France extended the dimensions of this art form also.

Picasso's work, as a feature of twentieth century art, is prolific, inventive and comprehensive: he unites the diverse traditions of international art with the changing values of the modern era. It is a statement of his exultation in life.

[258] Picasso: *Seated Woman*, oil on canvas, 1909. 92.7 x 61.6 cm. Tate Gallery, London

Georges Braque (1882-1963)

Like Picasso, Braque first settled in Paris in 1900. His first contacts there were with the young Fauves, notably Dufy and Friesz; using brilliant and exciting colour he painted with them during the years 1906-7. Then he met Picasso, and from 1910 until Braque entered the army in 1914 the two artists expounded in paint their Cubist theories. Braque found Cubism well suited to his intellect and temperament. The violent line work and disorderly composition of many of his Fauve friends disturbed him; even when he exhibited with them his powerful colour was laid on in squares and rectangles which gave an indication of the disciplined geometry of his future work.

When Braque exhibited a picture in 1908, one of the critics seized on a scoffing remark by Matisse about the 'cubes' of colour, and he used the term 'Cubism' in his comment on the works of Picasso and Braque. Although not a meaningful description of the style, the name has persisted. As noted in the treatment of Picasso, the Cubist style was largely a Negroid-Cézanne amalgam. *The Mandolin* [260], depicting as it does the breakdown of the subject and space surrounding it, is an example of Braque's compositions, which were highly complex in their analysis

[259] Picasso: *Girl before a Mirror*, oil on canvas, 1932. 162.6 x 130.2 cm. Collection, The Museum of Modern Art, New York. Gift of Mrs Simon Guggenheim

of form. The sober colours create a remarkable unity, and despite their lack of brilliance have a quietly compelling glow. It is interesting to note that the Cubists were the first art group to use musical instruments as the main subjects for painting.

In the years after *The Mandolin* Braque's work approached abstraction. Although he gave titles to his pictures the subject matter was nearly lost in the reorganization of the elements of the subject. Braque countered this trend in his work by the use of letters of the alphabet, and these letter shapes became a widespread feature of Cubism. He imitated wood-grained and marble surfaces with paint and ultimately, in 1912, he began to paste textured and patterned papers on to the picture surface; these sections of collage became integral parts of the composition. As the 'synthetic' period of Cubism developed, Braque's focus of concentration moved from form, space and volume to the treatment of the surface: the line work became simpler and the planes of the shapes much broader. *Guitar and Jug* [261] is typical of the many still-lifes which Braque painted in the 1920s. The pictures were small and the colour generally in low key, while the subject matter, invariably taken from the everyday objects of the middle-class home, was projected with simplicity and vigour in shape, line and colour. For the next forty years of his life, Braque's paintings encompassed a wide variety of techniques and subject matter, yet his works were always both dynamic and intellectually controlled, a remarkable combination of harmony and boldness.

125

[260] Braque: *The Mandolin*, oil on canvas, 1909-10. 72.4 x 59.7 cm. Tate Gallery, London

Braque's activity in art extended to ballet design, limestone and bronze sculpture, and designs for stained glass windows. His notebooks, covering the period 1917-52, reveal Braque as one of the great intellects of the twentieth century.

Juan Gris (1887-1927)

Juan Gris was born in Madrid and received a classical art training there: he went to Paris in 1906, and although he would have liked to return to his native country he had no passport — he had evaded military service by going to Paris — and he was never able to leave France.

Gris was attracted to the early analytical Cubist work of Picasso and Braque: he painted in their manner until the movement changed into its synthetic period, and then proceeded to develop his own style. His pictures assumed an architectural quality; in *Still-life in Front of Open Window* [262] there is an ingenious combination of the new Cubist concept of space in the foreground and the semi-traditional rendering of space in the background. Furthermore, the painting has most of the synthetic Cubist paraphernalia — newspapers, wine labels, fruit dishes, decorative wallpaper panels — as well as the intriguing open-window 'naturalism'.

[261] Braque: *Guitar and Jug*, oil on canvas, 1927. 81 x 116.2 cm. Tate Gallery, London

[262] Gris: *Still-life in Front of Open Window*, oil on canvas, 1915. 116.5 x 89.2 cm. Philadelphia Museum of Art. Louise and Walter Arensberg Collection

Over the next ten years Gris painted many beautifully ordered compositions of Cubist still-life forms — sheet music, mandolins, books and jugs — using colour that was austere and subdued but strongly harmonious. The accomplishment of Juan Gris was highly significant despite his untimely death at the age of 40.

126

FUTURISM

In 1909 an Italian poet, F. T. Marinetti, wrote a statement on the future of poetry and the other arts, in which he extolled the glories of mechanization, militarism and scientific achievement, and foresaw a future with qualities surpassing those of the classical past — 'a racing car . . . is more beautiful than the *Victory of Samothrace*', he said. Futurism in fact proceeded to reject the old cultural ideas and glorify movement and speed. In 1910 two Futurist manifestoes, signed by several painters, led to a fascinating art movement in which painting attempted the seemingly impossible — the representation of a dynamic sensation on a static surface! The Futurists, as a group, only painted in this way until the beginning of World War I, and the chief exponents of Futurism were Boccioni, Severini, Balla and Carrà.

Umberto Boccioni (1882-1916)

The Italian painter and sculptor Boccioni studied Seurat's Pointillist style early in his career; at the beginning of 1910, carried away by the Futurist ideals of Marinetti, he composed a *Manifesto of Futuristic Painters*, followed later in the year by the famous *Manifesto of the Techniques of Futuristic Painting*. Along with the other signatories to these documents, he began to exhibit pictures demonstrating the new dynamic paint sensations. *The City Rises*

[263] is a picture dating from 1910. It symbolizes the harnessing of the forces of the new era, with men and horses in a frenzy of movement against growing industrial might. (An unhappy outcome of the Futurist theories and their glorification of militarism was the spur they gave to Fascism in Italy and elsewhere.) Boccioni's picture shows elements of the Pointillist technique, and his colour and texture combine to give a sense of urgency.

On page 145 is a photograph of a sculpture by Boccioni entitled *Unique Forms of Continuity in Space* [296], in which we see an extension of the artist's concepts of dynamic sensation. Within a few years of the creation of these works, Boccioni was accidentally killed at the age of 34.

Gino Severini (1883-1966)

Severini, after his early art studies in Italy, went to Paris in 1906. He was enthralled by the work of Seurat, and met Picasso, Dufy, Braque and other young artists and intellectuals. With his former teacher Balla, and Boccioni, he exhibited in the first Futurist exhibition in 1912. *Dynamic Hieroglyph of the Bal Tabarin* [264] illustrates Severini's contribution to Futurism. This painting of cabaret dancers is actually a pictorial representation of movement, with a series of arms, legs and heads in successive positions of

[263] Boccioni: *The City Rises*, oil on canvas, 1910. 199.3 x 301 cm. Collection, The Museum of Modern Art, New York. Mrs Simon Guggenheim Fund

motion: flashes of fabric and even the decorations in the cabaret move in and between the dancing forms. There are elements of fantasy in the picture as well as devices (for example the printed names of dances) derived from the Cubist experiments of Picasso and Braque.

Giacomo Balla (1871-1958)

The Italian painter Balla had a strong influence on the formative painting years of Severini and Boccioni: he joined in their 1912 Futurist exhibition and *Dog on a Leash* [265] is a work of that year. It is pictorially simple, and although lacking the underlying intellectual intentions of Severini and Boccioni, it has wit and charm: there is a delightful fussiness in the representation of the foot movements, paw padding and leash swinging; the fact that there is an inadequate amount of body progression for both dog and owner is of academic interest and does not detract from its visual humour.

[264] Severini: *Dynamic Hieroglyph of the Bal Tabarin*, oil on canvas with sequins, 1912. 161.6 x 156.2 cm. Collection, The Museum of Modern Art, New York. Acquired through the Lillie P. Bliss Bequest

[265] Balla: *Dog on a Leash*, oil on canvas, 1912. 89 x 107.8 cm. Buffalo Fine Arts Academy, New York. George F. Goodyear Collection

128

EXPRESSIONISM

Any painting which projects the deep inner feelings and emotions of an artist and which results in heightened colour and deliberate distortion of form can be called Expressionist: perhaps the works of El Greco and Vincent van Gogh can explain this term more effectively than such a compressed, simplified statement. Expressionism in the twentieth century had its origins in two German movements — *Die Brücke* ('The Bridge') and *Der Blaue Reiter* ('The Blue Rider') — in the pre-World War I era.

Edvard Munch (1863-1944)

The Norwegian painter Munch first studied painting in Oslo. During a visit to Paris in 1885 he met van Gogh and this meeting was to have a profound effect on his work: like van Gogh, Munch suffered from mental illness, and his works were highly emotional personal statements which concerned themselves with the pressures and fears of the city dweller. A recurring theme in his pictures was the loneliness and alienation of man, and in many of his works we see the isolation of individual figure shapes. *The Dance of Life* [266] — actually the centre panel of a frieze called *The Frieze of Life* — is not so desperate in its projection of man as a solitary animal: here, loneliness is overcome and

man is involved with his environment, but despite this, fear and isolation continue to threaten him.

Early in the twentieth century Munch met many of the young German painters while he was carrying out art commissions in Berlin and other centres. His influence on Emil Nolde and the other members of *Die Brücke* played a part in the development of the German Expressionist movement.

Emil Nolde (1867-1956)

The German artist Emil Hansen took the name by which he is best known from his birthplace, Nolde, and he studied art in Germany, France and Denmark.

In 1905 a group of young painters in Dresden formed *Die Brücke*, a 'bridge to link all the revolutionary and surging elements' in the arts of painting and architecture, and they invited Emil Nolde to exhibit with them in 1906. Nolde's contribution to this Expressionist development lay in the strength — sometimes the violence — of his colour and the complementary quality of his brushwork with swirling, slashing rhythms that recall van Gogh.

The emotional power of his work was stimulated by a visit to the South Seas in 1913-4; *The Mill* [267] is a striking union of a romantic subject and heavy dramatic colour applied with forceful, primitive brushwork.

[266] Munch: *The Dance of Life*, oil on canvas, 1899-1900. 125 x 190 cm. National Gallery, Oslo

[267] Nolde: *The Mill*, oil on canvas, 1924. 73 x 78 cm. Nolde Museum, Seebüll

[268] Marc: *The Fate of Animals*, oil on canvas, 1913. 195 x 263.5 cm. Kunstmuseum, Basle

[269] Macke: *The Shop Window*, oil on canvas, 1912. 267 x 216 cm. Niedersächsische Landergalerie, Hanover

Franz Marc (1880-1916)

Marc, a native of Munich, felt that he had to escape from 'the artistic desert of the nineteenth century that was our nursery'. After his initial art training he visited Paris and was inspired by the first works of the Cubists and the Fauves. Returning to Germany, he met August Macke and Wassily Kandinsky and they joined forces with a group of young Munich painters. Late in 1911 the first Blue Rider exhibition was organized, and in the following year Marc and Kandinsky edited the book *Der Blaue Reiter*. (Incidentally, the unusual name was the outcome of Marc and Kandinsky having a special liking for the colour blue and a mutual interest in horses and riding.)

Marc used all kinds of animals to make his statements about life. He painted animals as symbols of the basic animate qualities — the tenderness of the deer, the vigour of the horse, and the menace of the tiger — and he also used colour for its symbolic value: blue was the masculine factor and yellow was the corresponding feminine one, while red signified brute force. (This is an oversimplification of Marc's intentions, and there are exceptions to it in his works.)

Unlike Kandinsky, Marc never abandoned the use of specific subjects for his pictures: he enjoyed the abstract works which Kandinsky created and himself left behind some abstract drawings of great charm, but the animal motif in his major works endured. *The Fate of Animals*

[268] has a dynamic quality which suggests the Futurist experiments, while its colour has the force of the Fauves, and the structure of its forms displays Cubist elements. This amalgam, nevertheless, has a strength and lyricism uniquely that of Franz Marc, whose contribution to art was made tragically brief by his death in the trenches at Verdun.

August Macke (1887-1914)

Macke studied art at Dusseldorf and later toured Europe extensively. After contact with the new movements in Paris, he met Marc and exhibited with the Blue Rider group. *The Shop Window* [269] is largely representational, but it incorporates elements of Matisse and certainly some aspects of Cézanne. The subject matter relates to Macke's love of city life, and this is one of the many pictures he made of the citizens strolling in the park and studying the merchandise in shop windows; the reflected patterns of the street are indicative of his technical dexterity with paint.

Macke joined Paul Klee on a trip to Tunisia in 1914, and on his return he began to paint with a new exciting abstract technique; but the fulfilment of this work was thwarted by the artist's death in World War I a few months later.

130

[271] Soutine: *Child with a Toy*, oil on
canvas, 1919. Collection of Charles
I. M. Obersteg, Geneva

[272] Kokoschka: *Woman in Blue*, oil
on canvas, 1919. 75 x 100 cm.
Staatsgalerie, Stuttgart

70] Beckmann: *The Dream*, oil on
nvas, 1921. 182.5 x 91 cm.
ollection of Morton D. May,
t Louis, Missouri

Max Beckmann (1884-1950)

Beckmann was born in Leipzig and studied art in Germany,
France and Italy: his early painting style was somewhat
Impressionist, but his experiences in World War I affected
him so profoundly that his work became Expressionist;
in this style of painting he depicted the harsh realities of
life in Europe after the war. He selected the involved
subject matter of his pictures from the dejected beings in
the city streets and the tired performers of the seamy
entertainment world. His figures have a nightmarish
quality which symbolized the tragedy of postwar Germany.
In 1933 the Nazis declared him a 'degenerate' and four
years later he left for Holland; finally in 1947 he migrated
to the United States of America.

Beckmann's Expressionist work included many portraits
painted in a rich colour range which gives a singular
vitality and a paint quality which is forceful and often
dramatic. *The Dream* [270] was painted in the aftermath
of World War I: it is a disturbing picture peopled with
pathetic aimless figures, who are involved in a horrible
fantasy which is difficult to interpret. It expresses bewilder-
ment and chaos — the distinctive qualities of Beckmann's
country in 1921.

Chaim Soutine (1894-1943)

Soutine came from a poor Russian Jewish family; he went
to Paris in 1911 and met Chagall and Modigliani, who
were both members of the international art settlement
which was to be called the 'School of Paris'. Soutine lived
a precarious, impoverished existence and his work reflected
his constant despair. The anguish he experienced is visually
expressed in the intensity of his colours and his distortion of
form.

Child with a Toy [271] portrays a subject that is generally
treated with tenderness, but Soutine endows it with colour
of such strength and with form of such distortion that a
powerful emotional impact is created: the child becomes a
symbol of human suffering. Soutine also used animal and
bird carcasses to interpret death and misery.

Oskar Kokoschka (*b.* 1886)

Kokoschka, an Austrian, showed strong Expressionist
qualities in the work of his early twenties; the Expressionist
attitudes were strengthened by his experiences in World
War I, in which he was wounded. His self-portrait from
this period (1917), painted in swirling greens and blues, is
remarkable for its emotional impact as the gaze of the
figure fixes the spectator with a look that is both searching
and bewildered. *Woman in Blue* [272], painted just after
World War I, gives an indication of the spontaneous
brushwork and colour strength that make Kokoschka's
early Expressionist style unique.

Between 1924 and 1933 Kokoschka travelled widely,
and he painted a series of vivid, expressive scenes of most
of the world's great cities. On his return to Germany he
was denounced by the Nazis and was forced to flee;
eventually he reached London, where he lived until he
made his home in Switzerland in 1953.

131

THE SCHOOL OF PARIS

The School of Paris is a term that has been applied to the international group of artists who assembled in Paris after the retrospective exhibitions of the Post-Impressionists, and those who joined the *avant-garde* movements in Paris prior to World War II. It is merely a convenient grouping of those artists who, because of the unique quality of their work, belong to none of the Parisian art movements such as Cubism or Fauvism. However, while it is possible to include artists like Picasso, despite his Cubist and other associations, the School of Paris generally comprises personalities such as Modigliani and Utrillo.

Maurice Utrillo (1883-1955)

Utrillo's early life in Paris was marked by desperate instability: illegitimacy, school expulsion and an early addiction to alcohol made his adolescence chaotic, but eventually, through self-training and encouragement from his mother, the artist Suzanne Valadon, he developed into a painter of considerable merit. With a technique somewhat reminiscent of Pissarro (see page 111) and some of the naïve, primitive elements of Rousseau le Douanier (see page 118), he painted between 1905 and 1915 hundreds of masterly canvases on the subjects he knew best — the streets of Montmartre. Utrillo gave the suburbs of Paris a unique glow: the churches, houses, courtyards and lanes assumed a fresh simplicity under his brushstrokes. In some of his works he attempted extraordinary effects: for example, he mixed glue, sand and plaster with his paint to achieve the actual quality of wall surfaces.

Rue de l'Abreuvoir, Montmartre [273] was painted in Utrillo's so-called 'white' period: the charm and strength of his composition are obvious, but today it seems strangely like an echo from the nineteenth century instead of an expression of an age about to embark on the mechanized horror of World War I. Although Utrillo lived until 1955, his work in the last forty years of comfortable middle-class existence lost the creative brilliance of his pre-1916 period.

Amedeo Modigliani (1884-1920)

Modigliani was born of a poor but well-educated Jewish-Italian family; he received a substantial academic training and studied art in Florence and Venice, and it is significant that his Italian ancestry and Florentine training are reflected in the Botticelli-like qualities of his nude studies.

[273] Utrillo: *Rue de l'Abreuvoir, Montmartre*, oil on carton, *c.* 1910-2. 66 x 75.2 cm. Royal Museum of Fine Arts, Copenhagen

In 1906 he became a member of the growing art colony in Paris; like Picasso, Modigliani was excited by his first contact with Negro sculpture and its fascinating distortion. He was to incorporate this simplified elongation of shape in his basically romantic style of painting, and in his own sculpture.

Modigliani's life in Paris was one of reckless poverty, and the effects of alcohol, drugs and eventually tuberculosis made his life tragically short. However, between 1908 and 1920 he painted portraits possessing a magnificent linear quality that is both decorative and graphic: the pictures have dignity, elegance and a distortion which, as Modigliani willed, heightens tenderness or sensuality. *Alice* [274] is typical of the gentle and poignant qualities with which he painted children, and demonstrates his mastery of line.

Georges Rouault (1871-1958)

Rouault spent all of his long life in the city of his birth, Paris. As a youth he was apprenticed to a stained-glass

[275] Rouault: *The Old King*, oil on canvas, 1916-37.
77 x 54 cm. Museum of Arts, Carnegie Institute, Pittsburgh

[274] Modigliani: *Alice*, oil on canvas, *c.* 1917. 78.7 x 39 cm.
Royal Museum of Fine Arts, Copenhagen

maker, but he later undertook formal art education. His pictures first made an impact at the Fauve exhibition of 1905, and in the following decade he developed a quality which linked his works with those of German Expressionism. The subjects of his paintings were people in states of oppression and suffering: Rouault was a religious man who wanted to expose the decadence of society, and in some of his works there is evidence of an affinity with Daumier (see page 105). His pictures of unhappy clowns, corrupt judges and prostitutes were painted in sombre tones with heavy areas of black; however, his palette later brightened and the colour assumed a jewel-like quality, with a heavy dark outline that gave the effect of stained glass, as well as making the structure of the pictures extremely powerful. A compassion and profundity of feeling is evident in all his mature work, which included religious paintings featuring Christ as well as various saints, and depicting old kings, prisoners and other symbols of his troubled social conscience.

Rouault, when an established and renowned painter, wisely destroyed many works which he felt did not measure up to his high standards of technique, expressive qualities and pictorial unity. *The Old King* [275] testifies to these attributes of Rouault's work — the power of the composition, the vibrancy of the colour and the intensity of his concern for humanity.

133

THE DADA MOVEMENT

The Dada movement began in the 1916-7 period in Europe and America, when young intellectuals practising the arts of the novel, poetry, drama, painting and sculpture began to express their horror at the seeming endlessness of World War I. The newspapers of every nation involved in the conflict carried a daily list of the names of thousands of young men killed or wounded in trench warfare; the futility of this destruction of life in the Western countries demanded expression, and Dada became its form. It condemned the social, economic and political structure of the age by attacking the prevailing culture, the contemptuous assault on conventional norms ranging from humorous absurdity to savage satire. Dada was frankly anarchistic, deliberately ignoring accepted subject matter and techniques in all the art forms, and even sometimes aiming at the deliberate destruction of the achievements of Western culture.

Among the artists involved in this movement were Marcel Duchamp, Francis Picabia and Max Ernst; apart from the immediate effect these artists had on the art 'establishment' after World War I, they influenced the Surrealist movement in the 1920s and continued to exert influence on movements in the middle of the century — the origins of Assemblages, Environments, Pop Art and Junk Sculpture can all be traced back to Dada.

Although the actual meaning of the word Dada has no artistic significance — a literal translation from the French is 'hobby horse' — its irrelevancy denotes the purposelessness of European life and culture in the eyes of the young artists of the period.

Marcel Duchamp (1887-1968)

Duchamp came from a family of artists, two of his brothers being Raymond Duchamp-Villon, the sculptor, and Jacques Villon, the painter; his sister, Suzanne Duchamp, was also a painter.

Duchamp achieved international fame at the age of 25 with *Nude Descending a Staircase* [276]. In this picture, Duchamp combined aspects of analytical Cubism and Futurism as he depicted the movements of an undulating female form in a sequential action: after its exhibition in 1913, this picture became notorious as a symbol of the 'craziness' of modern art.

In the following years in the United States, Duchamp became friendly with Francis Picabia, and together they helped to found the Dada movement in New York in 1915. Duchamp proceeded to shock the art world with his attitudes of anarchy: he was 'anti-art', and in 1919 he exhibited a print of the *Mona Lisa* on which he had drawn a moustache and a small beard, and to which he gave a title of vulgarity, symbolized by the letters *L.H.O.O.Q.* He produced more shocks with his submissions of 'readymades' as sculptural pieces — a bicycle wheel mounted on a kitchen stool (1913), and a white porcelain urinal signed 'R. Mutt' (1917). It was Duchamp's contention that the 'discovery' of the article gave it an artistic worth: he was concerned that people were unaware of existing objects and took art far too seriously, and thus removed it from its everyday application. It has been said of Duchamp that 'he used art to question art and life'.

[276] Duchamp: *Nude Descending a Staircase, No. 2*, oil on canvas, 1912. 147.3 x 89 cm. Philadelphia Museum of Art. Louise and Walter Arensberg Collection

Duchamp's influence on contemporary art forms is readily apparent in movements such as Pop Art and Junk Sculpture.

Francis Picabia (1879-1953)

Picabia, of Spanish-French parentage, spent his early life in Paris but later lived in New York and Barcelona.

After an early Impressionist period, Picabia experimented with Cubism, but his first significant works were made in the Dada period in the later years of World War I. He had met Marcel Duchamp in 1915, and together they proceeded to attack traditional attitudes to art and culture. In 1917 Picabia painted *Parade Amoureuse* which shocked the Parisian art world when it was first exhibited. The picture is carefully painted in a traditional technique, and depicts a finely detailed piece of machinery which contains all the necessary elements for effective functioning, but is designed to accomplish nothing! Was Picabia satirizing the 'establishment' and making his comment on the futility of a society which over the preceding four years had killed several million of its young men in trench warfare? Was this the 'display of love'? Although Picabia continued painting over the next twenty years, his work in Surrealist and Abstract painting never achieved the influence of his anarchistic Dada works. An intriguing example of this later period is represented in [277].

Max Ernst (*b.* 1891)

Ernst, born near Cologne, Germany, studied at the University of Bonn, became interested in painting, and after World War I worked with the Dada movement: he was one of the organizers of the first wild Dada exhibition at which axes were hung from the walls so that people could destroy what they didn't like — an exhibition that resulted in closure by the police. Later he went to Paris and became associated with the Surrealists. Ernst painted pictures of incredible fantasy, and he developed techniques that involved collage and 'frottage' (rubbing pencil over paper placed on the surface of a leaf, a board or some other textured object). His experiences of life between the two world wars and during the wars themselves (he escaped from a Nazi concentration camp in 1940) have provided the material for the horror and degradations of oppressed, suffering humanity which he portrays in many of his works. *The Little Tear Gland that Goes Tic-tac* [278] belongs to the Dada period, and is a satirical comment on post-World War I society and the dehumanizing of life; it is somewhat gentler than his later work, but is indicative of Ernst's philosophy and the technical excellence of his painting.

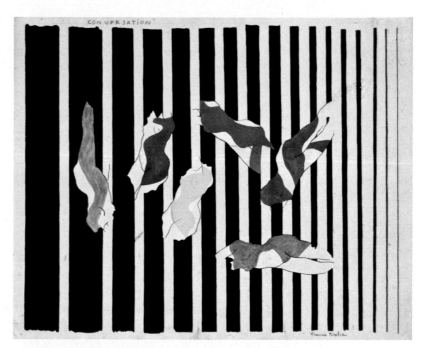

[277] Picabia: *Conversation*, watercolour on board, 1922. 59.4 x 72.4 cm. Tate Gallery, London

[278] Ernst: *The Little Tear Gland that Goes Tic-tac*, gouache on wallpaper, 1920. 36.2 x 25.4 cm. Collection, The Museum of Modern Art, New York

SURREALISM, FANTASY and METAPHYSICAL PAINTING

Surrealism means 'beyond or above realism', and was the name given to a twentieth century art movement concerned with the projection of the subconscious mind and dreams. In many of its aspects Surrealism looked back to the inventive imagery of artists like Hieronymus Bosch (see page 66), but a significant part of the theory of Surrealism comes from the work of Sigmund Freud and his research into the nature of man's mental life. It concerned itself with traditional techniques, and indeed the painting was usually extremely naturalistic in the single elements depicted, but it was far removed from reality in the shock association of these various elements: thus the artists depicted cannons in living rooms, giraffes on fire, and cartilage and bone abstracts in desert environments. Historically, Surrealism, like Dada, was a reaction against the horror of World War I; it was initiated in 1924 by the publication of *A Manifesto of Surrealism* by a French artist, André Breton, and flourished until World War II. Its main exponents were Max Ernst, Yves Tanguy, Joan Miró and Salvador Dali.

Joan Miró (*b.* 1893)

Miró is a native of Barcelona. After his early art training, he went to Paris in 1919 and experimented with Picasso's Cubist theories, but his temperament reacted against the restraint imposed by 'theories' of art. Miró became involved in the artistic furore which followed the publication of the *Manifesto of Surrealism*, and he exhibited in the first Surrealist show in 1925. André Breton, the originator of the movement, described Miró as 'the most Surrealistic of us all': this personal tribute might be ascribed to the pervasive sincerity that characterizes the projection of Miró's own inner fantasy life, coupled with his keen understanding of the works of primitive people like the Eskimos and Red Indians, and above all those of young children. The symbolism of his pictures has a naïve beauty and he executes his work with delicate line work and strokes and spots, using the primary colours and black.

[279] Miro: *Women and Bird by Moonlight*, oil on canvas, 1949. 81.3 x 66 cm. Tate Gallery, London

[280] Dali: *Soft Construction with Boiled Beans: Premonition of Civil War*, oil on canvas, 1936. 100.3 x 100.3 cm. Philadelphia Museum of Art. Louise and Walter Arensberg Collection

136

[281] De Chirico: *Mystery and Melancholy of a Street*, oil on canvas, 1914. 85.1 x 69.2 cm. Collection of Mr and Mrs Stanley Resor, New Canaan, Connecticut

[282] Klee: *The Twittering Machine*, oil, watercolour, pen and ink, 1922. 41.3 x 30.5 cm. Collection, The Museum of Modern Art, New York

Women and Bird by Moonlight [279] is not of the early Surrealist period but was painted in Miró's maturity: it is a charming combination of innocence and fantasy, with amusing symbolism which is almost child-like in its vision.

Salvador Dali (*b.* 1904)

Dali was born in Catalonia and studied at Barcelona and Madrid, where he was expelled from the Academy of Fine Arts. In 1928 he went to Paris and proceeded to paint in the Surrealist manner, bringing great technical skill in the traditionalist manner to his pictures of dreams and sub-conscious activity. The sensational aspects of his Surrealist period drew wide international publicity. *Premonition of Civil War* [280] is a Surrealist work based on the Spanish Civil War: the biblical story of Cain and Abel is used in the symbolism, but much of the symbolism remains private. Despite the poignancy of the theme, the artist's technique seems based in sensation rather than sincerity.

Dali settled in America in 1940 and for the last thirty years his life has attracted wide attention from the news media. It is difficult to distinguish the artist from the showman in the many statements he makes, and critical assessment of his religious paintings is varied indeed.

Giorgio de Chirico (*b.* 1888)

De Chirico, an Italian painter, spent his early years in Greece; he studied art there and later in Munich and Paris, before settling in Italy. Here he helped to establish a movement called Metaphysical painting which, like Dada, depicted the hollowness and wastefulness of life in the early decades of the twentieth century. Through his works de Chirico projected the gulf between modern man and the great symbols of the past. In *Mystery and Melancholy of a Street* [281], we see the artist painting in a style that is Surrealist: the pictorial assemblage of strangely assorted objects comments on the anti-life forces of the city streets and the solitary nature of modern man. Pictures like this had a considerable influence on the young Surrealists, and de Chirico was invited to exhibit with them at their first show in 1925. After this period he became traditionalist in style and since then has had little impact on international art.

137

[283] Chagall: *Over Vitebsk*, oil on canvas, 1915-20. 67 x 92.7 cm. Collection, The Museum of Modern Art, New York. Acquired through the Lillie P. Bliss Bequest

Marc Chagall (*b.* 1887)

Chagall was born into a poor Jewish family in Vitebsk, Russia, and after a brief period of art study in his native country, he won a scholarship to Paris. He returned to Russia during World War I, and after the revolution in 1917 he helped to establish art academies and painted a series of murals for the Jewish theatre in Moscow. He left Russia in 1922, and has spent the rest of his life in France and the United States of America.

On his first visit to Paris, Chagall began to paint fantasies of his past and present existence: Russian-Jewish village life, the city life of Paris, his courtship and marriage are all combined in compositions which resemble the visualizing of dreams.

Chagall developed a technique which contained elements of Cubism and Expressionism, and he organized the objects in his works in a manner that was to influence the Surrealists. *Over Vitebsk* [283] was painted between the years 1915 and 1920 — the period of the Russian Revolution. The structure of the buildings and the surface planes of the snow are distinctively Cubist, the floating figures and the general dream-like atmosphere are Surrealist, and the poignant quality of the artist's memories of his ghetto existence is Expressionist. During the 1930s and 1940s, Chagall produced a series of dramatic paintings in which he used the theme of the Crucifixion as a symbol representing the attempted Nazi genocide of the European Jews.

Chagall's artistic life has a breadth which few artists in the twentieth century can match: he has acquired a considerable reputation for his book illustrations, theatre design, ceramics, sculpture and murals. His work decorates the ceiling of the Paris Opera House and the walls of the Metropolitan Opera at the Lincoln Centre in New York; one of his finest accomplishments is the set of stained glass windows at the Hadasseh Hospital in Jerusalem.

Paul Klee (1879-1940)

Klee, born in Switzerland and of part-German ancestry, is one of this century's outstanding artists. After studying art in Munich he contributed to the first *Blaue Reiter* exhibition with Marc, Kandinsky and Macke; later he travelled to Tunisia and was thus impelled into new attitudes to colour. After World War I, he was invited to teach at the Bauhaus school in Weimar, and later in Dessau, but his career as a practising artist and teacher in Germany ceased when Hitler assumed power; Klee returned to Switzerland, where he died in 1940.

Over the thirty-year span of his painting career, Paul Klee's work defies category: at times the influence of Dada may be apparent, at others that of Surrealism, but it is Klee's method of painting which makes his creations so significant. His intuitive approach to painting and his self-projection into the act of creation are reflected in the overwhelming variety of his work — a variety which is comparable to nature itself. He recorded natural form ceaselessly in his notebooks, and from this activity came the seemingly 'artless' yet insightful statement of his imagination. Although his scintillating colour is not demonstrated, there is evidence of his fanciful line work in *The Twittering Machine* [282]. The medium is peculiarly his own: a conglomerate of oil paint, watercolour and ink on paper pasted to cardboard, it can be interpreted as a witty thrust at mechanization.

The insight evident in Klee's work is tragically apparent in the paintings of his last years: their colour and line work contain forebodings of the outcome of his long fatal illness.

ABSTRACT ART

All paintings, in a sense, are abstract: no matter what the subject, be it a person or an apple, the artist can never paint a *real* person or a *real* apple. The artist can create an illusion of reality, but since a painting has only two dimensions, it is necessary for the artist to 'abstract' from the natural three-dimensional form.

However, since the first decade of the twentieth century, abstract art — variously called non-figurative, non-naturalistic or non-representational — has been painted and sculpted without regard for the representation of real or natural objects: it has concerned itself purely with colour, texture, tone, line, shape, mass and space, and the disposition of these elements in the selected art form.

Kandinsky produced the first non-figurative paintings around 1911, and about the same time a group in Russia led by Kasimir Malevich banded together to found a movement called Suprematism, espousing a form of purely geometric painting in which the elements of shape were circles, triangles, squares, crosses and so on. Malevich's most famous work was his picture of a black square on a white background.

A little later the *De Stijl* ('The Style') group of painters in Holland advanced their theories emphasizing an art form based on the rectangle as the dominant shape and a colour range restricted to the primary colours. Mondrian developed the concepts of this group into his theory of Neoplasticism.

Wassily Kandinsky (1866-1944)

Kandinsky, born in Russia, was 30 years old before he decided to take up painting instead of continuing to practise law. He went to Munich to study art, and visited other centres in Europe before spending a year in Paris in 1906. His Impressionist style of painting underwent almost immediate changes; he experimented in the Fauve manner and exhibited in the first *Die Brücke* exhibition in Germany. He went to Munich in 1908 and in the next few years collaborated with Marc, Klee and Macke, an association which gave rise to *Der Blaue Reiter*. With this group, Kandinsky showed his first abstract pictures; this was the beginning of a style of painting which was to occupy his life for the next thirty years.

This period had three distinct phases of activity. *Romantic Landscape* [284] is from the first phase, and is a form of Expressionism which, although in this case called a landscape, is almost non-representational. It is certainly romantic and lyrical in its colour and form, with brush-strokes that make linear patterns on the massed colour of

[284] Kandinsky: *Romantic Landscape*, oil on canvas, 1911. 94 x 130 cm. Städtische Galerie, Munich. Gabriele Münter Foundation

[285] Kandinsky: *Softened Construction*, oil on canvas, 1927. 100 x 50 cm. Collection of Mr and Mrs Nathan Cummings, Chicago

139

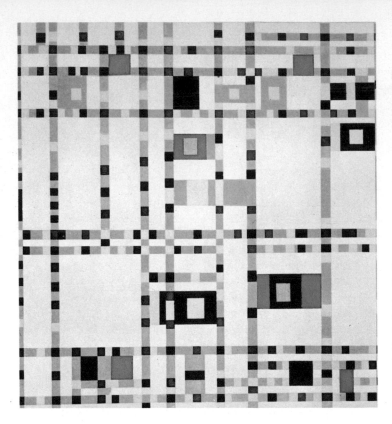

[286] Mondrian: *Broadway Boogie-Woogie*, oil on canvas, 1942-3. 127 x 127 cm. Collection, The Museum of Modern Art, New York

the background. The three 'horsemen' are little more than a token gesture to representation, and the picture has a special fascination in that it demonstrates the transition to complete abstraction.

Kandinsky returned to Russia after war broke out in 1914, and there, until he left for Germany in 1921, he was influenced by Malevich and Suprematism. Kandinsky was to develop this style of abstract painting in his ten-year stay at the Bauhaus, which he joined in 1922. In this second period his work became more geometrical, with a constant emphasis on circular shapes. *Softened Construction* [285] is from the Bauhaus period and shows a subdued colour harmony; it contrasts sharply with *Romantic Landscape* in that the composition has a remarkable tension.

In the 1930s, Kandinsky's work lost its angular and circular geometric form; his colour range generally was more gentle, and although his work encompassed a wide variety of motifs there is an intellectual grace present in all his paintings, which rank among the finest achievements of the first half of the twentieth century.

Piet Mondrian (1872-1944)

Mondrian spent the first forty years of his life in Holland, studying art, training to be a teacher, copying old masters and painting formal landscapes; at the end of 1910 he settled in Paris and was strongly influenced by analytical Cubism. He pursued the study of this style until he had reduced his compositions to what he considered the essentials — a rhythmic organization of lines and colours. Mondrian returned to Holland in 1914 and persisted with his experiments until the lines in his compositions were exclusively horizontal or vertical, and the colours were restricted to the primary range of red, yellow and blue — with the addition of black, white and grey. This particular style became known as Neoplasticism — pure plastic art — and in 1917 he was co-author of a magazine, *De Stijl*, in which he set down his ideas on abstract art. He followed this with other written statements on his philosophy of art, which he said was concerned with 'the pure relationships of lines and pure colours, because only the pure relationships of pure constructive elements can achieve a pure beauty'. This emphasis on purity was basic to Mondrian's work: there was no indication of brushwork, no illusion of three-dimensional space, no curved lines — in fact, nothing but the essential relationships of the right-angular meeting of lines, and the statement and careful disposition of rectangles of pure primary colours on a grey or a white ground.

Mondrian lived in Paris after World War I, his home becoming a centre for the international art personalities of the 1920s and 1930s; he went to London in 1938 and eventually settled in New York in 1940, where he spent the remaining four years of his life. In this period he introduced new elements into his painting: the black lines of his earlier work became patterned ribbons of coloured squares; but above all, he made an unprecedented statement of sentiment in works like *Victory Boogie-Woogie* and *Broadway Boogie-Woogie* [286]. The verticals and horizontals remain, as do the primary colours of *De Stijl*, but here Mondrian presents an abstract symbol of the excitement of American city life.

Mondrian's work has had a strong influence on the mid-twentieth century, in the fields of domestic interior decoration — carpets, linoleums, the painting of woodwork and walls — and architecture in particular: the simplification of design, the emphasis on relationships between space, line and colour, and the general concern for harmony and logic all reflect the impact of his philosophy of art.

ABSTRACT EXPRESSIONISM

Abstract Expressionism was a movement which began in the United States after World War II. It drew on the main art movements of the early part of this century, with colour from the Fauves, space concepts from the Cubists, the individual nature of the picture from the Expressionists, and 'subject matter' from the non-objective or abstract painters. An immediately prior influence was the later work of Kandinsky, with its 'spiritual' organization of abstract shapes. The innovation of the American artists was twofold: firstly, their works were of an enormous size, and secondly, they devised new methods of paint application. The actual 'doing' of the act of painting and the effect created were one, because the action of applying the paint determined the outcome — hence the term 'action painting'.

Among the exponents of this painting style were Jackson Pollock, Willem de Kooning, Mark Tobey and Franz Kline. The work of these artists reflected the post-World War II period: the diversity of the age, with the uncertainty of its ideals and aspirations, demanded new and different forms of expression.

[287] Pollock: *Yellow Islands*, oil on canvas, 1952. 143.5 x 182.9 cm. Tate Gallery, London

Jackson Pollock (1912-1956)

Jackson Pollock was the first American painter to initiate an international movement and promote a new art revolution; his contribution has been considerable, particularly so in view of his tragic death at the age of 44.

After training in Los Angeles and New York, Pollock studied the mural painters of Mexico and the old masters of Europe. In the mid-1940s, he challenged the notion that a picture was the end result of a planned design, carefully transferred to wood, paper or canvas. He made paintings an all-over surface affair, placing the work on the floor and using a wild tracery of lines and spots of colour, which trailed and dripped in accordance with his physical painting action. As abstract painting, his compositions differed from the mathematically balanced work of Mondrian, in that Pollock's organization of swirling patterns and patches of colour achieved strong pictorial unity from the intuitive control he exercised over his paint. The emotional act that sustains Pollock's work establishes its Expressionist quality: the spectator is involved in the life of the surface of the picture as lines react on each other, moving together and then separating, as spots of colour advance and then recede, as patches of white link up and then dissociate;

ultimately, because of the inescapable, overwhelming size of the work, the spectator feels drawn into the picture's rhythm.

Yellow Islands [287] represents a period late in Pollock's life — between 1951 and 1953 — when he used little colour, concentrating almost entirely on black and the pattern of line and shape on his picture surface.

Willem de Kooning (*b.* 1904)

De Kooning, born in Holland, went to the United States in 1926, and until 1940 his interest lay in portraiture and figure work. His painting slowly lost its representative appearance and a harsh, agitated line work dominated his largely abstract pictures, creating an intensely passionate quality. His work over the last thirty years has moved between his Expressionistic studies of the female form and pure Abstract Expressionism. In this latter style he was considered to be the leading exponent after Pollock's death.

1948 Painting [288] is not as chaotic in its structure as some of de Kooning's other works: its colours are almost a monotone of brown, and the forms which merge and overlap have a control that is somewhat akin to a drifting melancholy. De Kooning's abstract shapes give fleeting

141

[288] De Kooning: *1948 Painting*, enamel and oil on canvas, 1948.
108.3 x 142.6 cm. Collection, The Museum of Modern Art, New York

[289] Rothko: *Light Red over Black*, oil on canvas, 1957. 232.7 x 152.7 cm.
Tate Gallery, London

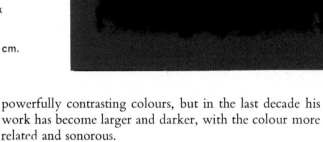

suggestions of human forms which seem to be struggling to the surface of the canvas, but there is a quiet confidence that the life force will survive.

Mark Rothko (*b.* 1903)

Rothko was born in Russia and went to the United States when he was 10; after studying at Yale University, he enrolled at art school in New York. He passed through a series of painting phases — from early figurative 'city scapes' of New York, to Surrealism, and in 1947 to a form of abstract painting based on rectangular shapes of enormous proportions. At first these abstracts were in powerfully contrasting colours, but in the last decade his work has become larger and darker, with the colour more related and sonorous.

The painting *Light Red over Black* [289] displays Rothko's typically large, simple forms and powerful colour: the enormousness of the shapes and the emphatic quality of the contrast in colour demand the spectator's participation in the work. Rothko explained the significance of the large dimensions of his works when he said in 1951, 'I want to be very intimate and human. To paint a small picture is to place yourself outside your experience. . . . However you paint the larger picture, you are in it. It isn't something you command.'

142

OP, POP, HARD EDGE
AND KINETIC ART

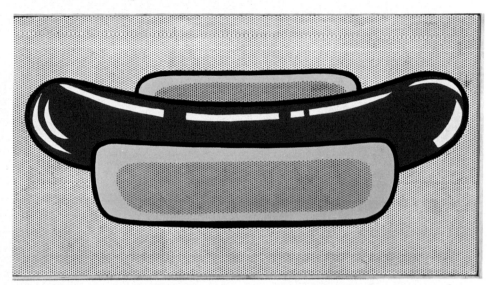

[290] Vasarely: *Nives II*, oil on canvas, 1949-58. 194.9 x 114.3 cm. Tate Gallery, London

[291] Lichtenstein: *Hot Dog*, oil on canvas, 1963. 50.8 x 91.4 cm. Collection of René de Montaigu

Op Art had its beginnings in the abstractions of Mondrian and his followers, but was not established as a movement until after World War II. It attempted to create from non-objective painting the sensation of movement caused by the optical effects of colour and shape. This theory was based on the physical properties possessed by the human eye which make it capable of projecting an after-image to the brain, as well as conveying an illusion of change created by colour relationships.

Victor Vasarely was born in Hungary in 1908; his earliest paintings were very formal, but after studying the theories of Mondrian and Kandinsky, he began to enunciate his own ideas on theories of perception and optical illusion, studies which he defined in his *Yellow Manifesto* of 1955. Vasarely sees the role of art in a technological society as integral to all the media of expression and all methods of

mechanical reproduction; in fact, he feels that art is only valid in this age if it is capable of representation by all the agencies of mass communication and mass production.

In *Nives II* [290], painted during the period 1949-58, Vasarely has used tone and colour to achieve an optical interplay of the abstract forms in his composition. The effect is subtle and gentle compared with the dynamic, even bewildering patterns in some of his other works.

Pop Art, a movement of the 1950s and 1960s, is based on 'popular' culture and is concerned with such phenomena of modern life as commercial posters, packaged foods, traffic signs and comic strips. The movement began in England in the 1950s and became significant in the United States in the following decade. However, the origins of this attempt to link gallery-type art to an age of mass production might in fact be traced back to Marcel Duchamp's exhibitions of ready-made factory articles during World War I.

Hot Dog [291] is by Roy Lichtenstein, who was born in the United States in 1923; in this painting he uses an enormous hot dog to represent one aspect of the current American way of life. The picture is larger than life — apart from its size — in that it is a statement of the 'perfect' hot dog, with a polished surface on the frankfurt that

143

[292] Smith: *Riverfall*, oil and acrylic on canvas, 1969. 198.1 x 685.8 x 40.6 cm. Kasmin Gallery, London

resembles a car's duco finish, and a structural perfection in the bun which is akin to conveyor-belt precision.

The application of the term 'Hard Edge' became current in the 1960s to distinguish between abstract painting that was Expressionistic and that which was deliberately Optical. Hard Edge involved flat, pure-coloured shapes with precise outlines, which often were not geometric. An extension of Hard Edge was the 'package' picture, in which the traditional frame shape was ignored and the surface of the canvas was structured to physically exist in a three-dimensional sense. This art form has led to a breakdown between separate areas of sculpture and painting. One such 'picture' is *Span* by the English artist Richard Smith (b. 1931), who stretched the canvas for his Hard Edge painting over shaped wood to create a 'span' form.

Smith's 1969 work *Riverfall* [292] has three dimensions: its width is 686 cm, its height is 198 cm, and its depth is 41 cm! Thus the middle section of the five making up this 'shaped' canvas is 41 cm from the wall, and the artist achieves an actual contour effect.

Kinetic art is a mid-twentieth century art form which can be both pictorial and sculptural, and which depends on the creation of movement in some of its parts by either the action of a machine or natural air currents. It follows the aims of Op Art, but substitutes the reality of movement for a mere illusion.

Light Dynamo [293], an example of this style, is by Heinz Mack, who was born in Germany in 1931 and now lives in the U.S.A. In Dusseldorf, he was a member of the

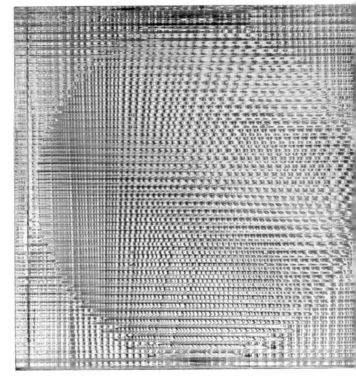

[293] Mack: *Light Dynamo*, mixed media, 1963. 57.2 x 57.2 x 31.1 cm. Tate Gallery, London

Kinetic Art Zero Group which group-created anonymous works. Mack has placed a small machine in an aluminium and glass construction so that the moving source produces a constantly changing series of patterns of reflected light.

MODERN SCULPTURE

Auguste Rodin (1840-1917)

While there were many artists who contributed to the resurgence of European painting in the latter part of the nineteenth century, the comparable achievement in sculpture is attributable to one man — Auguste Rodin.

Rodin was born in Paris and studied drawing, painting and sculpture. He encouraged the efforts of the young Impressionist painters in their struggle against the official Salon, for he too experienced constant rejection of his early works by the Parisian establishment. However, in 1877 his work was afforded some recognition, and over the next forty years he executed a series of sculptures which were to revitalize three-dimensional art. The works of this era include *The Thinker, The Prodigal Son, The Kiss, The Burghers of Calais* and *Balzac*.

Rodin was a creator in every sense, and broke from the emotionally frigid and sleek academic statuary of the nineteenth century. He made the human form the main subject of his works, but in so doing he did not idealize the human body — he humanized sculpture. His work achieved a combination of force and spirituality, as well as a dynamic sensuality. The conflict of shapes made an interplay of light and shadow which achieved the same vitality as colour does in a painting, and it was this organization of light which created a sensation of movement. He said, 'I do not represent all the parts of my figures in the same moment of their existence. Anyone looking over one of my statues from one end to the other, will be watching the unfolding of their movements through all the different parts of the work, from its birth to its completion.'

The bronze figure of Vaslav Nijinsky [294], the outstanding male dancer of his time, was cast from a plaster study — only 18.5 cm high — made by Rodin in 1912. He has captured the animal quality — what the critics called the 'unleashed, demonic quality' — of the faun, the role that Nijinsky created for the ballet of Debussy's *L'Après-midi d'un Faune*. The surging energy of Nijinsky's dancing is manifest, and this tiny study is indicative of the vitality of Rodin's work.

Just as Shakespeare is assured of universal greatness, so is Rodin: he has taken his place beside Michelangelo as a great sculptor for all times and for all places.

Aristide Maillol (1861-1944)

Maillol, born in France, began his art career as an easel painter and later became a designer of tapestries; he experimented with other art forms, but in 1909 a visit to Greece confirmed his interest in sculpture. The Greek sculpture of the Archaic and Transitional periods was to remain the stimulus for his later achievements. Maillol looked to the simple, organic construction of Greek

[294] Rodin: *Nijinsky*, bronze, 1912. Height 18.5 cm. Rodin Museum, Paris

[295] Maillol: *Torso of the Monument to Blanqui*, metal, c. 1905-6. 120.7 x 69.2 x 52.7 cm. Tate Gallery, London

[296] Boccioni: *Unique Forms of Continuity in Space*, bronze, 1913. 111.4 x 88.6 x 40 cm. Collection, The Museum of Modern Art, New York. Acquired through the Lillie P. Bliss Bequest

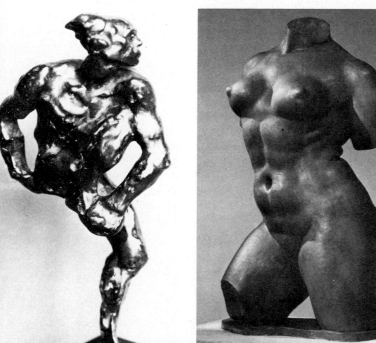

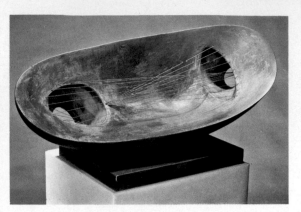

[298] Hepworth: *Landscape Sculpture*, bronze, 1944 (cast 1961). Length 66 cm. Tate Gallery, London

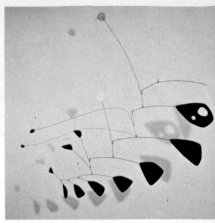

[299] Calder: *Antennae with Red and Blue Dots*, metal, 1960. 111.1 x 128.3 x 128.3 cm. Tate Gallery, London

[297] Moore: *Family Group*, bronze, 1948-9 (cast 1950). 150.5 x 118.1 cm. Collection, The Museum of Modern Art, New York. A. Conger Goodyear Fund

statuary, with its inherent strength and formal dignity, for his inspiration.

Torso of the Monument to Blanqui [295] is typical of his work: there is humanity and warmth in Maillol's sculpture, partly achieved by the interplay of light throughout the figure. Significant as the life quality is in the nude figures of Maillol, his accomplishment is notable for the absence of sentimentality, which was prevalent in other works in this genre by his contemporaries.

Umberto Boccioni (1882-1916)

Boccioni's contribution to Futurist painting has been mentioned on page 127. After parting with Severini and Balla, he travelled widely in Europe and in 1912 wrote a *Technical Manifesto of Futurist Sculpture*, attacking the academic traditions in sculpture, particularly the sentimental obsession with the female nude. Boccioni spent much time in Paris during the years immediately preceding World War I; the first works he exhibited in the tradition of Futurism caused a sensation, and one was smashed by members of the public.

Unique Forms of Continuity in Space [296] demonstrates the dynamic quality he was introducing to sculpture: like his painting, this work curves and sways back and forth in an illusion of movement. Boccioni projected successive stages of action in this one single shape; Futurist as the sculptor's intentions were, the work, in essence, is reminiscent of the classical past, taking us back to the soaring movement of the 'Victory of Samothrace'. Here, too, is the tension between space and mass which Boccioni sought.

Henry Moore (*b.* 1898)

Moore was born in Yorkshire, England, the son of a coalminer. He trained extensively in England, France and Italy, and the earliest influences in his career came from the sculpture of primitive and ancient cultures, particularly those of Pre-Columbian Mexico and west Africa. Other influences determined Moore's sculptural attitudes — the works of Michelangelo, Rodin and Maillol, and the anonymous stone carvings of English Medieval churches.

It is difficult to generalize about Moore's wide and varied achievements; however, many of his works begin with the human form and are transformed by the sculptural process into non-human objects — shapes which suggest caves and water-worn stones, or even non-representational geometric solids. Whether close to or far from natural or human form, Moore's work has the qualities of monumentality, massiveness and nobility. He has stated that the first time he pierced a hole through a stone it was a revelation to him. The hole or void in his work became an integral feature of his sculpture: Moore felt that the hole could have as much shape and meaning as the solid mass, and he likened its effect to the mysterious fascination of caves in hillsides and cliffs. The interplay between the mass and the void (or the positive and negative forces) is intrinsic to the rhythm in Moore's sculpture, whether the work be in stone, bronze or wood.

The subject of *Family Group* [297] — mother, father and child — was explored many times by Moore; the monumental dignity of the group is supplemented by the warmth expressed in the figure relationships. Although the figure proportions are freely treated, there is a quality of pre-Classic Greek simplicity in the work. Moore's constant recourse to human and natural forms and his versatility as an artist can be seen in the series of drawings he made of the English people during his years as an official artist in World War II.

146

[300] Brancusi: *Magic Bird (Pasarea Maiastra)*, Version I, white marble, 1910. Height 55.9 cm. Collection, The Museum of Modern Art, New York. Katherine S. Dreier Bequest

[301] Archipenko: *Woman Combing her Hair*, bronze, 1914-5. 35.6 x 9.5 x 8.3 cm. Tate Gallery, London

[302] Zadkine: *Statue in Memory of a Destroyed City*, bronze, 1953-4. Rotterdam

Barbara Hepworth (*b.* 1903)

Barbara Hepworth was born in Yorkshire, England, and she studied art there and in Italy; with her fellow country-man Henry Moore, she was ranked among sculptors of international reputation before World War II.

Hepworth's work is dominantly abstract, although suggestive of natural forms. She has found her inspiration in the rocks, foliage and shell creatures of the English Channel coastline, as well as in the Cornish countryside where she has lived for many years. The strings which are integral to much of her sculpture in wood are 'the tension I felt between myself and the sea, the wind and the hills'.

Landscape Sculpture [298] was originally sculpted in elmwood and string in 1944. Later Hepworth became interested in bronze sculpture, and in 1961 the work was cast in bronze: this version is the one reproduced here.

In the last ten years Hepworth has undertaken a variety of monumental works in marble and bronze which demonstrate both the delicacy and the power that are characteristic of her sculpture.

Alexander Calder (*b.* 1898)

Calder was born in Philadelphia, U.S.A., and trained to be an engineer, a fact that was to be significant in his future career as a sculptor. In 1926 he went to Paris, where contact with the current movements excited his experimentation with new sculptural forms; by the use of wire he made sculptures such as his *Josephine Baker*, in which a vibrating form anchored to a base made sinuous movements in space (these structures were later to be known as stabiles). In 1932 he introduced wire sculpture in conjunction with flat or rounded metal shapes which hung from a ceiling — sometimes they stood on a base — and moved under the impact of air currents. These suspended lines and shapes, called mobiles, swung rhythmically, creating new space expressions in art.

Antennae with Red and Blue Dots [299] is typical of Calder's mobiles. The forms subtly contrast in shape and size, and the sculpture conveys the impression of both lightness and strength.

During the 1950s and 1960s Calder made some enormous sculptural works, many of which were structurally involved with architecture. At Expo '67 in Canada, his metal constructions, 18 metres high, were designed so that cars could drive through them. At the University Hall in Caracas, Venezuela, Calder designed a huge mobile which not only decorates with its moving colour and shape patterns, but functions as an integral part of the acoustic engineering of the auditorium.

Calder's understanding of his materials and his artistic sensitivity have created a twentieth century art form which is gently lyrical, logical and strong.

Constantin Brancusi (1876-1957)

Brancusi was born in Rumania, and after his art training in Bucharest he travelled extensively throughout Europe. He settled in Paris in 1904, where he came under the influence of Rodin (Brancusi refused his offer of an assistantship) and the newly discovered Negroid sculpture. He soon abandoned modelling and began direct carving, developing a formal simplicity in his treatment of such themes as the human head, birds, fish and, eventually, the egg. He said, 'Simplicity is not a goal, but one arrives at simplicity in spite of oneself, as one approaches the real meaning of things.' Thus Brancusi reacted against romanticism and

147

[303] Lipchitz: *Figure*, bronze,
1926-30. Height 216.5 cm.
The Joseph H. Hirschhorn
Collection, New York

[304] Giacometti: *City Square*,
bronze, 1948. 21.6 x 64.4 x 43.8 cm.
Collection, The Museum of
Modern Art, New York

[305] Marini: *Horse and Rider*,
bronze, 1949. 180.3 x 124.5 x 81.3
cm. Walker Art Centre,
Minneapolis

classical naturalism as he eliminated all unnecessary detail from his work. The revolutionary quality of Brancusi's work was highlighted in the 1920s, when the United States customs service wanted to charge duty on his sculpture *Bird in Space* for its weight in metal, disallowing it as a work of art. Brancusi won the ensuing court case, a triumph for the modern art movement in its battle against conservative antipathy and ridicule.

Maiastra [300] is an early work in marble of which Brancusi made a polished bronze copy. The sculpture, based on a Rumanian fairy tale, depicts the fabled bird which led a lost lover to his beloved, and is an example of the bird symbol that Brancusi used so often in his works. The balance is brilliantly achieved, and the bird has a quality of essential purity, symbolic of its nobility of purpose. This work embodies the warmth, the eloquence and above all the power that have made Brancusi one of this century's most stimulating sculptors.

Alexander Archipenko (1887-1964)

Archipenko was born in Kiev, Russia, where he trained in art before travelling to Paris to study in the years preceding World War I. He developed a sculptural form which was both Futuristic and Cubist in style, and he pioneered the interplay of the void and the mass within his figure shapes: the hollowed-out areas and the relationships he devised between the convex and the concave forms created new rhythms in sculpture, which were to have a considerable influence on other sculptors. *Woman Combing her Hair* [301] was created in the period 1914-5, and should be inter-preted in the context of the analytical Cubist paintings of Braque and Picasso immediately preceding it.

In 1923, after a sojourn in Germany, Archipenko settled in the United States, where he taught sculpture and experimented in new materials and techniques.

Ossip Zadkine (1890-1967)

Zadkine, a fellow-countryman of Archipenko, was an early explorer of Cubist sculptural techniques. The Rotterdam memorial illustrated in [302] is a mature work which typifies the open forms of the Cubist sculptors. This style of sculpture seems particularly appropriate in its portrayal of the agonized destruction of Rotterdam in World War II: it symbolizes violence and destruction, as it pleads the case of humanity against barbarism.

Jacques Lipchitz (b. 1891)

Lipchitz, who was born in Lithuania, settled in Paris when he was 18. He studied both painting and sculpture and came under the influence of Picasso, Archipenko and Negro sculpture. He accomplished some fascinating works in the Cubist sculptural manner, in which the volumes of his sculptures were disintegrated by mass and void. His work over the next thirty years falls into phases of the represent-ational and the abstract.

Illustrated in [303] is a 1930 bronze figure reminiscent of monumental pagan symbols and in particular those of the Easter Islanders. The structure of the form, with its extraordinary stone 'links', creates a primitive forceful rhythm, and there is an aura of mystery and majesty in the

148

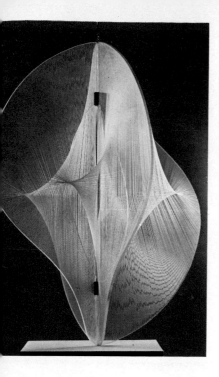

[306] Gabo: *Linear Construction in Space, No. 2*, perspex and nylon thread, 1949. Height 91 cm. Stedelijk Museum, Amsterdam

[307] Smith: *The Banquet*, welded steel, 1951. Height 134.9 cm. Private collection

oval head shape with its circular staring eyes. At this stage of his development Lipchitz was involved in the Surrealist art philosophy, and although this did not persist, his work remains symbolic. Lipchitz's contribution to so many twentieth century sculptural movements ensures his position in the history of modern art.

Alberto Giacometti (1901-1966)

Giacometti, the son of a Swiss landscape painter, lived his life in Italy, France and Switzerland. As well as practising the arts of painting, drawing and sculpture, he wrote prose and poetry. In 1922 he settled for a time in Paris, and there he was influenced by the fantasy writings and paintings of the period; the gruesome and macabre sentiments of these works were predictive of the barbarism of World War II, which was to influence Giacometti's work. He proceeded to make sculptures which reflected the frailty and remoteness of contemporary existence and which sharply contrasted with the smooth, simple forms of his earlier works. The men and women with their tall slender limbs and elongated heads are lonely beings who are isolated even in a crowd. *City Square* [304] illustrates Giacometti's fascination not only with these wraith-like figures, but with the spaces between them, and the work projects his vision of the nightmarish emptiness of life in the twentieth century.

Marino Marini (*b.* 1901)

Marini was born in Italy and after early art training he went to France. Although he was excited by the various post-World War I movements in Paris, he sought his inspiration in his own country and looked back to the sculpture of the Etruscans (see page 21). Over the next thirty years, he made portraits in bronze which, through his use of broken surface, have tremendous vitality. The recurring theme in Marini's work is that of the horse and rider: in his first development of this theme, the animal and human forms were depicted with a roundness that over the years became sharper and more angular, until finally in 1960 the horse and rider became one semi-abstract unit. The sculpture illustrated in [305] is from the middle period when the horse and rider, Marini's symbol of vitality and the basic life force, are still in the ascendancy; but eventually, in the plunging horse and rider symbol of the 1960s, humanity fell to its doom. Marini's work has a primitive strength that has had considerable impact on twentieth century sculpture.

Naum Gabo (*b.* 1890)

Gabo was born in Russia and his brother was Antoine Pevsner, also a sculptor. After his schooling in Russia he studied in Munich and travelled widely. He returned to post-revolutionary Russia and in 1920 he posted his theories of Constructivism in his *Realist Manifesto*; in this statement he said that space and time are the only real things in life and that art therefore must have these two factors as its basis. In the same year he exhibited his first Kinetic (moving) sculpture, and he proceeded to incorporate contemporary materials like metal tubing, glass and plastic in his work. He left Russia in 1923 and has lived in Berlin, Paris, England and now the U.S.A. Gabo's work ranges from enormous monumental pieces — as in the shopping centre at Rotterdam, Holland — to the translucent abstractions exemplified by *Linear Construction in Space, No. 2* [306]. Gabo's genius for structuring a geometrical harmony in plastic and nylon, with its rhythmical flow

149

[308] Tinguely: Wall sculpture, Studio Theatre, Gelsenkirchen

over the strings of light which link the folds and convolutions, is typified in this sculpture. The luminosity and the translucency create a drifting sensation which is determined by Gabo's use of contemporary media.

David Smith (1906-1965)

Smith was born in the United States and after graduation from university he worked in a car factory, where he was involved in riveting and casting steel. He studied art in New York, originally intending to be a painter, but he began to sculpt in abstract form in the 1930s. During World War II he worked as a welder in a factory and after the war he became one of the innovators of welded metal sculpture. His work, which contained elements of both Cubism and Surrealism, had a wide variety of theme. Just as his technique is peculiar to this century, so are the subjects of his work: he said that his themes were those of this era — 'power, structure, movement, progress, suspension, destruction, brutality'. In projecting the American scene he made works which ranged from the very slight to the monumental. Sometimes this work is full of humour, and *The Banquet* [307] demonstrates his capacity to make a line statement in metal, in which the geometric open pattern

contrasts with the representation of fish shapes and the strange assortment of banqueting objects. David Smith's contribution in welded metal sculpture opened broad new areas in twentieth century art.

Jean Tinguely (*b.* 1925)

Tinguely was born in Basle, Switzerland, and specialized in sculpture in cut and welded metal. Then, in the 1950s, he began to make kinetic sculptures that do more than merely move in space — they work! A kinetic he made in Paris in 1959 was geared like a robot to 'make' paintings, each of which was different — at the end of two years, 38,000 pictures had been produced by the 'sculpture'. Tinguely has also used sound in his works, and in New York in 1960 he made a self-destroying machine, which was designed to demolish itself automatically, bit by bit. (However, the work's efficiency in the field of destruction has never been put to the test.) Tinguely used it as a symbol of the horrors of mechanization.

In [308] we see Tinguely in a less dramatic situation; here he demonstrates his qualities as a sculptor who can contribute to architecture works of great charm which are functionally integral, and which, as in ancient cultures, link the role of the sculptor to that of the architect.

SCULPTURE IN THE 1960s

Some sculpture in the 1960s paralleled painting in its Pop expressions, with 'environments' and 'boxes'. Life-size figures made of plaster, fibre-glass, plastic and other similar substances, 'using' authentic contemporary utensils, were arranged in actual bathroom or kitchen settings, seated beside cocktail bars or swimming pools, or even lying on prison bunks or motel beds. The sculptors of these 'environments' made comment on contemporary society using techniques similar to those of the commercial window dresser, but invoked a personal statement in terms of the stylization of the figures.

MODERN ARCHITECTURE

The Crystal Palace [309], built in London's Hyde Park for the International Exhibition of 1851, was designed by the British landscape gardener and architect, Joseph Paxton (1801-1865), and is generally considered to mark the beginning of modern architecture. In this structure, Paxton used prefabricated sections of iron in conjunction with glass and timber, and achieved new concepts in space, light and speed of construction which anticipated architectural trends in the following century.

Nearly forty years after Paxton's achievement, Gustave Eiffel (1832-1923), the French engineer and bridge-builder, designed a tower over 300 metres high for the International Exhibition in Paris in 1889. His use of steel bonded by a riveting process was an innovation in its combination of strength and soaring lightness. Although not designed to fulfil any architectural function, the concept of an open structural skeleton instead of the traditional closed, disguised mass was the precursor to technological adventures in architecture in the twentieth century, and Eiffel's tower became the international symbol for the city of Paris.

For its full significance to be appreciated, the work of Paxton and Eiffel has to be considered relative to European architectural attitudes of the nineteenth century. The 'establishment' was generally opposed to change: the authorities found it difficult to separate revolutionary movements in painting or architecture from the revolutionary movements in social, economic or political spheres, and discouraged change for this reason. Thus the architecture of the nineteenth century was generally a curious amalgam of the new functions of public buildings — post offices, railway stations, police stations, banks, hospitals — and the ancient traditions of Greece and Rome, the Gothic period, or Renaissance Italy. Many buildings combined features of some or even all of these architectural styles, and this extraordinary eclecticism can still be seen in many Victorian-era buildings in the cities of Australia and New Zealand.

However, in the United States of America, architectural change was more dramatic in this period than elsewhere. The manufacture of rolled steel and its use in the construction of a steel skeleton for high-rise buildings was to eliminate the problem of excessive masonry weight, which had always been the limiting factor on building height. The invention of the elevator by Elisha Otis in 1854 overcame the second limitation on high-rise buildings — the necessity for easy transportation of people from floor to floor. The first buildings to incorporate the steel skeleton

[309] Paxton: Crystal Palace, London, 1850-1

[310] Sullivan: Guaranty building, Buffalo, New York, 1894-5

[311] Wright: Avery Coonley house, Riverside, Illinois, 1908

and the elevator were erected in the middle 1880s, but the first significant constructions came from the finest exponent of the 'Chicago School', Louis H. Sullivan.

Louis H. Sullivan (1856-1924)

The Guaranty building [310] in Buffalo, New York State, dates from 1894-5, and is considered to be one of Sullivan's most outstanding architectural accomplishments: by using the steel skeleton and combining the structural basis with wall mass and windows, he achieved a unity of design which basically defined the functional quality of much twentieth century architecture. He believed that 'form follows function' and that a skyscraper should be 'a unit without a single dissenting line': the interrelation of form and function in the Guaranty building achieved a uniformly organized surface pattern of masonry and window openings which is intrinsic to the monumental grandness of the building. For Sullivan, decoration was a necessary adjunct to architecture, and he used terracotta moulded decorations [310] in the Art Nouveau manner* on the masonry surfaces; as well as adding interest and charm, these decorative panels achieved strong surface continuity.

Sullivan's achievements in architectural functionalism were lost to the following generation in the United States: the majority of American architects dressed their buildings in classical academic decoration, and Louis Sullivan's attempts to create poems in stone' were overlooked by the architectural world. After 1900 he received few commissions and he died in almost complete poverty in 1924.

* Art Nouveau was a decorative style of the 1890s and early 1900s, whose characteristics can be seen in the flowing line of the terracotta moulded decorations on the façade of Sullivan's Guaranty building, the early lithographs of Munch, the posters of Toulouse-Lautrec, the flowing masses of some of Rodin's sculpture and the architectural works of Gaudí. A reaction against the historically-inspired decoration of the first three-quarters of the nineteenth century, it had its basis in the structural patterns and forms of nature: trees, water and land forms, and particularly plants — their leaves, tendrils, stems, roots and flowers. Much of this interest derived from research into early cultures, such as those of the Cretans and the Celts, who had developed natural forms for decorative purposes; another source of interest was the decoration of Japanese artifacts, which were widespread in Europe in the latter part of the nineteenth century. The quality of the decoration in these early cultures was at variance with the tasteless, inappropriate design of most of the machine-made products of the period; despite new materials and new methods of production, designers continued to look back to classical periods for the source of their design and decoration, which generally were motley combinations of dishonesty and sterility.

Over-commercialization caused Art Nouveau to decline as an art movement in the early years of the twentieth century; although in eclipse for more than half a century, its revival in the 1960s was of significance, and its role in helping to break the meaningless repetition of the past at the end of the nineteenth century was considerable.

152

Frank Lloyd Wright (1869-1959)

In 1893 Wright worked on a world architectural exhibition in Chicago, and he was particularly impressed by the Japanese exhibition with its deep roof overhangings, the simple contrasts of dark framework and light-toned panels, and above all, the complete co-ordination of the building and its natural environment. This experience was to have a profound effect on Wright's domestic architecture.

At the time of the Chicago exhibition, Wright already had ten years' architectural work behind him, six of them spent as a draughtsman in the office of Louis Sullivan. He now proceeded to place the organic unity of the Sullivan-type structure in its total environment—thus he envisaged the design of a building as inseparable from its natural setting. 'No house,' he said, 'should be "on" any hill . . . it should be "of" the hill.' In keeping with this theory he advocated the architectural incorporation of natural materials like wood and stone, thereby ensuring the co-ordinating effect of natural textures and patterns.

The Avery Coonley house [311], in Riverside, Illinois, demonstrates the fundamentals of Wright's domestic style, later to be called 'prairie architecture': the extended horizontal lines link the ground to the house, while the planes of masonry and the planes of the roof seem to 'move' into a series of relationships, which in turn relate to the varied areas of walls and window recesses. There is a dramatic tension in the compositional quality of this 1908 work which is reminiscent of the contemporary analytical Cubist paintings of Picasso and Braque. Architecturally, Wright attempted to solve the problem of the movement of space within the organic whole of this family house: he linked internal and external space with the horizontal windows under the eaves and the long vertical glass recesses.

Wright's domestic architecture is considered to have reached its culmination in his 1936 design for 'Fallingwater', the Kauffman house in Pennsylvania; this building is one of the finest examples of a man-made creation in conjunction with natural forms. Wright's own home (serving also as a school and an administrative unit), built in 1938 at Taliesin West near Phoenix, Arizona, ranks with 'Fallingwater' in the majesty of its conception: in this project Wright combined the desert environment with towering timber trusses and concrete and boulder walls to produce a monumental experience of space and form.

Two of Wright's major enterprises in his late maturity were the Johnson Wax building in Wisconsin (1936-9, with the tower added in 1949) and the Guggenheim Museum in New York (1943-59). The Wisconsin building is a brilliant exposition of space, achieved by the dynamic use of mushroom-shaped reinforced columns. The Guggenheim Museum, however, is Wright's major 'sculptural' achievement in his public buildings: a continuous circular ramp,

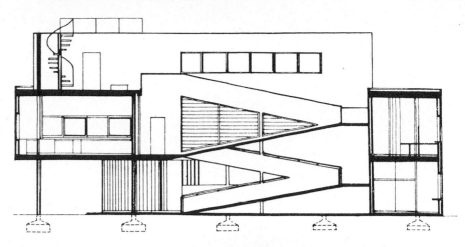

[313] Le Corbusier: Cross-section of the Villa Savoye, Poissy-sur-Seine, 1929-30

[314] Le Corbusier: Unité d'Habitation, Marseilles, 1947-52

[315] Le Corbusier: Notre Dame du Haut, Ronchamp, 1950-5

[316] Le Corbusier: Interior of Notre Dame du Haut

12] Gaudí: Sagrada Familia, Barcelona, begun 1884

[317] Gropius: The Bauhaus, Dessau, 1925-6

[318] Mies van der Rohe: Crown Hall, Illinois Institute of Technology, Chicago, 1952-6

deriving its form from a shell, serves as both a gallery and the means of moving through the building. Unlike the domestic architecture which he wedded to its environment, Wright makes the Guggenheim Museum a startling contrast to the towering skyscrapers around it. Wright was actively engaged on the final stages of this building at the time of his death — testimony to the retention of his artistic creativity into his ninetieth year.

Antonio Gaudí (1852-1926)

Gaudí's early architectural studies in his native Spain developed in him a strong affinity with Medieval Gothic architecture; this inclination was amalgamated with his attraction to the style of Art Nouveau (see note, page 152) at the turn of the century, and Gaudí's highly personalized, luxurious style largely evolved from these two sources.

Although much of Gaudí's work was begun in the nineteenth century, his stature as an architect was reassessed in the middle of the twentieth century — twenty-five years after his death — as a reaction against the anonymity of the International Style. The 1950s were the period of the architectural sculpturesque aspirations of Le Corbusier and Niemeyer, and the highly personal projection in Gaudí's work seemed pertinent.

Gaudí's designs had a quality of fantasy which, within the setting he created, was Surrealist. One of his most famous works is the church of the Sagrada Familia (Holy Family) [312], which he began in 1883 and on which he continued to work until his death nearly forty years later. This building defies categorization in any known style: it contains influences of Moorish origin, as well as those of Gothic architecture and Art Nouveau, but above all it expresses the audacious spirit of its architect. The fanciful spires have apexes with curvilinear planes of massed coloured ceramic, interspersed with cubes and spheres. Gaudí supervised the designing of every aspect of the building, from the ironwork of the entrance gates to the candelabrum before the altar, and each item reflects his extraordinary style.

Other Barcelona works of Gaudí, such as the Casa Milá apartment house with its remarkable spacelessness and intense vitality, have been a source of study for architects over the last twenty years: the influence of the undulating curves and general geometrical luxury has been reflected in the designs of many architects — Niemeyer being a notable example. Gaudí's work defies imitation in the detail of his style, but the broad principle of personal expression, which he so fascinatingly expounded in his buildings, has been an antidote to the International 'glass box' of the mid-twentieth century; the incorporation of local cultural and spiritual traditions in Gaudí's work has helped to break the cult of anonymity and has given architecture fresh impetus.

Le Corbusier (1887-1965)

Le Corbusier, born Charles Édouard Jeanneret in Switzerland, became one of the most significant forces in twentieth century architecture.

The Villa Savoye [313], built at Poissy in Paris in 1929-31, is typical of the so-called 'International Style' which Le Corbusier helped initiate in the 1920s. This plan incorporates a 'boxed-in' living area and central service area under a flat roof, supported by thin steel stilts. The building seems to be released from its earthly ties, and gives to domestic architecture a new concept of weightlessness; it demonstrates the functional precision of Le Corbusier's work and is a broad illustration of his famous statement: 'La maison — une machine à habiter' — ' the house is a machine for living in.' This dictum has often been interpreted too coldly and over-clinically; in the Villa Savoye, the 'machine' involves both a terrace and a hanging garden in an open courtyard, and space moves from below, above and through the middle of the house, while a gently sloped ramp effects movement within.

Twenty years later, Le Corbusier designed the Unité d'Habitation [314] in Marseilles, as part of a mass-housing project. This 1947-52 building contrasts in its massiveness with the suspended lightness of the Villa Savoye, although it, too, is suspended. The building provides accommodation for 1600 people, and each apartment has two storeys of living area with a private balcony; within the structure are shops, a day nursery, a cafeteria and a gymnasium. The rugged concrete exterior of the building has a textured surface which is the result of both the deliberate and haphazard effects of the timber shuttering in which the concrete has been poured. This architectural effect employed by Le Corbusier was to become the characteristic feature of 'Brut' buildings in the post-World War II period.

The chapel at Ronchamp in France [315], built by Le Corbusier in the years 1950-5, is considered to be one of the outstanding architectural achievements of the century. It is at variance with the principles of Le Corbusier's earlier works, but it is indicative of the adaptability and flexibility of mind that characterizes genius. He cited the philosophy which determined the design of the chapel: 'I wished to create a place of silence, of prayer, of peace and spiritual joy . . . strong in its means of expression, but extremely sensitive and informed throughout by mathematics . . . built of staunch concrete, treated perhaps over-boldly, but certainly with courage . . .'

This architectural creation is sculptural in character: poised upon a hilltop, it has ruggedness and yet creates a floating, ethereal effect. There is a dramatic quality in the organization of light and mass, as well as in the use of colour and texture. Inside the chapel [316], light glows through small, deeply recessed, coloured windows which

[319] Nervi: Palazzetto dello Sport, Rome, 1956-7

[320] Niemeyer: Parliamentary Buildings, Brazilia, 1957-60

[321] Mendelsohn: Schocken department store, Chemnitz, 1928

[322] Saarinen: T.W.A. Terminal, Kennedy Airport, New York, 1956-61

are asymmetrically placed in the heavy, rough-cast concrete walls: the result is an extraordinary combination of intense vitality and quiet contemplation.

Walter Gropius (1883-1968)

Gropius was born in Berlin in 1883 and studied architecture in Berlin and Munich. He began to practise architecture in the pre-World War I period, and his factory designs showed new concepts of function in the linking of external and internal space by glass curtain walls. In 1919, in the midst of Germany's postwar chaos, Gropius formed the Bauhaus from the Design and Fine Arts Schools in Weimar; in this centre he assembled a group of architects, designers and painters (including Paul Klee and Wassily Kandinsky) to promote creative activity and to link technology with art, not only in the designing of buildings, but also in the fields of furniture, weaving, ceramics, photography and theatre décor, as well as painting and sculpture. Gropius directed this centre of ideas in Weimar until 1925, when he moved it to Dessau; here he designed a great new complex [317], considered to be one of the finest examples of the International Style.

155

The Dessau Bauhaus consisted of three separate buildings — classrooms, workshops and small studio-apartments — all of which were designed for their specific functions, but which were joined in space by overhead 'links'. The combination of functionalism and aesthetic excitement was achieved by the asymmetrical balance of solid walls of masonry broken by ribbons of glass, and curtain walls of glass set in the reinforced concrete skeleton. The architectural concept of the Bauhaus gave a new approach to the International Style, and the work which emanated from its teachers and students influenced every area of design in the period between the World Wars.

Gropius left Germany during the Hitler régime and finally settled in the United States, where he maintained his international influence as professor of architecture at Harvard University.

Ludwig Mies van der Rohe (*b.* 1886)

Mies van der Rohe was born in Aachen, Germany, a city of great Medieval architectural character. In 1905 he moved to Berlin and worked with the architect Peter Behrens, who also employed Le Corbusier and Gropius. After World War I, Mies became involved in glass-wall skyscraper construction, as well as in International Style domestic architecture. His work first attracted world-wide attention with the pavilion he built for the 1929 Barcelona Exposition; the free floating space, organized with functional simplicity, was contained by architectural materials of traditional opulence, and his use of marble and onyx achieved an elegant, formalized nobility.

Mies became director of the Bauhaus in 1930, but left this position in 1933 because of the Nazi government's political antagonism. In 1938 he went to the United States and became director of the school of architecture in the Illinois Institute of Technology at Chicago, exerting wide architectural influence in this capacity.

The design for the Illinois Institute [318] was executed between the years 1942 and 1958. Each building of the vast complex embodies proportions and relationships of architectural sensitivity, and each of the buildings in turn relates integrally in the overall complex of the institute. The illustration shows the nature of some of the architectural relationships: the glass planes, the steel structure and the concrete make a pattern in space akin to a Mondrian painting.

Mies' later achievements — the Seagram building in New York, and the National Gallery in Berlin — are further attestations to his contribution to twentieth century architecture.

Pier Luigi Nervi (*b.* 1891)

Nervi was born in Sondrio, Italy, and trained as a civil engineer at the University of Bologna; he had many years experience in cement construction and this background enabled him to develop new techniques in reinforced concrete. In the 1930s he began to design public and commercial buildings; his daring innovations for spanning space were based on new roofing techniques, involving sweeping, intricately organized areas of concrete. Nervi's first major achievement was the building of the Italian air force hangars in the 1936-41 period; with a minimum of steel construction, he used skeletons of prefabricated concrete beaming and created a new tradition in architecture.

Nervi was invited to design stadia for the Rome Olympics of 1960; he devised three magnificent sports arenas, one to accommodate small crowds, the other two to accommodate 16,000 and 50,000 spectators respectively.

The small stadium, the Palazzetto dello Sport [319], was built in collaboration with Vitellozzi to seat 5000 spectators. The 'scalloped' roof is only 13 cm thick and is made from 1600 pre-cast pieces; it is supported by Y-shaped concrete buttress-pillars and surmounts a continuous band of windows to create a floating effect, an architectural sensation which is repeated inside the building. The diamond-shaped sections of the roof create a pattern of singular elegance, and the central ring provides natural lighting.

Nervi's imaginative genius is seen in the Pirelli Tower, Milan, built in 1958-61; this building (on which he collaborated with Gio Ponti) is one of the masterpieces of skyscraper architecture, with a dramatic tapering effect at each end of the building, and a roof that hovers in space like a floating lid.

Oscar Niemeyer (*b.* 1907)

Niemeyer was born in Rio de Janeiro, Brazil, in 1907. His work reflects the Baroque traditions that were manifest in the bold extravagance of eighteenth century Brazil, as well as the twentieth century influence of Le Corbusier, who worked in that country from 1937 to 1943. The Parliamentary Buildings in Brazilia [320], built between 1950 and 1960, are part of one of the greatest architectural concepts in history — the construction of a capital city, designed to unite a giant, largely undeveloped country, on a plateau over 900 km inland. The buildings illustrated contain the elements of functionalism and anti-functionalism — sculptured masses of reinforced concrete in combination with soaring glass towers. The Parliamentary Offices are contained in the two glass-walled structures linked by glazed bridges, and beneath the two domes are the Legislative Houses; the curved dome is the roof of the Senate Chamber, while the inverted dome surmounts the House of Representatives.

Previous to the gigantic commission for the public buildings of Brazilia, Niemeyer designed schools, churches, housing blocks, hospitals, museums and recreation centres. Each of his solutions to these various projects was an embodiment of both power and lyricism: sweeping, graceful curves would often dominate the form of walls or roofs and achieve a lightness rarely attained in buildings of such enormous bulk.

Eric Mendelsohn (1887-1953)

Mendelsohn was born in East Prussia and studied architecture in Munich. After a period designing conventional architecture in pre-World War I Germany, he began to design buildings in the postwar era which had a definite affinity with the Expressionist movement in the painting of the period. One of the most effective examples of this architectural style was the Einstein Tower built at Potsdam in 1921: concrete was used in dramatic sweeps to make hollowed recesses and scooped wall areas in the base structure, while the enormous pillar shape with curved windows combined the dual function of a monument and a laboratory-observatory. This building was destroyed in World War II.

Mendelsohn's most celebrated — and most imitated — works were his four department stores, built in the German cities of Nuremberg, Stuttgart, Chemnitz and Breslau between 1926 and 1929. The Schocken department store in Chemnitz [321] was typical of the daring and vitality of Mendelsohn's architectural approach to the needs of a contemporary commercial enterprise of this type. Instead of merely providing ground floor display windows, Mendelsohn designed ribbons of windows from ground level to the top floor; these horizontal lines of glass ensured effective lighting by day and made for fascinating advertising displays by night.

When the Nazis came to power, Mendelsohn was confronted with the choice of death or exile; he went to England in the 1930s and later lived in Palestine and the United States. During his residence in these countries he created many outstanding hospitals, community centres, churches and synagogues, and his final work was the designing of a dramatic, towering memorial for the six million Jewish victims of Nazism, to be built in New York. Models still exist, but construction was never begun.

Eero Saarinen (1910-1961)

Eero Saarinen was born in Finland, the son of the internationally famous architect Eliel Saarinen, and he went with his father to live in the United States in 1923. After training in Paris and America, Saarinen entered into partnership with his father. After Eliel's death in 1951, Eero Saarinen independently proceeded to design a series of buildings which displayed an amazing variety of architectural approaches; he saw each architectural problem as requiring different technological and structural solutions, and he maintained that a so-called 'style' could inhibit the unique architectural fulfilment of the locational, functional and material potentials of a building. Thus the Bell Telegraph Research Centre, the dormitory blocks and skating rink at Yale University in Connecticut, the T.W.A. Terminal at Kennedy Airport in New York, and the enormous, 25-building complex for General Motors in Michigan, are strikingly dissimilar in architectural concept.

The T.W.A. Terminal [322] symbolizes the aeroplane, with its aircraft-wing profile and the interlocking reinforced concrete vaults of its interior: it is an architectural counterpart of Brancusi's sculptural symbols of flight. Saarinen extended this symbol into the design of the terminal signposts, reception desks and telephone booths, and the totality is one of architectural Expressionism.

Because of both the 'lack' of consistency in his style and the magnitude of his accomplishments — in a tragically brief period of time — Saarinen's work is an amazing composite of the diversities in twentieth century architecture.

NEW ZEALAND ART

Hamish Keith

For most of the first half of the twentieth century, the related problems of cultural isolation and national identity dominated New Zealand art. Isolation created a sense of alienation among artists; English art and culture were preserved, as a pale, nostalgic reflection, in the society, architecture and art of a colonial generation who continued to think of England as 'Home'.

To a large extent, the first generation of New Zealand born artists were able to accept the idea that New Zealand could only be a provincial version of Britain. They discovered a simple solution to the problems of location and identity — by removing themselves physically from the cause, and travelling to the homeland their fathers had pined for. The generation that followed them, or at least those who had to remain in New Zealand, did not find this solution so acceptable. They faced the problem of defining their own cultural and national identity. While they could see that an imitation of English art was alien to their immediate experience, it was difficult for them to imagine any real alternative. The dilemma of this generation is neatly summed up in the short story *The Making of a New Zealander*, written by Frank Sargeson in 1939.

Sargeson had his main character see the problem in terms of a Dalmatian settler: 'Nick and I were sitting on the hillside and Nick was saying he was a New Zealander, but he knew he wasn't a New Zealander. And he knew he wasn't a Dalmatian anymore. He knew he wasn't anything anymore.' The publication of this story coincided with New Zealand's centennial, and it fairly outlines the cultural situation after 100 years of European settlement. In fact, that first century had been one of considerable achievement, but to the artists, writers and architects of the 1930s New Zealand's cultural history was far too close in time to provide the basis of a tradition, or to be used for defining future directions.

Cut off from any direct contact with European art and lacking an established tradition, the New Zealand artist was forced to consider his own resources. Out of personal experience and out of the New Zealand light and landscape, the artists of this generation had to face the problem of making an art that would satisfy their growing concern with their own identity. Inevitably, the prevailing style in all the arts was a more or less self-conscious regionalism. Some of this found expression in an interest in New Zealand history, but its principal subject was the landscape and the imaginative relationship of the New Zealander to it. As one painter of the period put it, 'to turn the stark facts of life in this country . . . into a unit of living design' became a major cultural aspiration.

At its best this artistic nationalism produced a genuine reflection of the distinctive qualities of New Zealand life and the New Zealand landscape. At its worst it fostered an aggressive regionalism which seized on the immediately obvious facets of the New Zealand scene and rejected all other possibilities.

During the 1950s, as New Zealand's cultural isolation began to lessen and the influence of European art became more frequent and more direct, it was inevitable that internationalism and regionalism would conflict. Out of this clash of styles, the major trends in contemporary New Zealand art have developed. The conflict was productive: it did not produce any bitter rejection of regionalism or the immediate past, but an interaction between the two alternatives. The effects of international influence were conditioned and directed by attitudes established through regionalism.

[323] McCahon: *Victory over Death No. 2*, acrylic on canvas (non-chromatic), 1970. 206 x 602 cm. Barry Lett Galleries, Auckland

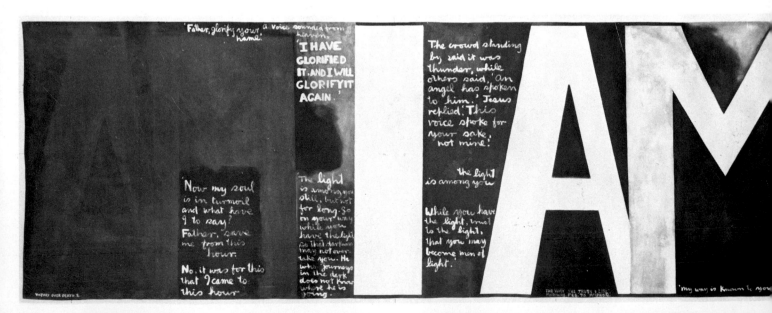

Painting

To an eye conditioned by paintings that are expressive as much for their handling of paint as they are for their imagery, the hard formal images and techniques of New Zealand painting are likely to seem cold and intellectual. The physical environment of New Zealand has, to a very great extent, encouraged an approach to painting that is primarily concerned with a clear-cut linear or planear imagery. The Pacific light, emphasized by the narrowness of the country's two main islands, is harsh and clear. The landscape itself tends towards a formal geography of clearly defined divisions between plains, hills and mountains.

Although the content of New Zealand painting is often Romantic or Expressionistic, it has generally been stated in a formal way. This is not only true of the regionalist painters who have drawn directly on images of the landscape, but also applies to contemporary abstractionists, who have been more influenced by Hard Edge and Minimal painting than by Abstract Expressionism.

Impressionism, for instance, was never a significant influence on New Zealand painting, unlike the Australian situation. As a style it enjoyed a brief period of fashion, but only in a superficial way, and the earliest productive influences on contemporary New Zealand painting were the more formal aspects of Cézanne and the early phases of Cubism. None of this impact was direct. It came at second hand through the occasional reproduction. This kind of influence, through mechanical printing processes rather than by direct experience, is also likely to have made a significant contribution to the New Zealand artist's formalism. There have been, of course, individual painters who have worked very successfully in Expressionist styles, and many important contemporary painters have moved through an Expressionist phase. In general, however, the major directions have been formal, expressed in a concern for the making of images rather than an involvement in the qualities of paint or gesture.

Twentieth century New Zealand painting, like any other modern school, has reached its highest achievements in the work of individual painters such as Colin McCahon (*b.* 1919) [323], M. T. Woollaston (*b.* 1910) and Rita Angus (1908-70), whose personal vision defies simple categories. Despite this it is possible to isolate some general directions.

The regionalism which emerged in the late 1930s has continued to develop. In the work of Rita Angus it matured into an intense realism bordering on Surrealism, and during the first years of the 1960s it took on new life in the work of

[324] Smither: *Rocks with Mountain*, oil on board, 1968. 122 x 160 cm. Auckland City Art Gallery

[325] Walters: *Tamatea*, acrylic on canvas, 1969. 152 x 114 cm. Govett-Brewster Art Gallery, New Plymouth

[326] Hotere: *Black Painting*, acrylic on canvas, 1969. 112 x 91 cm. Robert McDougall Art Gallery, Christchurch

[327] Twiss: *A Group of Athletes*, bronze, 1964. Height 34·3 cm. Auckland City Art Gallery

[328] Narbey: *Real Time*, light and sound environment, 1970. 560 square metres. Installed Govett-Brewster Art Gallery, New Plymouth

younger painters like Don Binney (*b*. 1940) and, later, Michael Smither (*b*. 1939) [324]. Currently it continues as one of the major directions in New Zealand painting, as a kind of super-realism which is, in some ways, a regionalist variation of Pop.

Parallel to this but as a minor theme, the broad Expressionist approach to landscape painting, obvious in the work of Woollaston, has also been extended. It was considerably refreshed at the end of the 1950s by the influence of West Coast American Abstract Impressionism, but with the exception of a few individuals it largely persists as an acceptable mannerism rather than any more significant direction.

In the same way, Abstract Expressionism has failed to develop in New Zealand painting. In 1958 the style had a liberating influence on New Zealand painters, largely through a single exhibition of contemporary British painting, but most of those who then responded to the influence have since moved on to the stylistically more comfortable directions offered by Hard Edge and Minimal abstraction. Currently, these are the strongest international influence in New Zealand painting. In the work of painters like Don Peebles (*b*. 1922), Milan Mrkusich (*b*. 1925), Gordon Walters (*b*. 1919) and Ralph Hotere (*b*. 1931) these styles have been reinforced by the general tendency of New Zealand painting towards a formal imagery (see [325] and [326]).

Sculpture

While the development of contemporary New Zealand painting has been reasonably continuous since early in the century, that of sculpture barely covers two decades. Sculptors were active before the 1950s, but their output was small and it alternated in style between a war-memorial realism and an imitative modernism.

The absence of a strong tradition in sculpture, or any tradition at all, is surprising in a country where the original inhabitants, the Maori, had developed it as a major form of expression. Maori carving, however, has had little productive influence on European New Zealand sculpture and any potentially enriching cross-fertilization has not occurred.

Since the end of the 1950s and particularly during the last ten years, sculpture has rapidly developed. Like painting, it initially emerged in a regionalist style drawing largely on a direct visual experience of New Zealand life. This particular development is best illustrated by the bronze athletes and protest marchers of Greer Twiss (*b*. 1937), which he began to exhibit in 1964 (see [327]).

Also as in painting, international influences progressively became more direct. Exhibitions of European and English sculpture, brought to New Zealand during the 1960s, coincided with the emergence of a new generation of sculptors who were able to use and adapt what they saw.

A few sculptors had worked in an abstract style previously, but their contribution did not become significant until it was reinforced by the work of the new sculptors. Abstract sculpture developed, again like painting, in a formal, space-defining style, rather than in the more organic directions of earlier European modern sculpture.

Colour and new materials — vinyl, sheet plastic, welded and inflatable polythene, neon lighting — have led New Zealand sculpture into a logical extension of its concern with the modulation of space — environmental sculpture. From its original beginnings, in the conception by some sculptors of an exhibition in which their works related as units rather than individual objects, this direction developed during 1969 into the construction of fully integrated environments. Early in 1970, Leon Narbey (*b.* 1947) was commissioned to carry out a large-scale environment to mark the opening of a new provincial art gallery (see the two views in [328]). His construction spread over three floors of exhibition space and involved a total articulation of space, light and sound. The success of this particular work is likely to have a marked effect on the future development of New Zealand sculpture.

Architecture

Three main factors have shaped the development of New Zealand architecture in the twentieth century: a small population, a largely rural economy, and a colonial tradition of simple structures built from basic materials. Colonial New Zealand built mainly in wood, only very

occasionally relieved by brick and stone, and its architecture at all levels was conceived on a small scale. Not surprisingly, the major trends in modern architecture were developed through domestic architecture.

The first significant developments occurred in the mid-1920s when the largely Victorian tradition succumbed to fresh influences from abroad. The Californian bungalow and the 'Spanish Mission' style of stucco and tile were particularly influential. The design of public buildings of this period contributed little to architectural development, the prevailing style being bank and insurance company neo-classicism with the occasional unsuccessful excursion into a more fanciful conception.

The most important influence of all was the English style of house design, which had its origins in the Arts and Crafts movement established by William Morris. When private building practically ceased during the early years of the Depression, this approach to domestic architecture formed the basis, although on a reduced scale, of the housing projects undertaken by the State. It was recognized as 'quality housing', and the intention of the then Labour government was that this standard of housing should be available to all.

Throughout the Depression and the war years following, government building dominated architecture in both domestic and public areas. In hydroelectric schemes, schools, hospitals and State flats, a simple functional style was developed. While this could have declined into a functional sterility, the philosophy of the government, as well as the fact that most of the best architects were employed by the State, ensured that the human element was retained.

After World War II, a new generation of architects, influenced by the principles of the major contemporary European architects and the approach to housing design developing in America, took the first steps towards the creation of a significant New Zealand style. The functional approach to building design continued, but it was reinforced by new uses of wood and glass and a much more flexible conception of space.

During the last decade, a second generation of post-war architects has carried this initial direction further. The imaginative use of concrete block construction and a reassessment of the simplicity of colonial domestic architecture laid the basis of a style which could be extended to architectural design on a larger scale. Simple formal elements, the use of flat, unrelieved wall surfaces against deeply articulated spaces, and an inventive use of roof structures (often as a direct reference to colonial architecture), are the principal features of the best new public buildings (see [329]).

As in the other arts, the successful grafting of international influence on to regionalism is a major element in contemporary New Zealand architecture.

[329] Canterbury Building Society, Auckland, 1968 (architect Peter Beavan, *b.* 1925)

AUSTRALIAN PAINTING

Ken Reinhard

The earliest Australian paintings were either topographical or scientific records of the newly discovered continent, and were often the work of a ship's artist or botanist. While such artists produced an interesting historical documentation of the early days of settlement, they are undeniably within the tradition of European and English art; many of their works possess an obvious charm and lyricism, but rarely do they capture the light or atmosphere of the Australian bush.

One of the first artists to make a genuine attempt to modify his style to meet the requirements of local conditions was the Englishman John Glover (1767-1849). Glover had enjoyed a degree of fame in England, exhibiting regularly with the Royal Academy and holding several successful one-man exhibitions. His style of painting shows a predilection for the romantic qualities of Claude Lorraine (see [188]), but upon settling in Tasmania in 1831 he set about recording with accuracy and tranquillity the inhabitants old and new, the landscape, and the flora and fauna of this ancient land of new opportunity. His interpretation of the eucalypt captures the characteristic rhythm of its sprawling limbs.

Conrad Martens (1801-78) was the last of the itinerant artists employed on voyages of scientific discovery. He arrived in Sydney in 1835 and settled permanently there. As with Glover, his work became an advertisement for Australia, and he recorded in watercolours and small oil paintings various aspects of the thriving settlement that Sydney had become. He made several sketching expeditions throughout New South Wales, but is generally considered to be at his best with his romantic views of scenes in and around Sydney, in which the mood created by clouds and cloud shadows recalls Turner or Ruisdael, the great Dutch landscape painter.

S. T. Gill (1818-80) was born in England and first settled in Adelaide in 1839, later moving to Melbourne where he died in obscurity. His drawings, lithographs and watercolours present a more humanistic record of the life of the early settler. Here we see a marked shift of interest; no longer is there an emphasis on botanic specimens or topographical records, but rather a concern with the people who panned for gold, the diggers and the overlanders who were to carve out the heritage of early Australia. Such a painting is *The New Rush* [330]; here we find a delightful immediacy and spontaneity that is not evident in the work of his artistic predecessors.

Perhaps the greatest single stimulus towards an Australian style of painting was derived from the work of Louis Buvelot (1814-88), a Swiss-born artist who settled in Australia in 1865. Previously he had spent eighteen years in Brazil, where he enjoyed the patronage of the emperor, but returning briefly to Switzerland he found the cold too severe and moved permanently to Melbourne, where he worked for a short time as a professional photographer to supplement his income. He quickly established himself as one of Victoria's leading artists, putting into practice the *plein-air* technique of the French Barbizon school, of which his work is strongly reminiscent. Evidence of this may be found in *Water Pool at Coleraine* [331], which displays a delightful feeling of tranquillity; the rich golden light that pervades the canvas had a profound influence on subsequent Australian painters.

Among the many other artists to exert considerable influence were the Tasmanian-born William Piguenit (1836-1914), a close observer and detailed transcriber of atmospheric effects, and the Italian, Girolamo Nerli (1863-1926), who painted in Australia for four years (1886-90) and who had a marked influence on Charles Conder and

[330] Gill: *The New Rush*, lithograph, *c.* 1865. 25.4 x 17.8 cm. Mitchell Library, Sydney

[331] Buvelot: *Water Pool at Coleraine*, oil on canvas, 1869. 106.7 × 152.4 cm. National Gallery of Victoria, Melbourne

[332] Roberts: *Bailed-up*, oil on canvas, 1895. 134.6 x 182.9 cm. Art Gallery of New South Wales, Sydney

[333] Streeton: *Fire's On, Lapstone Tunnel*, oil on canvas, 1891. 183.8 x 122.5 cm. Art Gallery of New South Wales, Sydney

[334] De Maistre: *Rhythmic Composition in Yellow Green Minor*, oil on pulpboard, 1919. 86.3 x 141.5 cm. Art Gallery of New South Wales, Sydney

others of the Australian Impressionist school through his broad, direct approach to painting.

Between the years 1885 and 1895 a distinctive school of painting evolved, later to be called Australian Impressionism. This form of Impressionism borrowed some of the features of French Impressionism, but there were major differences: the two forms may be compared but never equated, for the French Impressionists used subject matter, mainly landscapes, to explore the effect or quality of light, whereas the Australian Impressionist used light qualities to interpret the true visual nature of the Australian scene.

Tom Roberts (1856-1931) spent four years abroad from 1881 to 1885 and came under the influence of French Impressionism in his studies; on his return to Australia he was anxious to share his new-found knowledge and saw the possibilities of applying it to the Australian landscape.

First Fred McCubbin (1855-1917) and later Arthur Streeton (1867-1943) and Charles Conder (1868-1909) came under his influence, and the Heidelberg school (as it was later to be known) was born. These painters followed directly the *plein-air* maxim of their European predecessors, and had an enormous influence on Australian painting in the last decade of the nineteenth century.

Although these men had gained their inspiration and borrowed much from European artists, the problems of rendering the effects of light and colour peculiar to the Australian atmosphere were not European, and the techniques which they discovered to solve these problems were their own. The efforts of the Heidelberg school represented the culmination of a century of endeavour by painters to interpret realistically the special qualities of the Australian landscape. Their works, however, were not mere pictorial records as such, but the results of an artistry born of a creative attitude and deeply-felt personal vision.

Bailed-up by Tom Roberts [332] is a realistic reconstruction of a robbery by bushrangers, in which the artist has used technical methods gleaned from overseas — a broad colour range, free handling of paint, and transparent shadows — to record a scene common in the Australia of the goldfields. Besides being as carefully composed as many of the larger French Impressionist paintings, *Bailed-up* is an important historical record, for it depicts a human drama of Australian life enacted during a significant phase in the country's development.

Arthur Streeton was inspired by Roberts whom he met when he was nineteen, and became famous for his romantic pictures which expressed his respect and love for the Australian scene. His works, ranging from small studies to huge vistas, are visual essays in which he attempted to solve the problem of recording atmospheric effects from sunrise to twilight. *Fire's On, Lapstone Tunnel* [333] was painted in full sunlight, and in it man's labours are dwarfed by the dazzling sandstone boulders and walls of the huge gully.

Between 1900 and 1920 Europe had felt the full impact of the French Post-Impressionist giants — van Gogh,

163

Gauguin and Cézanne — and the movements that emanated from that source — Cubism, Fauvism, German Expressionism, Futurism — but these developments passed practically unnoticed and unwanted in Australia. Poor communication with Europe was one impediment, but the chief reason was that the Australian public and most artists had been conditioned to the Heidelberg ideal of expression. Apart from a few adventurous young painters whose efforts were derided, it was not until the end of World War I that paintings influenced by Post-Impressionism and the movements that proliferated from it were openly exhibited.

Roy de Maistre (1894-1968) and Roland Wakelin (*b.* 1887) were two of the artists to show the influence of Cézanne and early Cubist experiments, particularly through geometric composition and application of paint. Together they evolved a scheme for harmonizing sound and colour. *Rhythmic Composition in Yellow Green Minor* by Roy de Maistre [334] exemplifies the application of this colour theory to interior decoration, and was one of the first experiments in Australian abstract painting. Although a few artists, mainly Grace Cossington Smith (*b.* 1892), Grace Crowley (*b.* 1896) and Rah Fizelle (1891-1964), experimented with the effects of Cubism and other European influences, the modern movement had little impact in Australia, and it did not bring the same sense of discovery to the artists of the time that Impressionism brought to the Heidelberg painters and their contemporaries.

However, the 1930s manifested a more tolerant and exuberant attitude and the first real onslaught of modernism was felt. The threat of a second world war brought back many expatriate artists, among them William Dobell, John Passmore (*b.* 1904), Eric Wilson (1911-46) and Godfrey Miller (1893-1964), together with refugee professional artists from Europe like Desiderius Orban (*b.* 1884) and Sali Herman (*b.* 1898). This sudden infusion of talent had an invigorating influence that was to transform art in Australia when it challenged ideas that had been accepted for thirty years. However, despite the influence of these artists from Europe, the public were mainly unsympathetic to the modern movement; the Melbourne Herald Exhibition of 1939, which was the first fully representative collection of contemporary European painting to be seen in Australia, was an exciting event for young Australian artists, but generally a source of ridicule to the general public.

Frank Hinder (*b.* 1906), who returned from the U.S.A. prior to World War II with his American artist wife, Margel, had come into contact with Cubism, Futurism, the Bauhaus and Mexican mural painting during his studies abroad: both he and his wife proceeded to further the modern movements in the visual arts in the late 1930s in Sydney. *The Bridge* [335] is a dynamic, geometrical analysis of the Sydney Harbour Bridge and its movement of traffic.

[335] Hinder: *The Bridge*, watercolour, 1957. 61 x 91 cm. Sydney Teachers College

[336] Gleeson: *The Agony in the Garden*, oil on canvas, *c.* 1948. 152.4 × 121.9 cm. Sydney Teachers College

[337] Drysdale: *Sofala*, oil on canvas, 1947. 71.8 x 93 cm. Art Gallery of New South Wales, Sydney

James Gleeson, born in Sydney in 1915, became interested in the writings of the Surrealists in the late 1930s: in 1938 he was one of the few Australian artists to exhibit work in the manner of Dali, Max Ernst and Yves Tanguy, and he is the only Australian to have persisted with this style of painting. *The Agony in the Garden* [336] combines super-real symbols in unexpected combination which, unlike a traditional picture, allows many readings. Normally an image allows one reading in its context, but Gleeson's painting, which projects the subconscious mind, demonstrates that one symbol can often produce multiple effects. Man is the central theme, with the Garden of Eden and Gethsemane involved in Freudian imagery.

World War II impeded contact with Europe, but after 1945 more students arrived from abroad and with them came a number of important painters, teachers and designers, most of whom were professional artists— Michael Kmit (*b.* 1910), Stanislaus Rapotec (*b.* 1912), Judy Cassab (*b.* 1920) and many others.

Russell Drysdale was born in England in 1912 and settled permanently in Australia in 1923. He became interested in art in the 1930s, and during the following decade, being country born and bred, developed a preoccupation with themes based on life on the land. His paintings of the effects of a disastrous drought in New South Wales, graphically depicting the resultant devastation, were vastly different from the romantic images of earlier painters. Drysdale does not seek the beauty spots or the picturesque, and his subjects often depict the never-ending struggle and isolation of farming folk or Aborigines in drought-stricken and eroded areas. The gaunt inhabitants and even the country towns like *Sofala* [337] are often placed on a Surrealistic plain in a vast setting where one can almost feel the intensity of heat and light, and despair at the loneliness.

Just before World War II, William Dobell, destined to become Australia's most famous portrait and genre painter, returned to Sydney from Europe. Dobell, who was born in Newcastle in 1899, had been articled to an architect before beginning art studies in Sydney. He won a scholarship to London and spent the thirties studying and painting in Europe. His work developed along basically conservative lines, with great freedom in the brushwork, allied to a sensitivity — often somewhat satirical — in his observation of the people in the immediate environment. His interest in the work of Rembrandt, Daumier and Renoir was manifest in his subject matter and technique. In 1939 his genre paintings were enthusiastically received by the comparatively small art group in Sydney, and within five years his name had become a household word throughout the country. Dobell won the 1943 Archibald Prize for portraiture, but the

[338] Dobell: *The Cypriot*, oil on canvas, 1940. 122.6 x 122.6 cm. Queensland Art Gallery, Brisbane

[339] Nolan: *The Quilting of the Armour*, ripolin on masonite, 1946-7. 91.4 x 121.9 cm. Collection of Mrs Sunday Reed, Melbourne

165

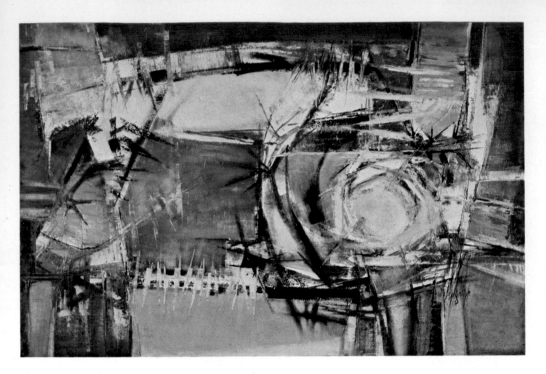

[340] Gleghorn: *Coast Wind*, oil on hardboard, 1959. 121.9 x 182.9 cm. Art Gallery of New South Wales, Sydney. Gift of Patrick White

[341] Lanceley: *Monsoon I*, paint and timber on canvas, 1969-70. 122 x 122 cm. Bonython Gallery, Sydney

uniqueness of statement which Dobell achieved. The organization of the structural forms in this picture is dramatically complemented by the sensitive depiction of the sitter's personality.

In the immediate post-World War II years and the early fifties, two divergent art groups dominated Australian art — one based in Melbourne, the other in Sydney. The Melbourne group had been concerned with painting the life of the city environment in the later war years, and continued in peacetime what they felt to be an authentic Australian style in direct development from the works of Roberts and Streeton: they were not interested in the gum-tree landscape, however, nor were they concerned with abstract painting, but were predominantly figurative in their work. Albert Tucker, Arthur Boyd and Sidney Nolan were artists in the Melbourne group, and each displayed powerful individuality in his painting.

Albert Tucker, born in 1914, was often spokesman for the Melbourne group and his work, in its vigorous depiction of the human form, has an affinity with German Expressionism. Arthur Boyd, born in 1920 into a distinguished Australian family of artists, painted the Australian environment in a strongly personal symbolic style. However, it was Sidney Nolan who achieved the distinction of becoming the first Australian of real international stature in painting. Born in Melbourne in 1917, Nolan, although he attended several art schools, was largely a self-taught artist. In 1946 he painted the Ned Kelly series of pictures [339]: the boldness of his imagination, in the fusion he made of history and the Australian environment, was widely acclaimed. He has continued to depict the Australian landscape with a primitive strength, in brilliant colour and with exciting imagery.

award was challenged in the courts on the grounds that his portrait of a fellow artist, Joshua Smith, was a caricature. The sensational nature of the legal proceedings and the verdict, which gave legal acceptance to contemporary art forms, created an interest in Australian art which had not previously existed. Ironically, the picture that created this furore was subsequently destroyed in a fire. Until his death in 1970, Dobell's portraiture and genre painting embraced a wide range of subject matter: his portraits are remarkable in their individuality, and *The Cypriot* [338] reveals the

The persistence with figurative painting continued in Melbourne throughout the 1950s, some of its finest exponents being Charles Blackman (b. 1928), John Brack (b. 1920) and John Perceval (b. 1923), and ultimately a manifesto was issued in 1959 by several leading Melbourne artists, the 'Antipodean' group, defending figurative painting against the Abstract Expressionism which then dominated the Sydney art world, and critical denigration of figurative work.

The development of painting in the fifteen years since World War II had differed profoundly in Sydney. The 'Sydney Group', formed in 1945, was a romantic movement which reacted against the social realism of the depression and wartime years: there was a strong influence of Byzantine and Persian colour and decoration, and in the later forties a growing interest in religious painting was apparent. Justin O'Brien (b. 1917), with his jewel-coloured Byzantine-influenced compositions, was significant in this revival of religious art, and in fact won the first Blake Prize for religious painting in 1951.

The early 1950s also saw the gathering momentum of non-figurative abstract painting, influenced by Godfrey Miller, John Passmore and Ian Fairweather (b. 1891). Although none of these painters were abstractionists, their works were so strongly formalized that they intensified the growing interest in abstract painting in Sydney. Young artists were entranced by the balanced unity in the tiny mosaic blocks of colour in Miller's paintings, the forceful Cézanne-like integration of natural forms into the abstract order in the work of Passmore, and the subtle, calligraphic harmonies of Fairweather's compositions — an amalgam of East and West. Added impetus to the growth of abstract painting was provided by the 1953 exhibition 'French Painting Today', and during the later 1950s young abstract painters including John Olsen (b. 1928), Elwyn Lynn (b. 1917), William Rose (b. 1930), Eric Smith (b. 1919) and Tom Gleghorn proceeded to dominate the exhibition scene. An example from this era is *Coast Wind* [340] by Gleghorn, who was born in England in 1925, came to Australia at the age of three and eventually trained as an engineer. With Dobell's encouragement, but no formal art training, Gleghorn proceeded to develop a style of Abstract Expressionism in his painting which combined dramatic impact with balanced harmony. His pictures, he says, 'are about events and remembered experiences related to "things" seen, felt, or heard . . .'

The years since 1960 have probably been the most diverse and internationally significant period in Australia's brief art history. With the universal escalation in speed and scope of communication, the country's previous physical isolation has now been almost eliminated. Vital and informative books, magazines, lectures, films and (most important of all) exhibitions have reached Australia almost as soon as the concepts were expounded overseas. Admittedly this information was comparatively limited, but it was sufficient to enable the local *avant-garde* to realize that they were part of an overall international development in the fine arts. There has been a dramatic increase in the number and range of art competitions sponsored by a variety of groups and organizations, and the prizes and scholarships offered provide a strong incentive to young Australian artists; the need for more exhibition space has resulted in the mushrooming of new galleries — and the refurbishing of old — in many centres of the Commonwealth. The advent of Pop, Op, Hard Edge, Assemblage and Kinetic Art movements, occurring in this country as a reaction to the urban environment and happening almost in unison with their counterparts overseas, made this a colourful, lively and controversial period.

Among the many young artists contributing to Australian painting in the sixties were Syd Ball, Robert Boynes, Alun Leach-Jones, Michael Johnson, David Aspden, John Coburn, Col Jordan, Gunter Christmann, Rodney Milgate, Brian Seidel, Brett Whiteley and Colin Lanceley. Lanceley, born in New Zealand in 1938, is represented here by his painting *Monsoon I* [341]. Initially his work reflected American Pop Art and then he turned to 'junk art' or Assemblage. Lanceley's aesthetic satire was both vital and original in concept: the shock tactics of his combination of various symbols representing the vulgarity of our materialistic age created a great deal of controversy and excitement. In fact, the picture for which he was awarded the Helena Rubenstein Scholarship for overseas study was critically challenged on the grounds that it was *not* a painting.

The role of art in the cultural life of Australia in the last decade is reflected in the new academic status it has been afforded: the Power Institute of Fine Arts at Sydney University was established in the late 1960s — Melbourne University created a Chair of Fine Arts shortly after World War II. The study and practice of all forms of the visual arts has become an integral part of most secondary school programmes.

AUSTRALIAN SCULPTURE

Margel Hinder

Art cannot be separated from its sociological and physical background, a fact very evident in the development of Australian sculpture. Early Australian painters, for the most part English born and trained, filled a need from the very first by recording the landscape and indigenous peoples, as well as the plants and animals for scientific purposes. The works they produced were small and easy to transport. Sculpture, on the other hand, was rare before the middle of the nineteenth century because of the limitations imposed by contemporary conventions of subject matter and the technical difficulties involved in its production.

Still working within the eighteenth century outlook, the sculptor's skills were confined to portraits, heroic monuments and memorials of the rich and famous, or to figurative and animal subjects that only a well-to-do society could afford or esteem. First modelling in clay, the sculptor then had his work cast in bronze or carved in wood or stone by craftsmen; these were skills not readily to be found in a new country. There were no galleries, public monuments or even illustrations available to stimulate the early colonial student; Aboriginal art made no impact, and the great cultures of India and the Orient were unknown or ignored.

However, the gold rush of 1851 altered every aspect of life. Expansion took place within the small groups of artists who had been working and exhibiting over the past decades. Art schools, societies and galleries were established, not only in the capitals but in some of the country towns as well. Two English academic sculptors, Thomas Woolner (1825-92) and Charles Summers (1825-78), drawn by the gold rush, arrived in Melbourne in 1852 and 1853 respectively; they were probably the first 'professionals' to carry out a substantial quantity of work. Woolner, during his two-year stay, modelled many portrait-medallions and the Captain Cook Memorial in Hyde Park, Sydney. Summers remained longer; the Burke and Wills group in Melbourne is one of his many works and the first large bronze to be cast in Australia.

The late 1880s found Rodin the dominating influence in Europe. Melbourne-born Bertram Mackennal (1863-1931) worked for a short time as his assistant, having studied earlier in Australia and England. However, he continued in

[342] Mackennal: *Shakespeare Memorial*, bronze and stone, commissioned 1914. Sydney, N.S.W.

[343] Lewers: *Camel's Head*, trachyte, 1946. Approx. 46 × 46 cm. Art Gallery of N.S.W., Sydney

168

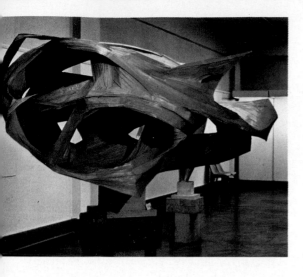

[344] Dadswell: *Paper Sculpture*, gummed paper over wire frame, 1967-8. 1.22 x 1.83 x 0.91 metres. Art Gallery of N.S.W., Sydney

[345] Parr: *Astra*, welded steel, 1970. 10.06 x 7.62 x 3.35 metres. Tullamarine Airport, Melbourne

[346] Klippel: *Junk Sculpture*, typewriter parts welded, 1961. 67.3 x 41.9 x 36.8 cm. Collection of Rudy Komon

the English academic tradition, one of his larger works being the Shakespeare Memorial in Sydney [342]. At the beginning of the twentieth century a group of sculptors in Sydney were well known for their works in plaster, and among others, C. W. Gilbert (*b*. Talbot, Victoria, 1869-1925) won recognition for his World War I bronze memorials.

The end of the nineteenth century saw great changes in the painting traditions of Europe, starting with Cézanne. By the early 1900s Maillol, Brancusi, and those sculptors allied with the Cubists, Futurists and Constructivists, were seeking differing solutions to the problems of volume and space, thus altering the course of sculpture. A few years later the Dadaists and Surrealists opened new vistas of expression. However, no indications of change were evident in three-dimensional work in Australia, although a small group of painters (1915-8) were beginning to explore the theories of Cézanne and the Cubists.

Paul Montford (1868-1938) and G. Rayner Hoff (1894-1937) came to Australia from England in 1923, the former settling in Melbourne, the latter in Sydney, and here they became prominent both as teachers and as practising artists. The Shrine of Remembrance in Melbourne by Montford, and the Anzac Memorial in Sydney by Hoff, are among the memorials and other works they carried out in the capital cities and country centres. Hoff was one of the first sculptors of note in Australia to carve directly, but both he and Montford continued to work in the English realist tradition.

In the early 1920s Daphne Mayo (*b*. Brisbane) began her overseas study. Later she played an important role in the development of art in her own city and in Sydney; some of her larger works include the tympanum for the Brisbane City Hall, which she carved directly, and the reliefs on one of the bronze doors for the Mitchell Library, Sydney. Dr Clive Stephen (1889-1957) and Ola Cohn (1892-1964), the first sculptors in Melbourne to show awareness of the contemporary movement, were both active in establishing modern art in the Victorian capital. After arriving in Sydney from Germany in 1930, Elenore Lange, through

her sculpture, lecturing and teaching, brought first-hand knowledge of the Continental contemporary outlook.

Gerald Lewers (1905-62) studied in Europe and worked with John Skeaping in England, before returning to Sydney in 1934. With his modern approach, direct carving and sensitive use of native wood and stone, he won early recognition. His animal and bird carvings (see [343]), and his abstract work in wood, stone and metal made him one of the few modern sculptors of the late 1930s and early 1940s.

Lyndon Dadswell (*b*. 1908) studied under Hoff and was a student-assistant to Montford. A trip overseas in 1935 brought him into contact with newer developments, and

[347] Walker: *Foreshore Group*, bronze, 1969. 0.96 x 0.99 x 1.57 metres. Artist's collection

[348] Redpath: *Fountain*, bronze and water, 1969. Height approx. 4.3 metres. Treasury Department, Canberra

[349] Meadmore: *Split Ring*, steel, 1969-70. Diameter approx. 3.7 metres. Max Hutchinson Gallery, New York

later as a teacher, educationalist and controversial sculptor he had considerable influence on students and laymen alike. Some of his larger works were fabricated for him in Sydney, or cast in bronze in Melbourne. During the 1960s he evolved a new direction, using paper as a medium. One of these sculptures is illustrated in [344].

Australian sculptors returning home at the beginning of World War II and migrant artists from Europe further stimulated artistic development: subject matter was greatly freed from the persistent tradition of representation by their enthusiasm for abstraction. Following the war years, numbers of students went overseas after completing their training in Australia, many enjoying the valuable experience of assisting Henry Moore. Among them was Lenton Parr (*b.* 1924) who, with his English-oriented welded sculpture, is now executing some of our finest and largest commissions in a strong personal style. *Astra* [345] is an example of his work.

Robert Klippel (*b.* 1920), with a more varied background, was not only a direct carver but one of the first of this generation to use mixed techniques. The Surrealist influence in his early work was rare in Australian sculpture of this period. During several trips to the U.S.A. his direction changed; the subsequent welded 'Junk' sculptures [346] are recognized as outstanding achievements.

The impact of European migrant sculptors has been most pronounced in Melbourne. Andor Meszaros (*b.* 1900 — Hungary) and Danila Vassilieff (1899-1958 — Russia) began working there before World War II, Vincas Jomantis (*b.* 1922 — Lithuania) and Julius Kane (1921-62 — Hungary) followed in 1949, and Inge King (*b.* 1918 — Germany) in 1951.

In 1961 Ernest van Hattum, the energetic and far-seeing director of the Mildura Art Gallery, initiated the Mildura Prize for Sculpture which has become a triennial event of national importance. Throughout Australia, sculpture societies, very generous prizes and scholarships from industry plus large commissions have also increased activity and done much to develop public interest and awareness. Fountains are becoming an important part of city environments. Of those belonging to the nineteenth century outlook, figurative sculpture dominated the designs. The abstract fountains of Gerald Lewers, amongst others, endeavour to use sculpture and water as integral parts of the composition, while water is the outstanding element in the El Alamein Fountain at Kings Cross, Sydney, designed by architects Woodward and Taranto.

Ranked among an increasing number of important sculptors in Sydney are Michael Nicholson (*b.* 1916 — U.K.), Tom Bass (*b.* 1916) and Alan Ingham (*b.* 1920 — N.Z.); in Melbourne, Clifford Last (*b.* 1918 — U.K.) and Ruth Adams (*b.* 1918); in Adelaide, Margaret Sinclair (*b.* 1918) and Owen Broughton (*b.* 1922); in Brisbane, Leonard Shillam (*b.* 1915) and Kathleen Shillam (*b.* 1916 — U.K.);

in Perth, Margaret Priest (*b.* 1922 — U.K.). Hobart and the provincial cities, because of small populations and isolation in varying degrees, are generally more restricted in opportunity.

A new generation of sculptors began to emerge in the 1950s, represented by Stephen Walker (*b.* 1927), Norma Redpath (*b.* 1928) and Clement Meadmore (*b.* 1929). With the exuberant organic approach exemplified in *Foreshore Group* [347], Walker is an excellent sculptor as well as an outstanding craftsman in the 'lost wax' process of bronze casting, carried out in his studio-foundry near Sydney. Much of Redpath's work is done overseas and cast in Italy. She is romantic in approach, but combines a restrained Expressionism with more formal relationships. Her Canberra fountain shown in [348] clearly demonstrates the compositional integration of water and sculpture that has been previously noted as a modern development. Clement Meadmore first worked in Melbourne and then in Sydney, where his uncompromising outlook brought little response. After finally migrating to New York, he is fast becoming one of Australia's leading sculptors. His large simple shapes, thrusting and twisting through space [349], are usually fabricated from maquettes.

During the 1960s there was a quickening in the number of overseas trends that were being adopted by younger artists. With better communications, more overseas exhibitions, and a proliferation of art books and magazines, changes were taking place. Pop, Op, Minimal, Environmental, Kinetic, Hard Edge and Wrap-ups emerged rapidly. Much of the current work stems from the revolutionary developments of the Cubists, Constructivists, Futurists and Dadaists, but with different directions and intents. The lines that had previously divided painting, sculpture and architecture were disappearing. Many painters turned to three dimensions and used colour in new ways, while sheer size took sculpture closer to architecture, with an increasing emphasis on 'total environments'.

Twentieth century technological and scientific processes are the underlying force in one direction of sculpture. Another seeks to re-present in visual terms the constant search for new understandings of life, using instant methods, throwaway materials and other innovations, a far cry from the age-old crafts and techniques of wood, stone and the 'noble' metals. Appreciation of these new trends in many cases demands that fresh thought be given to established beliefs, always keeping in mind that innovation and experimentation, while an essential part of development and change, do not in themselves constitute art.

[350] Coleing: *Wind Construction*, painted steel, 1970. Height 12.2 metres. Mildura Art Centre, Victoria

Younger artists of this period include Ron Robertson-Swann (*b.* 1941), Michael Kitching (*b.* 1940 — U.K.) and Tony Coleing (*b.* 1942) in Sydney, Ti Parks (*b.* 1939) and George Baldessin (*b.* 1939) in Melbourne, and Maxwell Lyle (*b.* 1935) and Nigel Lendon (*b.* 1944) in Adelaide. Coleing's *Wind Construction* [350] is a lively example of their work.

While many aspects of sculpture in Australia continue to develop in their various ways, each outstanding individual adding something to the sum total of work, Australians have not yet contributed anything original to sculpture as a whole, in the sense of breaking new ground or pointing a new direction, although there is little doubt that the potential is there.

AUSTRALIAN ARCHITECTURE

Peter Newell

Architecture is visible history

Throughout the evolution of man, his buildings have reflected a need for protection against weather and marauders in the most comfortable possible manner. Every building records in physical form the cultural, social and economic conditions of the time and place in which it was built; thus historians can trace the migrations of ancient peoples from the evidence of their arts and architecture.

However, the first settlers in Australia found no monuments left by ancient dynasties. There was not even an indigenous style of building, evolved from the hard school of experience, since the Aboriginal people had no need for permanent structures. Their casual grass or bark gunyas were sufficient shelter for a nomadic existence, unmolested by wild animals and largely free from the attacks of hostile tribes.

Convict builders and bush carpenters

The construction of barracks and public buildings in Australia began with convict tradesmen working under the direction of soldiers on colonial duty. They worked, as they had been trained, in traditional English building techniques, adding only one feature as a compromise with the climate — the verandah. This element of the early Australian house, which had shaded the buildings of the tropics from time immemorial, had been taken back to the counties of Devon and Cornwall by the Empire founders. When re-exported to the Australian colonies, it was not just a retreat from the sun: verandahs were extended along three or four sides of a building to function as an external passage linking a row of rooms, and providing protection against the weather for the saddle racks, shuttered wall openings and soft handmade brickwork. The Australian tradition of the low, single-storeyed house with its characteristic verandah began as early as 1793, when Captain John Macarthur, the father of the Australian wool industry, built what he described as 'a most excellent brick house' at Parramatta. Fortunately, Elizabeth Farm is still standing, proudly preserved by the National Trust of New South Wales [351].

Of necessity, the pioneer settlers reduced their bush shelters to the simplest form. A tomahawk, thrust under their belt, was the only tool they could carry when seeking their selections on horseback. With it they built a bark or 'wattle and daub' hut. As drays or trading schooners followed with axes, cross-cut saws, hammers, wedges and

[351] Elizabeth Farm at Parramatta, Sydney, 1793-4

[352] St Luke's church, Liverpool, N.S.W. Architect Francis Greenway, 1818

[353] Terrace houses in Campbelltown, Sydney, c. 1840

nails, the first earth-floored cottages were erected with walls of wide slabs split from straight-grained ironbarks, and roofs of wood shingles or flattened sheets of bark secured with saplings. When more permanent dwellings came to be required, the 'bush' carpenters and migrant tradesmen transplanted English building traditions to their strange new environment.

The designs of the more pretentious Colonial residences were obviously modelled on their Georgian English counterparts, except in the colder climate of Tasmania, where the verandah was not considered so important. There, excellent building stone and convict labour were readily available to create a heritage of formal two-storeyed mansions, almost Italian Classical in character. The Early Colonial style with its qualities of simplicity, symmetry and good proportions, whether it graced a humble artisan's cottage or proud homestead, reached its peak in the 1830s.

Much of the essential public building erected by the convict gangs around the early settlements was either primitive or makeshift. So much so that when the ambitious and much-travelled Governor Macquarie took up his duties in squalid Sydney Town in 1810, he assumed the role of Australia's first patron of architecture, but with no suitably trained architect to advise him! Fortunately, in 1814, Francis Howard Greenway, a Bristol architect who had been sentenced to fourteen years' deportation for forgery, arrived on a convict ship. This egotistical but able man was the expert Macquarie so desperately needed: after two years' valuable work he was pardoned and appointed official civil architect. In less than ten years, he had established himself as Australia's first great architect. Some of his sensitive and dignified designs, inspired by the late English Georgian style, can be seen in the restored St James's church in Sydney (1820-4) and St Matthew's at Windsor, N.S.W. (1817-20).

The battle of the styles

On 1 January 1838, a set of building ordinances was enacted in Sydney. These regulations, which were to have a profound influence on the history of architecture in Australia, had as their principal purpose fire-control in the growing cities. Since they were based on the London Building Act framed after the Great Fire of 1666, their effect was to stifle the development of a characteristically Australian style by implanting even more English traditions. Rows of narrow terrace-houses in their stark thousands spread throughout the inner suburbs of the cities to quickly and economically house the growing Australian-born and migrant populations. Public demand later resulted in the return of the verandah, however modest, to these city dwellings. See [353].

Where the cities became more prosperous, a new charac-

ter appeared: brickwork was plastered to imitate stone, and decorative elements borrowed from the Classical styles were added to windows, doors and parapets. Panels of lavish cast-iron filigree, used for ballast in the outbound wheat ships, were applied to the exteriors of buildings of all types, and cheaply imparted an impression of opulence to basically simple structures. As demand began to exceed the supply of these English cast-iron embellishments, foundries sprang up all over Australia to manufacture them, often with Australian motifs replacing the imported designs. When the use of cast-iron work or timber lattice panels was introduced into Queensland, it sometimes spread over an entire façade to screen the strong sunlight without obstructing cooling breezes.

As the nineteenth century progressed, the comparatively austere character of the Georgian-inspired Colonial style was replaced by yet another 'Old Country' influence — the Gothic Revival. Its most famous advocate in Australia was Edmund Blacket, an English-trained designer who in 1849, after a period as adviser to the Anglican diocese of Sydney, was appointed government architect. His evocative work can be seen at Sydney University and St Andrew's cathedral [354], two of his principal commissions after he resumed private practice in 1854.

After the heady days of the gold rushes abated, the city administrators set about improving their services and public buildings, while the merchants began planning more substantial stores and warehouses. The issue of whether they should instruct their architects to design in Classical or Gothic styles became so controversial that the 'Battle of the Styles' ensued. The protagonists of the former maintained, with some logic, that their choice was more appropriate because the Australian climate was closer to that of the Mediterranean, where the Classical styles originated; the Gothic Revivalists were more influenced by patriotism than reason, and insisted that Christian colonies of England should follow the English Gothic traditions! About this time, Gothic influences, such as steeply-pitched gabled roofs with bargeboards richly carved to simulate the stone window tracery of Medieval churches, even appeared in houses

[354] St Andrew's cathedral, George Street, Sydney. Architect Edmund Blacket, 1846-68

built for the wealthier citizens. Other architects did not have Blacket's restraint, and their buildings in the late Victorian period competed with each other in many guises borrowed from French chateaux, Viennese palaces and Eastern temples — or even an exuberant mixture of styles! In 1889, the editor of the *Jubilee History of Queensland* boasted that the arrival of each new architect in Brisbane enriched that fast-growing city with a greater wealth of architectural styles than any other colonial city!

Boom and bust

During the second half of the nineteenth century, the character of the Australian population was changing. Increasing prosperity promised such a bright future for the man of enterprise that each ship arriving from the 'Old Country' brought new types of migrants — professional men, merchants, skilled tradesmen and the sons of landed families sent out to enter the expanding pastoral industry. Thus the English traditions reflected in the architecture of the period became firmly rooted in the Australian way of life. The cities settled into mid-Victorian standards of middle-class respectability, which resulted in a spate of ecclesiastical building, ranging from humble chapels to imposing cathedrals. The majority of the churches built in this period differed little from their English Gothic models — which was only to be expected, for the architects commissioned to design them were either trained or practising in the United Kingdom. The great stone cathedrals of St Patrick and St Paul in Melbourne, St Peter's in Adelaide and St Mary's in Sydney were among those commenced in the 1860s.

In the following decades, prosperity increased to such an extent that the already lavish Classical buildings of the mid-Victorian period became even more ostentatious, as though their principal purpose was to impress the passer-by with the wealth of the owner. Italian craftsmen were imported to provide the skilled labour required for the elaborate brick, tiling and plaster work. There seemed no limit to the use of cast-iron decorations festooning balustrades, columns, beams, and even extending up the gables of the houses. Little heed was given to the protests of such architectural crusaders as the American-trained John Horbury Hunt, who practised in New South Wales. He described the flamboyant buildings of that time as 'vile . . . false . . . reckless piles revolting to the cultured taste and demoralizing to the public mind'.

All this exuberance was not to last much longer. Overseas financial depression in the 1890s spread to Australia, causing heavy withdrawals from the banks and building societies, which culminated in a major slump. Primary production was drastically set back by a severe drought and commerce was dislocated by a series of strikes. Speculative building and the construction of imposing mansions for newly-rich mining men, merchants and squatters came to a sudden stop. High Victorian architecture in Australia was dead, never to be revived.

Australian styles emerge

At the turn of the century, new trends emerged in Australian architecture. The sobering effect of the slump resulted in more rational and simpler structures. Also, new techniques and materials, such as reinforced concrete, became available and further influenced building design. Students entering the architectural profession to learn what their indenture papers described as 'the art and mystery of building' began seeking more logical designs for a new age and for different climates from those which had moulded the Classical styles. For a while, Art Nouveau, with its gracious lines inspired by the natural beauty of plant forms, had its adherents among Australian designers. Among them was the eminent teacher Robert Haddon, who adapted Australian motifs to Art Nouveau elements in his buildings, and stressed the chaste beauty of plain surfaces to his students of architecture at the Melbourne Technical College.

The dictates of climate were causing regional variations to appear in houses, those of Queensland developing the most distinctive character. As had some Pacific Island tribes, builders in the hot, humid areas found that if they raised their timber houses the occupants were above the level of seasonal flooding and low-flying insects. Moreover, living conditions were made more comfortable by cooling breezes circulating beneath, and useful space was provided under the house. In 1894, when the distinguished architect Robin Dods returned from overseas to practise in Brisbane, he was dismayed at what he described as 'the unsightly houses set on a forest of black stumps'. He developed a successful combination of the verandah of the Indian bungalow with elements derived from the traditional Colonial and elevated Queensland houses, and so made a significant contribution to that state's regional residential architecture.

Elsewhere, the use of stone and plastered wall surfaces gave way to exposed brickwork, invariably tuckpointed and patterned. Manufacture of terracotta tiles, which were previously a product of southern France, began in Melbourne and spread to the other capital cities. As these tiles supplanted slate and corrugated iron roofing, red became the dominant colour of the sprawling suburbs and remained so for the next half-century.

After World War I, steeply gabled and somewhat involved 'Queen Anne' brick and tile houses were too expensive for the average home builder. The answer came with the Californian bungalow, which achieved great popularity in all states. At least this latest importation, with its

[355] Contemporary house at Brookfield, Brisbane. Architect John Dalton and Associates, 1965

[356] Residence at Toowong, Brisbane. Architect John Dalton and Associates

[357] University of Sydney Law School, Phillip Street, Sydney. Architects McConnel, Smith and Johnson, 1969

[358] Water Board building, Bathurst Street, Sydney. Architects McConnel, Smith and Johnson, 1965

builders strove to overcome the lag and yet keep pace with a heavy demand for houses in the new suburbs, which because of increasing motor car ownership were spreading into the empty land between and beyond the railway lines. As prosperity mounted, another 'Battle of the Styles' began. Social status determined which garb a house should wear. There was a wider choice than before as Tudor, Georgian and the first bold experiments in the International Style made their appearance in the fashionable suburbs.

The International Style

The so-called International Style, which had its origins in Britain during the world-wide financial slump in the 1890s, received its greatest stimulus in Germany in the depressed decade which followed World War I. It was characterized by a reaction against the florid styles that then reigned, as buildings were shorn of decoration and reduced to a simple statement of function, relying on their 'massing' and proportions, and a rational use of building materials, for integral rather than applied aesthetics. It was during this period that the eminent French architect, Le Corbusier, propounded his famous statement that a house is merely a machine to live in.

lower roofs, generous eaves and verandah porches, was more suited to Australian conditions. In time the bungalow was challenged by yet another Californian transplant — the Spanish Mission style — characterized by low-pitched 'Cordova' tile roofs and arches supported off columns. The external walls, usually textured with cream-coloured stucco, enclosed much the same plan-form as the bungalow.

In the early 1930s, another severe depression virtually closed down the always vulnerable building industry. In the few years between this depression and World War II,

[359] Assembly Building, Academy of Science, Canberra. Architects Grounds, Romberg and Boyd, 1959

[360a & b] Sydney Opera House. Architect Joern Utzon, begun 1959

[361] Stained-glass ceiling by Leonard French in the Great Hall of the Victorian Arts Centre, St Kilda Road, Melbourne, 1967 Architect Sir Roy Grounds

capital city property forced councils to relax their ordinances, and buildings shaped by the latest technology rose to thirty storeys on land which previously supported only low-rise developments. Even in the suburban districts of the capital cities, construction of high-rise office blocks was necessary to satisfy the needs of the expanding economy, while avoiding the mounting car parking and traffic congestion problems in the central city areas.

The generation of architects trained just before and after World War II were so thoroughly indoctrinated with the 'form follows function' creed that in the post-war period they discarded their books of architectural rules and history and began designing in the 'Contemporary' style with an almost evangelistic fervour. They created new forms, expressive of the purpose of their buildings, yet tempered by the climate and materials in which they worked.

By mid-century the new architecture was no longer new. Even the conservative insurance companies and banks, which previously projected an image of solidity and permanence through the classical colonnades on the façades of their buildings, accepted modern architectural philosophy. This led to the development of such structural techniques of the glazed 'curtain wall': a building's frame was designed to carry the loads and so reduce the external surfaces to translucent weather protection for the artificial environment created inside by the lighting, air-conditioning and

The skylines of the cities were also changing. As early as 1854, Elisha Otis invented the passenger lift in America. Although visionary architects began talking about the 'skyscrapers' of the future, it was not until 1885 that the first steel-framed twelve-storey building was built in Chicago. The following year, the brick Australian Building in Melbourne became the highest building in the world, rising to 46 metres. However, most Australian cities set a height limit of 40 metres. After World War II, the enormous demand for urban accommodation on expensive

[362] 'Cluster' housing, Mount Ommaney, Brisbane. Architect P. J. Moroney, 1970

acoustic engineers. The post-war period ushered in an enormous industrial expansion throughout Australia. Factory buildings, which were once reduced to the cheapest utilitarian protection for the machinery and stock, took on a new significance as some industrialists realized that an efficiently designed plant set in landscaped grounds was an acquisition to their communities and, as such, good public relations.

Blueprint for the computer age

The backlog of house, factory and office construction resulting from depression and war, combined with an urgent need for new buildings to serve a growing population and expanding economy, was largely overcome by the 1960s. To provide facilities for the cultural life of the communities, major projects with strong individual characters such as Sydney's Opera House and Melbourne's Arts Centre were commissioned. The architect now finds himself involved in matters of total environment, with the community rather than the individual as his client.

The rapid development of technology is influencing every phase of building, and such techniques as prefabrication must reduce construction time and costs. We even appear to be returning to the communal living pattern of the Middle Ages, as high land and building costs are shared in 'cluster groups' of houses or vertical villages of home-units. More holiday resorts, motels and caravan camps will be built to accommodate the increasing leisure hours of an affluent society.

It is now accepted that, owing to the enormous and complex problems of housing the world's fast-growing populations, rebuilding the blighted cities and arresting the pollution of our environment, there will have to be more new construction in the remainder of this century than the previous constructional achievements of the whole history of mankind! As individual buildings become merely elements of new towns and regional developments, the architect whose training has prepared him for the creation of a total human environment will expand his traditional role to bring order and beauty into this environment, and so make a significant contribution to the wellbeing and advancement of the human race.

In seventeenth century England, Sir Henry Wootton summed up the creed Vitruvius propounded some two centuries earlier, when he stated: 'Well building hath three qualities — commodity, firmness and delight.' Today, as new structures are shaped to changing conditions, we evaluate them by their efficiency — both functional and economic — their structural sufficiency, and the quality of design: Wootton's three basic criteria of good architecture are just as pertinent now as they were in the past.

Index

Figure numbers of illustrations are in **bold** type